THE DRIVEN BILLIONAIRE

ERIN SWANN

SWANN PUBLICATIONS

Cover image licensed from Shutterstock.com

Cover design by Swann Publications

Edited by Jessica Royer Ocken

Proofreaders: Donna Hokanson, Tamara Mataya, Rosa Sharon

ISBN: 978-1072519096

The following story is intended for mature readers. It contains mature themes, strong language, and sexual situations. All characters are 18+ years of age, and all sexual acts are consensual.

Find out more about the author and upcoming books online at:

WWW.ERINSWANN.COM

If you would like to hear about Erin's new releases and sales join the newsletter. We only email about sales or new releases, and we never share your information.

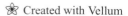 Created with Vellum

ALSO BY ERIN SWANN

The Billionaire's Trust - Available on Amazon, also in AUDIOBOOK

(Bill and Lauren's story) He needed to save the company. He needed her. He couldn't have both. The wedding proposal in front of hundreds was like a fairy tale come true—Until she uncovered his darkest secret.

The Youngest Billionaire - Available on Amazon

(Steven and Emma's story) The youngest of the Covington clan, he avoided the family business to become a rarity, an honest lawyer. He didn't suspect that pursuing her could destroy his career. She didn't know what trusting him could cost her.

The Secret Billionaire – Available on Amazon, also in AUDIOBOOK

(Patrick and Elizabeth's story) Women naturally circled the flame of wealth and power, and his is brighter than most. Does she love him? Does she not? There's no way to know. When he stopped to help her, Liz mistook him for a carpenter. Maybe this time he'd know. Everything was perfect. Until the day she left.

The Billionaire's Hope - Available on Amazon, also in AUDIOBOOK

(Nick and Katie's story) They came from different worlds. She hadn't seen him since the day he broke her brother's nose. Her family retaliated by destroying his life. She never suspected where accepting a ride from him today would take her. They said they could do casual. They lied.

Previously titled: Protecting the Billionaire

Picked by the Billionaire – Available on Amazon, also in AUDIOBOOK

(Liam and Amy's story) A night she wouldn't forget. An offer she couldn't refuse. He alone could save her, and she held the key to his survival. If only they could pass the test together.

Saved by the Billionaire – Available on Amazon

(Ryan and Natalie's story) The FBI and the cartel were both after her for the same thing: information she didn't have. First, the FBI took everything, and then the cartel came for her. She trusted Ryan with her safety, but could she trust him with her heart?

Caught by the Billionaire – Available on Amazon

(Vincent and Ashley's story) Her undercover assignment was simple enough: nail the crooked billionaire. The surprise came when she opened the folder, and the target was her one-time high school sweetheart. What will happen when an unknown foe makes a move to checkmate?

The Driven Billionaire – Available on Amazon

(Zachary and Brittney's story) Rule number one: hands off your best friend's sister. With nowhere to turn when she returns from upstate, she accepts his offer of a room. Mutual attraction quickly blurs the rules. When she comes under attack, pulling her closer is the only way to keep her safe. But, the truth of why she left town in the first place will threaten to destroy them both.

Nailing the Billionaire – Available on Amazon

(Dennis and Jennifer's story) She knew he destroyed her family. Now she is close to finding the records that will bring him down. When a corporate shakeup forces her to work with him, anger and desire collide. Vengeance was supposed to be simple, swift, and sweet. It was none of those things.

Undercover Billionaire – Available on Amazon

(Adam and Kelly's story) Their wealthy families have been at war forever. When Kelly receives a chilling note, the FBI assigns Adam to protect her. Family histories and desire soon collide, causing old truths to be questioned. Keeping ahead of the threat won't be their only challenge.

Trapped with the Billionaire – Available on Amazon

(Josh and Nicole's story) When Nicole returns from vacation to find her company has been sold, and she has been assigned to work for the new CEO. Competing visions of how to run things and mutual passion collide in a volatile mix. When an old family secret is unearthed, it threatens everything.

CHAPTER 1

BRITTNEY

I DIDN'T DARE OPEN THE INTIMIDATING GRAY ENVELOPE. INSTEAD I slipped it under the orange folder, grabbed my keys, and departed for my date. This was the only night of the week I didn't work and could fit in a social activity.

I arrived five minutes late after intentionally parking three blocks away, behind the restaurant. My date for the evening, Jeffrey, was already here. I passed his BMW out front as I hurried up the walk to the Tres Pinos entrance.

He'd suggested this place after our first meeting last week over coffee, and I didn't want to jinx anything by objecting to his choice, so I told him I'd love to try it. The food here was great, and the prices were reasonable. As an added bonus, the bowl of chips would occupy me enough to not fidget, and maybe keep my mouth full enough to prevent me from saying something stupid— at least I could hope.

Jeffrey smiled from beside the ficus tree as I pulled open the door. He kindly didn't check his watch. "I was hoping I didn't get the time wrong."

I smiled. His button down shirt and blazer were more formal than average for this area, but I attributed that to him working in marketing.

"No. I'm just running late. Traffic on Pico."

His hand at my waist guided me to the hostess station, where he whispered something to the cute young thing.

His touch reminded me this was a date. I fingered the heart-shaped gold medallion around my neck. It had been long enough since Todd, hadn't it?

Cute Young Thing beamed a smile back. She showed us to one of the primo tables by the front window. "Will this one do?"

Jeffrey nodded. "*Perfecto, señorita.*" He slipped a bill into her hand and pulled out a chair for me.

"*Hablas español,* Jeffrey?" I asked after the hostess left.

"No. You just heard it all, if you don't count asking for a Dos Equis. I had Spanish in middle school, but these days I couldn't even ask where the bathroom is."

"*Dónde está el baño,*" I told him.

"I'll take your word for it." He arched an eyebrow. "And, what did I do wrong to be demoted to Jeffrey?"

His correction caught me off guard. "Sorry, Jeff. Nothing at all."

His smile told me he was letting me off easy.

It had only been a week, but I shouldn't have made such an obvious mistake. Benji's harassment was screwing with my concentration.

So far I was finding Jeff's modesty refreshing after all the braggarts I'd met on the SuperSingles dating site—not that I'd had many dates. Somehow dating brought out the need to show off in men, which often translated into exaggerating everything in their lives. I was over having men try to impress me with the car they drove, their expensive taste in wine, or the latest concert tickets they'd snagged.

Jeff had showed up in a BMW, a million steps above the

Accord I drove, but he hadn't mentioned it once on our previous coffee date—ten points for him.

Our waitress arrived with chips and salsa, both hot and medium. They didn't serve mild here.

Eager to get past my embarrassment, I ordered a margarita on the rocks, no salt. I couldn't tell if Jeff was following my lead, or we merely liked the same adult beverage, when he copied my order.

"So, what do you think's good here?" he asked, ladling the milder of the two salsas onto his chip.

I chose the hotter salsa. "Pretty much everything."

"So you've been here?"

I maneuvered to escape my mistake. "No. But my friend Lillian eats here all the time, and she raves about it." That was a close one.

He switched to the hot salsa for his next chip. "I'm liking the looks of the burritos. What about you?"

I perused the menu slowly before answering. "I think I'll try the fajitas." That was my go-to order here when I didn't feel like an enchilada.

"Then maybe I'll try that too."

I inquired about his work, and he told me about some of his recent customer visits. At least he got to talk to his customers.

"I guess your clients don't talk much," he noted.

I laughed. "The jabs and scrapes of my instruments against their teeth keep their responses to mumbles when they aren't shrinking away."

I didn't drill teeth, but patients still cowered at the sight of curettes, scrapers, scalers, and probes. If a root canal was on someone's most-hated list, a visit to my chair was not far behind. Nobody ever moved a cleaning appointment up because they were looking forward to the experience.

He grimaced. "Ouch." A bead of sweat appeared on his forehead after another chip with the hot salsa. The hot stuff here was scorching hot.

I took pity on him and switched to the milder salsa.

The waitress interrupted us to take our orders, and once again I went first. Jeff copied my order of fajitas, even down to choosing chicken and no sour cream.

I raised my margarita. "I'm used to it. Nobody puts a visit to get their teeth cleaned at the top of their wish list."

He joined me with a sip of his drink, and his next chip went into the milder salsa.

"My dentist only works four days a week. Does that mean you get a lot of time off as a hygienist?"

"More than you might think. My dentist has us all under twenty hours a week so she doesn't have to provide benefits."

He grimaced in sympathy. "That's not fair."

"*Fair* isn't in Dr. Call's vocabulary. It is what it is."

Jeff finished the chip he was chewing. "Can you fill in with another dentist?"

"I wish, but she keeps moving our days around, so that makes it hard."

"That's tough."

I smiled. Jeff was the first of my dates to understand the unfairness of the way she treated us. "I fill in my other hours tending bar."

"Very ambitious of you."

I smiled and sucked down more of my margarita. "A girl does what she has to do to make ends meet."

"That must keep you pretty busy."

"Busy girl, that's me. What about you? I hear startup hours can also be on the brutal side."

He was detailing his most recent few days when our food arrived.

As always, the fajitas were served still sizzling on hot cast-iron plates.

Mine was as tasty as always, and Jeff seemed impressed with his.

"You said you had a sister?" he asked.

I had to finish chewing before I could answer. "And a twin

4

brother, Doug. Samantha is two years younger and getting her MBA at Wharton. Doug is in the Marines."

Just then my heart skipped a beat as I caught sight of a gray Charger driving by, which looked like it could have been Benji's.

Every time I saw one, my skin crawled as I wondered if it could be him.

I crossed mental fingers that Benji wasn't prowling for me. Jeff's brow creased. "Something wrong?"

I willed a fake smile onto my face. "Oh no," I lied. "Just trying to remember when her tuition is due." Picking up my drink, I tried to be casual about looking out the window in the direction Benji had disappeared.

"You're paying? That's an expensive school, I imagine."

I knew that better than anyone. Putting my younger sister through school had fallen to me and Doug, and he couldn't help much with the debts he was still paying off. Providing for Sam's education kept my bank balance hovering near zero, and sometimes below, even with all the overtime I pulled down at the Pink Pig.

"My mom passed away two years ago," I told him. My father's departure years before didn't warrant a mention. "It's my responsibility now to get her through school."

There were months I wouldn't have been able to feed myself if it weren't for credit cards.

"She's a grownup. She should take care of herself," he remarked.

That was a common feeling, I'd learned.

"It's not how I was raised. The older ones look out for the younger ones."

He nodded and smiled without offering an opinion of my family values.

I scooped veggies and chicken inside a tortilla and asked about his family.

That steered the conversation away from my plight, and had me longing for the simple situation he enjoyed.

All through dinner I kept a cautious eye out the window for Benji—without any sightings.

I finished the last of my fajitas, save the green bell peppers I never ate.

Jeff checked his watch again—the third time in the last few minutes.

This dinner was coming to a close soon. If the third date didn't improve from this, there likely wouldn't be a fourth.

I wasn't heartbroken about it. Jeff seemed nice, stable, almost normal—unlikely to be an axe murderer—but there was no spark. He was about as exciting as cream of wheat. I'd nearly nodded off listening to his description of his sister's latest venture—she was apparently the Waikiki hamburger queen—when I caught it.

Jeff lived with his parents. Though, at least, he probably didn't live in the basement, since almost no houses in California had basements.

Five minutes later, we'd both declined our waitress's dessert query, and I followed him out the front door into the warm evening air.

Jeff stopped at his car and unlocked it with his key fob. "Next week, would you prefer sushi, or perhaps a movie instead?"

The marketing guy was on his game. His question presumed a third date.

I considered my choices.

"Hey, get away from my girl." The yell came from down the sidewalk as Benji approached at a fast clip.

He'd been behind the hedge, probably for a long time. Sneaking around was his style.

Jeff backed up, looked first at Benji, then at me. Fear marked his face.

Benji's version of crazy could do that.

"Get out of here, Benji, and leave us alone," I yelled. I put my hand in my purse, feeling for my pepper spray, just in case.

Jeff disappeared around his car and climbed in. He didn't have any interest in an altercation with my crazy ex.

My heart galloped a mile a minute, but I stood my ground and pulled out my phone.

Jeff burned rubber pulling away from the curb.

Benji gave him the finger along with a "fuck you."

"Benji, get the hell out of here before I call the cops," I yelled.

He stopped.

I pulled out my phone.

An older couple that had just come out of the restaurant retreated back inside.

"You can't go out with him," Benji yelled.

The guy didn't get it. We weren't an item any more, and weren't ever going to be again. Not ever.

I lifted my phone with my finger poised over the emergency button. "I'm calling the cops in three… two… one."

Benji turned and ran back the way he'd come.

I couldn't take this shit.

As soon as he turned the corner, I left in the opposite direction, struggling to get my breathing back under control.

He got crazier every time.

Z_{ACK}

A SALTY BEAD OF SWEAT TRICKLED INTO MY EYE. WIPING IT AWAY with my gloved hand made it worse when a fleck of sawdust joined it.

"Shit."

Standing up and removing the glove, I blinked like crazy and coaxed the irritating particle out of the corner of my eye with a fingernail.

With two functioning eyes again, I located the last cold can of ginger ale, popped it open, and took a few long, stinging gulps. I reversed the towel that had covered the can to find a clean section. I wiped my brow and surveyed the dusty room.

After two evenings of work, I was only a quarter done with this room. I refolded the rag, dirty side out.

What idiot would glue crappy fake laminate like this over the marvelous oak flooring the house was built with? And the second layer glued down without removing the first was double sacrilege against this fine old mansion.

It would take a lot of work, but I could already envision walking on the warm golden strips of oak, dotted with tasteful area rugs, instead of the half-plastic crap the last two owners had glued down.

I gulped the rest of the can before tossing it in the corner garbage bag and kneeling down with my pry bar to attack the offending laminate again.

Three small sections later, the music started up next door.

Fucking punks.

I rose, brushed a layer of dust from my jeans, and walked back to the kitchen—one of the only two semi-clean rooms downstairs during this project of mine.

I wiped down my hair and torso with a clean towel and pulled on a T-shirt. The snub-nose pistol went into my waistband at the small of my back, and I grabbed a flashlight from the counter.

Neighborhood kids had taken to using the abandoned house next door as their occasional nighttime party spot, and I was sick of it.

Twice I'd tried calling the cops. But the cops had rolled up an hour later, turned on their flashing lights, and the kids dispersed out the back, only to return a few days later. The officers viewed scaring them off as the easy way to deal with it, and they never attempted to catch any of the buggers.

The moon lit the way as I moved toward the back porch door I knew to be open. One of the delinquents had broken the lock on the doorknob and removed the deadbolt for easy access. Tomorrow morning I'd get a replacement deadbolt on the way to work and be able to put an end to their parties.

God-awful music blared out of an open window. How they could even call that music was beyond me.

The back door was ajar. The squeak of its rusty hinges as I entered was drowned out by the cacophony coming from the boom box toward the front.

I passed through the old dining room to the front parlor. The kids had laid down their cell phones with the lights pointing to the ceiling for illumination. They were so busy dancing, none of them noticed as I approached.

A solid kick from my work boot, and the plastic boom box went quiet as it shattered against the wall. Simultaneous protests from the three couples replaced the music.

The tallest of the boys started toward me. "What the fuck, asshole?"

I pointed the pistol.

The click as I cocked the hammer was loud in the instantly quiet room.

"What did you call me?"

The boy backed up and the front of his jeans went dark with piss. "I didn't mean…"

The others grouped together and backed toward the wall. Piss Boy didn't have any rescuers in this group.

"I catch you creeps in here again, and there'll be hell to pay. Do you understand me?"

Piss Boy nodded and backed toward the others.

One of the others stooped to pick up a phone.

"Leave it," I yelled.

The girl dropped the phone.

I rounded the room toward the door. "The phones stay on the floor. Now, get over there." I motioned toward the corner with the gun.

The group shuffled toward the corner.

I counted and only saw five phones. "I said all the phones." I waved the gun at the group.

A girl in the back slid the missing phone to the middle of the room.

"Listen carefully. This is how this is going to go. You can come to my house next door after dinner time tomorrow…" I pointed toward my house. "…with a letter of apology, and I'll give you back your phones. Do you understand?"

The group nodded, even Piss Boy.

I unlocked the deadbolt of the front door and backed away from it. "Now out." I raised the pistol toward the ceiling and fired.

The loud report of the gun reverberated in the room as Piss Boy made it to the door first, with the rest of the pack only seconds behind.

It was only a starter pistol loaded with blanks, but it got the point across. Piss Boy and his crew wouldn't be back.

I locked the front door after them, gathered up the phones, and exited through the back. Tomorrow when they came back to retrieve their phones, they'd get another reminder not to return. Back inside my house, I locked my doors, set the alarm, and replaced my starter pistol in the drawer.

If I knew teenagers, the word would spread, keeping them from destroying the majestic house next door any further.

Fucking juvenile delinquents.

CHAPTER 2

BRITTNEY

I TURNED IN TO MY ASSIGNED PARKING SPACE BETWEEN THE TWO pickups and noticed it just in time. I hit the brakes, got out, and pocketed the nail—placed conveniently on end where my tires normally rolled—before getting back in to finish parking.

Fucking Benji.

He'd told me two weeks ago, *"What if you get a flat tire? You'll need me then."*

This was the third time I'd found a nail or screw in my parking spot since.

Safely upstairs in my apartment, I locked the door behind me. The orange folder on my desk taunted me.

I opened it to the printout of the last email from Detective Swenson I'd read and printed out. It suggested one more time that I'd be safer if I could remember what had happened to the key— the key I had no idea about. My sister, Samantha, had convinced me to stop checking the secret gmail account, and I hadn't since this had arrived nine months ago. Every previous message had only turned into an hour-long crying session with her over the issue. I couldn't remember something I never knew.

Would I ever really be safe?

I opened my laptop to log in and tell him one last time to leave me alone, so I could put the reminders of my plight behind me.

But I chickened out and closed the laptop's lid. He didn't need a message from me. Samantha's solution was simpler. I tossed the whole ugly folder back in the bottom drawer where it belonged— out of sight out of mind. What I didn't read couldn't bother me.

But when I did that, I was faced with the fucking gray envelope again. The envelope that detailed my real problem. Hovering over it for a few seconds, I resisted and stuffed it in my purse. It needed to be dealt with, but it was going to wait.

Saving me from my dilemma, my phone rang, with Samantha's pretty face on the screen.

"How'd your date go, Brit?" she asked.

Her saying the word *date* sent my fingers nervously to my medallion. I winced as the scene with Benji replayed in my head.

"Okay," I said.

Technically, the date had been okay; it was the ending that got all fucked up.

"Tell me about him. I think Jeffrey is an okay name, but not a leader."

She thought a lot of names were cool, as if you could judge a guy's character by what his parents had named him when he was mere hours old. Although she'd thought Derrick was a creepy name, and her theory had been borne out, and same with Norman before him.

But after watching Hitchcock's *Psycho*, I should have known better than to go out with anyone named Norman.

"We went to Tres Pinos," I told her as I sank into the couch.

"I bet he had the fajitas and a margarita on the rocks," she guessed. Some of these guesses were her superpower.

"What makes you say that?"

She laughed. "Simple. Jeffrey is a follower name. Like I said,

12

not a leader, and you always get a margarita on the rocks and the chicken fajitas."

She knew me too well.

"Sam, that was just a lucky guess."

"Was not. Bet it ended without a kiss. Jeffreys move slow."

She had guessed right again, but not for the reason she thought.

"Well, am I right?"

"No kiss," I confirmed.

"I knew it. Boring, huh? Brit, you deserve better. You deserve hot. You deserve tall, dark, and studly."

"He was okay."

"But no third date, right?"

She was likely right once again.

"I'm pretty sure that's not happening."

"I hear it in your voice. Spill, big sister. What happened?"

I sighed, caught again. I swear she must have hidden a webcam in my apartment last time she was here. "Nothing. I just don't think he'll be calling."

"Stop holding out."

"It was Benji. He accosted us outside the restaurant."

She gasped. "Worse than last time?"

"Yeah, a little."

I underplayed how I'd felt for my sister's benefit. She needed to concentrate on school instead of worrying about the drama in my life.

"That idiot's a dozen crayons short of a box. You better get a gun."

"That's one thing I'm not doing."

"He's dangerous, if you ask me," she retorted.

"He's got no balls. I know how to handle him. He'll get over it sooner or later."

My words were more confident than my feelings.

"He doesn't need balls to be dangerous. He can poison your cat, or burn down your house without having the guts to face you."

"I don't have a cat."

"Very funny. You know what I mean. Benjamin is a back-stabber's name. Better be careful."

She had warned me against Benji from day one. It was my fault for not listening to her. "He'll get tired of it sooner or later."

So far all my predictions of that had been premature. Sooner wasn't looking likely.

"You know Grams's house is empty, and it's half yours now."

Our grandmother had passed on last year and left Doug the tiny lake cabin and my sister and me her house in west LA. Doug had rented the cabin, so that wasn't an option—not that commuting from the mountains would work anyway. The thought of living at Grams's house would be tempting if it wasn't in LA, and also if she hadn't died in the house.

I dodged the suggestion. "Dealing with ghosts is not on my agenda."

"The house is just waiting for you. And you could save on rent."

Her mention of rent brought my gaze back to the gray envelope.

I'd never shared with her how hard it was keeping my nose above water financially with her tuition. If I could just handle it another two semesters, she'd be done and launched into a life with loads of potential. She deserved that.

But move back to LA? I didn't intend to ever go back.

"I like it better up here."

"Right. Well, keep the house in mind and don't turn your back on Benji. I don't trust him."

I changed the subject. "What classes are you signing up for?"

As she started to talk, I glanced across the room. The clock I kept on the counter was facing toward the kitchen instead of its normal orientation toward me on the couch.

After ten minutes discussing her upcoming semester and another ten on her non-existent dating life, we hung up.

I got up, repositioned the errant clock, and settled in for a little television.

CHAPTER 3

Zack

Tuesday morning, I took a deep breath as the red digits increased one by one, with a ding at each floor. The elevator doors finally opened on the top floor of Benson Corp.—Galactic HQ, as I liked to call it—where my father reigned supreme over all he surveyed.

I cinched up my tie and turned right toward marketing.

My ever-cheery assistant, Wendy, was at her desk ahead of me, as always.

"Good morning, Mr. Benson. Make much progress last night?"

Wendy understood my passion to get my old house restored to its former glory. There was something majestic about an old Victorian—the craftsmanship of the woodwork and the unique personality of each one. They'd been built in a time before cookie-cutter designs and mass production became popular. They were built lovingly by hand and exuded a warmth missing in the square McMansions of today.

"Slow and steady. Still arguing with the laminate those two idiots laid down. Any emergencies this morning?"

"Just the usual."

"Let me guess. Stanton from the London office?"

He needed something pretty much every morning, and the issues were almost always minor. He had the mistaken impression that phone time with me, just because my last name was Benson, would accelerate his career. He didn't get how Dad operated.

"One point for you. And your father wants to see you."

I schooled my face to not show the irritation I felt, but the cock of her eyebrow revealed I'd been unsuccessful. Wendy knew how much I enjoyed my father's interruptions.

Not.

Yesterday's breeze had cleared out the smog, and I took a moment to enjoy the view of the Pacific Ocean out my office window.

"Anything special?" I asked Wendy as I picked her coffee cup up off the desk and headed to the break room with mine in the other hand.

"The usual will be fine, thanks." She enjoyed a mocha with non-dairy creamer most mornings. On occasion, she'd change it up and ask for decaf.

My first and only argument with Wendy had been my insistence that it wasn't in her job description to get me coffee the way she had for Walt before me. Walt was old school in that respect.

I'd insisted on changing that dynamic, and it was my routine to make and bring coffee for each of us—black for me and mocha for Wendy. It seemed like the civilized thing, and Wendy wasn't wrong when she suggested I did it to be different. Different was good.

After a sip of the hot brew, I took off my coat, threw my keys on the desk, and settled in for the inevitably boring call with Stanton. I opened my cell phone to the timer screen and hit speed dial on my desk phone to Stanton's London office number. Dad insisted we use the landlines when communicating between offices to avoid interception of calls.

Stanton picked up after a few rings, and I started the timer on my cell. He wanted to review some customer quotes he'd emailed.

I pulled the messages up, and we went through them one at a time. Predictably, half of them were within his pricing authority and didn't require a call to get my authorization. I glanced at Vince Lombardi's face on the coin attached to my keyring. I considered giving Stanton one of Lombardi's quotes—"*The only place success comes before work is in the dictionary.*"—but decided he wouldn't get it.

We finished the last quote with two minutes to spare on my timer. I'd warned him often enough to keep the calls below fifteen minutes so I had time to call the Rome office before they went home for the day.

After a short call to Lucio in Rome, it was time to see the old man. I gathered my keys and a notepad before making my way to Dad's office on the other end of the floor.

My father was on the phone, but he waved me in as he finished up his call. "Zachary, how are you this morning?"

"No complaints."

"Great. I wanted to congratulate you on the Swankstead deal. That's another first-rate piece of business."

"Thanks, Dad, but it was mostly Franciscovich."

Swankstead had taken a month and seven trips to their head-quarters to put together, but hundred-million-dollar equipment sales didn't happen overnight. Franciscovich, the sales guy, had done most of the legwork.

"He'll get a fat commission check for this one. But either way, you handled that admirably."

I nodded.

"So well, in fact, that I think you're ready for your next challenge."

I knew exactly what he meant, and I didn't like the sound of it. "I'd like to spend more time in marketing before moving on."

"Nonsense, Zachary. A position is opening up in finance at the London office before long."

"London?"

"Sure. It's a great little town."

Only Dad could call London a *little town*.

"Why not here?"

"You'll have to get used to warm beer, and don't eat the mushy peas. Those mushy peas are awful."

Apparently, he'd already decided I was moving to my next rotation. All that remained in his mind was to set the date.

"I'll think about it," I told him.

"I think you could learn what you need to in less than two years there."

He evidently hadn't heard me.

"I said I think I need more time in marketing first."

My words finally registered, and the effect wasn't pretty. His brow furrowed, and his eyes bored into me.

I returned his glare in equal measure.

"Nonsense. Finance is next up for you. "

This conversation was reminiscent of the one we'd had three years ago when I'd agreed to take my current marketing position at the company. That time I'd folded quickly and agreed to move when he wanted. The departmental rotations were mandatory for family members, but I was trying to have some input on the timing, and not making a lot of progress.

He meant well. He was doing his best to train me, and all of us, for the futures he envisioned for us.

I was committed to supporting the family company, and I'd known what that entailed when I joined.

"Review it with Harold in finance," he said. "He has all the particulars. We'll talk about timing later."

"I will," I said as I stood to leave.

I felt in my pocket for the keyring Dad had given me. Family obligations came above all else—but London?

"Congratulations again on Swankstead. I mean that."

"Thanks, Dad," I replied as I departed his office.

Why London?

CHAPTER 4

BRITTNEY

I HADN'T SLEPT WELL, WORRYING ABOUT SAMANTHA'S BENJI warnings. It was the first time she'd been so adamant about him being dangerous.

I'd written him off as obsessive, but last night's encounter had been worse than anything yet. Still, sooner or later, he'd get tired of chasing me. He had to. Didn't he?

My ponytail didn't look quite right on the first try, so I redid it. Dr. Call was picky about her hygienists' appearance.

I opened the door and saw it immediately. The chill went all the way to my toes.

SLUT in big red letters, spray-painted on my apartment door.

Fucking Benji had gone too far—way too far.

I looked both ways down the hall before closing the door behind me and locking the deadbolt.

The nasty word was also painted on the wall next to my door, with the drips from the letters making it look like the letters were bleeding.

Mrs. Butterman exited her unit. Her mouth gaped, and she shook her head before scurrying for the stairs.

I waited a moment before following.

MY FIRST PATIENT WAS MR. SNODDER. HIS CHART SAID HE HADN'T been in since last year, and the tartar he'd accumulated took especially long to remove.

"I can tell you haven't been flossing as often as you should," I told him.

"Probably right."

"And you really should have a cleaning every six months," I encouraged.

"I come in as often as I can afford to," he said.

Dr. Call came in shortly after and told him the same things, and got the same responses.

"Your insurance covers it," she told him.

"Really?" he said, faking surprise.

A visit to our office was just something he wanted to avoid.

The rest of my appointments for the morning were pretty ordinary. I put my fingers and instruments in patient's mouths, and tried to avoid getting bitten. I was used to it: staring down at teeth and bleeding gums, and dealing with the occasional dose of bad breath. It wasn't glamorous, but the pay was good on an hourly basis. If I could get more hours, things might actually be manageable, but with Dr. Call, that wasn't likely.

I was in the middle of my last patient before my lunch break when I heard him.

"I'm here to take Brittney to lunch." It was Benji's loud voice coming from reception.

"You need to leave, sir," Rosa at the front desk told him.

"No. I'm not leaving without Brittney," Benji said, even louder.

Dr. Call came to my station. "You need to take care of this."

I got up and excused myself from my patient. I could feel the heat of the doctor's glare as I walked up front.

"Benji, you need to leave," I told him as I reached reception.

His eyes were wide and bloodshot. "Not without you."

Rosa rolled her eyes.

The two patients in the waiting area looked on apprehensively.

"I'm not going to lunch with you."

Benji kicked the reception partition. "Yes, you are," he said angrily.

One of the waiting patients got up and left.

"Call 9-1-1," Dr. Call said from behind me.

Rosa dialed.

I pointed to the door. "Get out of here, now."

He didn't move, but the remaining patient did.

Dr. Call followed him. "Mr. Carson, don't go."

It was a standoff for a half minute or so, with him pacing the waiting room and me demanding that he leave.

The wail of a police siren sounded outside and Benji bolted for the door.

Dr. Call poked her head in the door from outside and motioned for me to join her.

Once I'd stepped outside, she said, "Brittney, it's not acceptable for your boyfriend to impact the practice and scare patients, not to mention the rest of us."

"He's not my boyfriend," I explained.

Her countenance didn't soften. "I'm canceling your shifts for now."

My stomach clenched. "But..."

"Collect your things, and call me when you have your situation sorted out."

"Now?" This couldn't be happening.

"Right now."

The police cruiser pulled up in front, and Dr. Call went to talk to them while I walked back inside, stunned.

As I left, Dr. Call whispered to Rosa, who gave me the side eye.

When I stepped back outside, the police car was gone, and my life was a shambles. The gray envelope with Samantha's tuition bill loomed as an even bigger problem than it had been yesterday.

I drove back to my apartment in a funk. I'd have to start checking with other dentists for a hygienist opening right away.

Maybe I could explain that I needed more days than Dr. Call was willing to schedule me, but that was tenuous. If they called her, the truth would sink me.

Benji had fucked my life big time.

I must have looked odd to the other drivers on the road. I spent the drive home yelling at the windshield, telling Benji to fuck off a hundred times.

Upstairs, the paint had been removed from the door, and the wall had been repainted, with a wet paint sign taped up.

I let myself in and collapsed on the couch.

I'd barely caught my breath before the knock sounded on the door.

I braced myself for a confrontation with Benji through the closed door. It would be just his style to show up now to apologize and ask to be forgiven.

Fat chance.

The view through the peephole, though, showed Mrs. Honeycutt, the manager's wife.

I opened the door. "I'm sorry about Benji," I started.

She forced a folded up paper in my direction. "And I'm sorry about this. But we run a quiet, respectable complex here."

I opened the paper.

THREE DAY NOTICE TO QUIT.

I was being evicted. "But, I can't possibly find a place—"

"Three days. You can call later about where to send your deposit, if any is left," she said before she turned and walked away.

I couldn't breathe as I closed the door and let the ugly paper fall to the floor.

The first tears rolled down my cheeks.

A knot of dread formed in my stomach.

Find a place to live and a new job at the same time?

How?

What would I tell Samantha?

This was impossible.

I had to pull myself together. I tore open the gray envelope from the Wharton School of Business and took in the total. It didn't include books, and it was way too big for me to handle now.

I logged onto my bank account. The meager total almost made me sick.

I could ask for extra shifts at the Pink Pig, but the number was still insurmountable. And even if I could find a place in three days, Sam's tuition, plus first, last, and a security deposit was out of reach anywhere in this town.

"You know Grams's house is empty, and it's half yours now," Samantha had said.

But when I'd left, I'd told myself I would never go back to LA.

Now it was either that, or call Sam and tell her she couldn't finish her degree this year.

Getting help from Doug was out of the question. We'd talked last week, and he'd already maxed out his credit card sending me what he could.

I pulled a pen from my purse and started working numbers. If I got my job back at the Rusty Bucket in LA, and also managed to get a few shifts as a hygienist down there, it could work.

And, moving would provide a workable explanation for leaving Dr. Call's practice. Dr. Fosback might even have some open shifts. He'd take me back in a minute; I was sure of it.

LA was looking more and more like the solution to my money problems.

My phone said two in the afternoon. I pulled up Dr. Fosback's number and dialed.

Fifteen minutes later, I fist-pumped the air as I hung up.

He said he could get me up to eighteen hours a week in his practice, and maybe more later.

I could do this. I had to do this.

My clothes went into garbage bags as fast as I could fill them. In an hour, my car was filled to the brim. Not everything would fit, so I left some winter things in the closet.

I swept the jewelry on my bathroom counter into a plastic bag to keep from losing any of it. Then I remembered the heart-shaped, solid gold pendant my ex-boyfriend, Todd, had given me before he'd disappeared.

After Benji, I'd gone back to wearing it on occasion. It was pretty, but stupid, with a Klingon love quote on the back. It was heavy, so I planned to melt it down and make a proper gold ring and a pair of earrings, maybe two, when I got the chance. If I had to, I could sell it for the gold. I laughed to myself—my financial life preserver of last resort. I added the pendant to my makeshift jewelry bag and toted it, along with my bathroom items, to the car.

I put my key under the mat and pointed the car south on the freeway. My legs were jittery as I dialed my bartending buddy Lillian.

"Hey, what's up?" she answered.

"Lil, I've gotta leave town. You can have my shifts, if you want them."

"Sure, I could use the hours. How long will you be gone?"

I spit out the truth. "A long time."

"Why?"

I ignored the question for the moment. "I'll call Tony and tell him I can't come back, but I'm also calling about my place. You were interested in my couch last time you were over."

"Yeah."

"The key's under the mat. Take the couch and any of the other furniture you want. Could you do me a big favor and box up and send me the clothes that are left in the closet? But you gotta do it in the next three days, and you can't tell anyone where I went."

"Brittney, what's going on?"

"I'm getting kicked out of my apartment because of Benji, so I'm getting as far away as I can. And I don't want him finding me."

"I'm sorry about the apartment. Randy and I can go over Thursday night and get your stuff. Is that soon enough?"

"That's great. Thanks, Lil."

"Are you sure you're doing the right thing? I mean, just up and leaving?"

"It's the only thing I *can* do."

"What about a restraining order or something?"

She meant well, bringing up alternatives.

"That would cost money, and I don't think it would work with him. He's just crazy." I was too embarrassed to admit I'd also lost my job because of him.

"Where are you going?"

I kept my answer vague. "LA."

"Call when you get settled and let me know you're okay. I need an address to send your stuff anyway."

"I will, and thanks," I answered.

A bit later, I turned onto route 152 toward Interstate 5, which would get me into the LA basin in six hours, give or take.

Heading south on the interstate, I couldn't get past the feeling I'd forgotten something. When I finally figured it out, it was too late to turn around.

I redialed Lillian and asked her to add the contents of my desk to the care package she was sending me.

CHAPTER 5

ZACK

ALL DAY AT WORK, I'D ONLY WANTED TO GET BACK TO MY project.

This restoration kept me grounded. I was expending real sweat, creating something that would last. Working with Dad, nothing lasted. Each price negotiation gave way to the next, and would be forgotten a week later. No PR plan had any lasting impact. I couldn't point to a single lasting thing I'd done in the past year at Benson Corp.—nothing that was visible now. Nothing I'd accomplished withstood the tyranny of time. Swankstead was a win this week but would be forgotten with next week's impending deal.

I wanted something solid, something I could point to and say I fucking *did* that. I fucking *made* that.

"Fuck," I hissed as the section of floor I pried up splintered and hit me on the forehead. My safety glasses protected my eyes, and at least my glove came back without blood on it as I wiped my brow. Even more care was required on this section, with particularly difficult glue holding the stupid laminate to the beautiful oak below.

A glint of light caught my eye from next door. After a look out the window showed the neighboring house still shrouded in darkness, I refocused on the flooring.

A minute later I saw it again, upstairs this time.

Those good-for-nothing kids were back. Four of them had come by with apology letters to retrieve their phones earlier this evening—the three girls and one of the boys. The girls had come by in a group, likely too scared to approach the crazy man alone.

I stretched my legs after getting up and unclipped my knee pads. With my flashlight, I went out my back door and slid sideways through the hole in the fence and up to the back door of the old Victorian next to mine.

There wasn't any music tonight to mask my approach, so I climbed the stairs slowly. This might have been avoided if I'd stopped at Home Depot after work to get a new deadbolt for the door as I'd originally planned. Unfortunately, my father's words had rattled around in my head all day, crowding out my rational plans. In short, I'd forgotten.

I'd also neglected to put fresh batteries in the flashlight, and it was almost useless, emitting only a dim yellow glow.

The back door to the abandoned house opened with a squeak. I paused. Footfalls came from the second floor. Walking softly, I made my way to the stairs and started up.

"I warned you," I called.

The sound of scurrying came from above, but no voice accompanied it.

If this was Piss Boy again, I was going to drop-kick him across the street.

At the top of the stairs, I stepped over a garbage bag on the landing. I turned right down the hallway.

Then it happened.

The kid came from behind a door, kicked me in the shins, and sprayed me with pepper spray. My lips burned and my nose stung, but the safety glasses I still wore protected my eyes. I dropped the flashlight as I grabbed my injured leg.

He came at me again in the darkness.

I grabbed his hand and twisted it, wrenching the can loose from his grasp. I pointed it back at my attacker, giving him a long spray in the face.

He fell back, hands to his face, and let out a blood-curdling scream.

A woman's scream.

I picked up the flashlight. It was a woman all right, and not one of those teenagers.

She moaned and writhed on the floor.

I dodged a kick.

"Get the fuck out before I call the cops," I yelled. My lungs burned from the acrid mist.

"*You* get the fuck out. This is my house." The voice was oddly familiar. She moaned and rubbed at her closed eyes.

"Brittney?" I asked incredulously.

It was Brittney Spear, a vision from my past.

~

BRITTNEY

MY EYES CLAMPED SHUT WITH THE SEARING PAIN. IT WAS LIKE getting a hundred bee stings on my eyeballs. I rubbed them with my fists, but it did nothing to relieve the excruciating burning.

"Brittney?" the asshole asked, no longer yelling.

I kicked at him but missed.

"Stop that. It's Zack…Zack Benson."

I struggled to my knees. The voice came back to me in a rush. I couldn't believe it. Zack Benson, of all people. I tried for a deep breath and the burn made me regret it.

He pulled me up to standing. "I have to get you next door."

He wasn't making any sense. None of this made any sense.

Even shallow breathing stung. "I'm not leaving."

"Bullshit. The quicker we get this crap off you, the better." He picked me up, and I was over his shoulder the next second.

My eyes were on fire, and I couldn't open them. I beat on his back with no effect. "Put me down."

I bounced on his shoulder as he must have been carrying me downstairs. Every step hurt my stomach. I kept pounding on him.

"Put me down," I screeched again.

"Stop your bitching, for once."

"I can walk," I insisted, even though my lungs burned and I couldn't pry my eyes open one bit.

"Shut up. This is safer."

I gave in and stopped fighting. I heard the door opening, and the next second we were going down what must have been the front steps, then after a moment up another set of stairs before he stopped to open a door.

Finally, I could breathe without each inhale bringing flaming pain to my lungs.

A few moments later he set me down.

I tried to pry open my eyes, but they stung too much. I clung to his arm to steady myself.

"Give me your phone," he demanded.

I didn't have it. "I dropped it."

"Arms up so I can get your shirt off."

I'd wished to hear those words from him years ago, but not now. "No way."

"Stop being a baby. You're going into the shower clothed or not. Your choice."

I lifted my arms, and he pulled my shirt over my head. He guided my hand to what felt like tile.

"Hold on to the counter. Don't move. I'm going to untie your shoes."

He finished one shoe, urged my foot up, and slipped the sneaker off, followed by the other.

My eyes still burned and remained welded shut. Being

undressed like this without being able to see was the oddest feeling.

He pulled down my jeans, but thankfully left my underwear and bra.

I heard the water start.

"It's a tub shower. Step up and over." He held my forearm and guided my foot into place.

I completed the rest of the climb into the tub and braced myself against the far wall.

The showerhead started to spit, and the warm spray hit me.

"Get it off your face and out of your hair first," he commanded.

Inching closer to the shower, I let the water cascade over me. The acrid taste and smell around me slowly dissipated.

"Hold out your hand. Here's some shampoo."

I did, and I felt the cool gel fill my palm.

"Make sure to wash your hands as well. You don't want to rub your eyes and get it back in there."

I worked the shampoo into my hair, rinsed, and then blinked into the spraying water, slowly ridding my eyeballs of the vicious chemical.

"I'm putting your clothes in the wash. I'll be right back."

Slowly, the water cleared my eyes, and I could see enough to clean myself off. The shower curtain was closed. I pulled it aside and peeked around an old bathroom with a pink pedestal sink and pink tile halfway up the wall—very un-Zack. None of this made any sense. The door started to open, and I ducked behind the curtain again.

"Clean clothes are on the sink. I need to rinse off, too, so hurry up, unless you want me to join you."

I heard the door close. Turning off the water, I stripped off my wet underwear. After toweling off, I stepped into the hip-hugger panties he'd provided. They fit, but the bra was more than a cup size too big, so I skipped it and donned the sweatpants and sweat-shirt in the pile.

"You stock women's underwear?" I yelled.

"Don't ask," came back from the hallway.

I didn't ask anything further. I probably didn't want to know how many drunken women had left parts of their wardrobe here after a night with Zack. I'd missed a sock after one night out, but never lost track of my panties.

I grabbed the brush beside the sink.

As I opened the door, he said, "Wait in the room across the hall while I rinse off. Then we can talk."

I went across the hall and sat on the bed. I should have closed the door.

He walked past and into the bathroom—buck naked.

When I saw him, I couldn't look away, or I didn't want to. The sight of him after all these years halted my breathing.

The man was even more muscled than when I'd known him before, and in high school I'd thought he was the epitome of buff. His shoulders were even broader now, and I couldn't help noticing the back muscles that tapered down to that tight ass and powerful legs. Also, his dangly parts were on full display. The man was Adonis in the flesh, and I couldn't help but look—stare, really.

I shook my head and closed my eyes tight. It was a sight I wasn't going to unsee anytime soon. All the memories of afternoons with him and my brother, Doug, came rushing back. I'd hung out with my brother a lot, just to be near Zack—just to hear him talk, and to imagine what it would be like if he noticed me as a girl instead of merely Doug's twin sister.

The door closed, and the shower started.

I pulled the brush through my hair.

This evening had been such an emotional roller-coaster. When I first drove up, I was elated to see Grams's house again. But when I located the hidden key in the planter and opened the front door, I found the lights didn't work. It made total sense, in retrospect, that the utilities would be turned off after her death, but it hadn't occurred to me on the drive here.

I'm such an imbecile. Of course the house isn't as I remember it.

When I'd heard the intruder, I'd prepared to defend myself and thought my day couldn't get any worse. But having the pepper spray turned on me had proven that thought false and become the new low point of a completely shitty day.

Now I was sitting on a bed, having just seen my teenage dreamboat naked, waiting to talk to him after all these years. Zack Benson—I mean, how lucky could a girl get? I should have taken him up on his offer to join me in the shower. How sexy would that be?

Get real, girl.

He wasn't into me then, and it could only be worse now. I'd just kicked him and pepper-sprayed him.

I kept brushing my hair.

The water stopped, and a minute later Zack emerged from the bathroom with a towel around his waist. He ran a hand through the mane of sandy blond hair that was now darker for being wet. The slight bulge in the front of his towel had me imagining the magnificent man parts I'd seen minutes earlier.

I looked up, and his smirk indicated he'd caught me staring. I looked away, but couldn't control the heat in my cheeks. I heard him pad off down the hall, followed by the closing of a door.

A minute later he returned in a pair of jeans and T-shirt. He took a seat in the chair across from the bed. His deep blue eyes bored into me.

I handed him the brush.

He ran it over his scalp. "Thanks."

I couldn't help but admire his arms as he pulled the brush through his hair.

He handed it back to me. "Now you can tell me what you were doing sneaking around that old place." His words came out cold and accusatory.

"I told you, it's my place—well, me and Samantha. We own it now."

"Bull," was his one-word answer.

"Our grandmother left it to us when she died last year."

Surprise wrote itself across his face. "Wilma Gossnet was your grandmother?"

"Duh."

His voice hitched. "I'm sorry to hear that. I had no idea. When I bought this place six months ago, they told me she lived in Seattle. I've been chasing kids out of there lately trying to keep them from destroying it."

"You could have said who you were."

"I didn't hear you announce yourself," he shot back. "And I'm the one who's been keeping the place from getting any more trashed than it already is."

I stood. "I need to unload my car and get my stuff in the house. I've got work tomorrow."

"No," he said curtly.

"I beg your pardon."

He blocked my path to the door. "Is your car the gray one out front?"

I nodded. "Yeah."

He pulled my car keys from his pocket. He'd obviously gotten them from my pants. "Stay here, and I'll bring your stuff up."

"No way." I was unsuccessful in grabbing for my keys. "I'm staying in my own house, thank you very much."

He stepped toward me. "No. You're not. It's not safe. No electricity, no water, and no locks. You're staying here with me until it gets fixed up, and no arguments."

I hated the news, but his concern for my wellbeing warmed me.

"Bossy much?" I complained, although the thought of not having any water or a working toilet in the house had me happy to accept his offer to stay—at least until I got the utilities turned on.

"No. Just practical. Doug would kill me if I let anything happen to you."

He was probably right about that. He'd phrased it as though he was doing this for Doug, but his look gave me hope—for the first time ever—that he was doing it for me.

He pulled out a set of keys and worked one off the ring. "Here's a key to this house. You're staying here for now."

I took the key. "My purse is in the other house, in the kitchen." I followed him to the door.

He left down the hallway. "Stay here, Sunshine. I'll get it."

It was the first time I'd heard that name in years. I couldn't help but smile. Watching his tight ass walk away down the hall, I couldn't believe this turn of events. I'd crushed on Zack forever growing up, but he'd never noticed. He'd never asked me out, or given any indication that he cared to.

But tonight, that nickname gave me hope.

CHAPTER 6

ZACK

I BOUNDED DOWN THE STAIRS AND OVER TO THE HOUSE I WOULD now have to think of as Brittney's. Seeing her again had been a surprise of the tenth order. She'd moved out of state, and then to San Jose, and to hear Doug tell it, she was *never, ever* coming back.

The odor of the pepper spray in her house wasn't as obnoxious as it had been, but was still noticeable. I located her purse and, using my phone's flashlight, looked around for anything else she might have left. Finding nothing, I locked up and started carrying bags of things from her car to my house.

I noticed Piss Boy walking down the other side of the street. He watched as I pulled a bag of Brittney's belongings from her car.

Each trip back up the stairs with bags, to the room I'd put her in, brought back memories.

She smiled as I deposited another load. "Zack, you don't have to bring them all in."

Her smile now was even more gorgeous than when I'd first given her the Sunshine moniker in middle school. With every trip,

I noticed the curves under the sweatshirt that covered her delectable body. She'd had perky tits back then, and they looked even fuller now, begging to be held, fondled, and sucked.

The memory of her soft skin, and the mounds of her tits spilling out over the top of her bra as I'd undressed her in the bathroom a short time ago tortured me. It had taken monumental willpower to not unclasp the bra, pull down the panties, and take in the full sight of her. The girl had become a woman with true beauty.

"You don't have to," she repeated.

"Yes, I do—no telling what would happen to them if I didn't. This isn't the best neighborhood."

I didn't trust Piss Boy to leave the car alone overnight. But why bother her with details of our prior altercation? I headed downstairs for another load.

As kids, Doug and I had hung out together. And almost no matter what Doug and I had going on, Brittney would tag along. She had been a constant source of temptation, a lure I had to avoid. Rule Number One: you don't touch your best friend's sister. Rule Number Two: leave the country if you already broke Rule Number One. Neither of the rules said I couldn't think about touching her, though, and I'd done a lot of that in the past.

I'd spent many a night envisioning a lot more than touching her. I'd planned how I would kiss her, and yes, how we would do all the dirty things boys and girls did together. But all that was just mental exercise—most often while pumping my dick in the shower and releasing my pent-up frustration at the rules.

Doug never had any idea of my lurid thoughts about his twin sister, and good thing, because he would have beaten me to a pulp, or we would have bloodied each other up while he tried. I had two inches on him back then, but it probably wouldn't have made up for the fierceness he'd have brought against anybody who messed with Brittney—even me. Probably especially me.

I brought another bag up the stairs to her room, along with her lone suitcase. "I left some of it downstairs until you get this put away."

"I won't be putting it away." She turned and piled the last bag on top of the others. "I'll get the utilities turned on and move in tomorrow."

The bag fell, and she leaned down to pick it up, poking her ass out—one of the positions I'd always imagined for us.

I blinked back that image, went to her, and turned her around. That was a mistake. The electric shock of touching her, even clothed, was more than I'd bargained for. I wasn't ready for the heat of that touch.

"What?" she asked.

I backed away. "Not until I get a chance to fix the locks. You said you have work tomorrow. What time?"

"Eight."

I backed into the hallway. "I have work tomorrow as well. We'll talk about a plan tomorrow evening, then. You're staying here until the house is safe and the utilities are on."

A slight smile appeared. "How can I thank you, Zack?"

"I'll think of something." The words escaped before I realized the innuendo involved.

Her grin grew. She hadn't missed it.

"See you in the morning, Sunshine." I escaped to the stairs to move the laundry to the dryer before heading to bed.

"Good night, Zack" she called.

It had been a good night—not the pepper-spray incident, but what had followed. That hadn't been the way I would have imagined me undressing her, but the sight of her almost naked had been burned into my brain. I wasn't letting go anytime soon. For a sight like that, I had a photographic memory.

Downstairs, I moved the wet clothes to the dryer and started it. Closing my eyes for a moment, my skin heated and my cock surged. I saw her in front of me again...felt her skin as I raised the shirt over her head, putting me face-to-face with her cleavage— cleavage I wanted to nestle my face in.

I repositioned my swollen dick in my pants and took a deep breath before heading back upstairs.

Inviting her to stay here had been the right thing to do—the only thing, under the circumstances. But life would be a whole lot more complicated after tonight.

Living next to Brittney was going to be pleasure and torture all wrapped together. A constant temptation, but one I could manage. I could envision Friday night pizza and a movie with her—no, make that Thursday night, just like we'd done as teenagers, the three of us.

Only now it would be just the two of us, without Doug to keep us apart.

Complicated *is not nearly a strong enough word.*

CHAPTER 7

BRITTNEY

I WOKE UP EARLY WEDNESDAY MORNING. MORE CORRECTLY, I RE-woke for the umpteenth time since trying to fall asleep. The sky had started to brighten outside, and the sheer curtains wouldn't allow even an attempt at further sleep with the sun up. Between memories of Benji's harassment, thoughts of Zack's kindness had bounced my emotions from one extreme to the other, so sleep had come in fits and starts.

Rolling out of bed, I slipped into the sweats Zack had provided last night and a pair of black work shoes from my suitcase.

The house was quiet as I descended the stairs.

Last night, I hadn't seen anything of the downstairs, and I was surprised to find the first two rooms with construction debris and torn-up floors. One of the rooms had a wall out down to the studs. This place was a disaster zone. Passing through plastic sheeting covering a doorway, I found two rooms in back without any of the destruction of the other rooms: a room with a TV and the kitchen. A check of the fridge yielded the normal bachelor-living-alone situation: no veggies, a package of hot dogs, some containers that looked like leftover Chinese, beer and soda cans, bottles of wine, and an egg carton with one egg in it, but no milk.

I closed the fridge and checked the small pantry. Nothing worthwhile for breakfast in there except some protein bars and coffee.

After a return trip upstairs to grab my purse, I let myself out the front door. I'd passed a grocery store a few blocks from here, so I climbed into my trusty little car for a quick shopping trip.

My first order of business was the restroom in the store. I hadn't wanted to wake Zack at this ungodly hour by flushing in his house. Although Doug hadn't minded peeing and not flushing, it wasn't my style.

With that out of the way, I started filling my hand-held basket with real food. Dodging the early-morning employees restocking shelves, I needed a while to find everything in the unfamiliar layout.

At the checkout lane, I added an energy drink for later.

The elderly lady in front of me was counting out coins to pay for her apple, a dozen eggs, and three cans of cat food.

The cashier looked on nervously as she fumbled in her coin purse to come up with enough.

After pushing the coins around on the counter she glanced back at the screen and her face dropped even further as she recounted her coins. "Maybe if we take off one of the cans," she suggested to the cashier.

My stomach clenched for her. I fished two quarters out of my purse and placed them on the counter. "Please, allow me."

She turned to me with teary eyes. "I'm sure I've got it in here somewhere." She fumbled through her purse again.

"I insist," I said, pushing the coins forward. "I know how much our cats mean to us. I have one too."

I'd never had a cat. But I'd known people who had, and that was close enough.

She blinked back tears. "Thank you so much, dear."

The cashier swept up the coins and returned a nickel to her.

When it was my turn to pay, a few measly fives and a twenty stared back at me from my wallet, so I used my Visa. As I exited the store with my bag, the sunrise lifted my mood. Today was a new day, a new beginning. Benji and San Jose were behind me. LA and my new neighbor Zack, of all people, were ahead of me.

The thought made me grin—my neighbor Zack. I'd noticed the kitchen windows of the houses faced each other. With some luck, I'd get a glimpse of him eating his Wheaties or whatever every morning. I envisioned myself waving to him through the glass, and him smiling when he noticed me and waving back.

After closing the car door, I pulled mascara out of my purse and used the visor mirror. A few strokes before starting back to Zack's place wouldn't hurt.

~

Zack

I LISTENED FOR A MOMENT BEFORE ROLLING OUT OF BED. No noises indicated that Brittney had woken yet.

Downstairs though, I realized I'd been wrong. The aroma of bacon was unmistakable as I neared the kitchen.

The sight of her brightened my morning. Brittney was busy at the stove with her back to me. She hadn't noticed me enter as she swayed to music in her earbuds.

I noisily pulled a chair out at the table and sat.

"Breakfast is almost ready," she said as she turned to see me.

"My breakfast is just a protein bar or a Hot Pocket."

"No way." She waved the spatula at me. "Breakfast is the most important meal of the day." She turned back to the stove. "I didn't know what you liked, so I kept it simple. I've got French toast and bacon."

"Just a breakfast bar is fine."

She ignored my comment. "If you don't like the French toast, I can scramble some eggs."

I went to the pantry and pulled out two bars, tore off paper towel sections for napkins, and returned to the table.

Brittney arrived with two aromatic plates of breakfast, added bowls of raspberries, and took a seat across from me.

I lifted a bar, ready to open it.

She fixed me with a glare. "Don't you dare insult the cook."

I stopped. "Now who's being bossy?"

"You provided the roof. I'm providing the food. Now grow up, eat it, and stop complaining."

This sassiness was an adorable new side of Brittney.

I put the bar down, trying not to show a grin, and bit off a piece of bacon. The taste was perfect.

"Thank you. You didn't have to."

The warm smile she offered was as contagious as I remembered from before.

"You're welcome. I wanted to. And from the look of your refrigerator, I could tell you needed a regular meal."

I drizzled a little maple syrup over the French toast. "I eat out a lot."

"That's not healthy."

"Who are you? My mother?" I asked, suddenly annoyed.

She stared at me as I cut into my French toast. The corner of her mouth turned up ever so slightly. She thought she'd won.

The French toast melted in my mouth. "This is good," I mumbled, chewing.

She started in on hers.

"Long drive down from San Jose?" I asked between bites.

She rolled her eyes. "I've never seen so many trucks on the road, and there was an accident with a car fire on the Grapevine that took forever to get past."

I took a guess. "You must have started late."

She finished chewing before her answer. "A little after three, I guess."

"Had to skip dinner?"

"Yeah, I wanted to get here before it was too late."

"Why didn't you start earlier?"

She looked down at her plate and shrugged. Instead of answering, she filled her mouth with berries.

I didn't pursue it, but finished my bacon and French toast in silence. I glanced up at her after my last forkful, and for just a second imagined how those pouty lips would taste. Would I be able to separate the taste of her from the maple syrup and bacon? I settled on yes.

"What are you smirking about?" she challenged with a creased brow.

"Nothing."

Her fork came up and pointed at me.

"You suck as a liar, Zachary Benson."

I got up to leave before I painted myself into an inescapable corner. "I was just admiring...what a good cook you are."

Honesty was not the best policy here.

"You didn't eat your berries."

I took my plate to the sink, unable to look at her for fear she'd see right through me.

"I'm not a big fruit person." At least we'd changed the subject.

"You need fruit. Sit down and eat or I'll be insulted."

I took my seat again. "Well, we can't have that." I didn't dislike all fruit. Apples were okay. I spooned some of the tart, red berries into my mouth.

"I forgot to ask, where are you working?"

I forced another spoonful before answering, but the real reason for my delay was that smile.

"I'm part of the Benson Corp. team."

"How is working for your dad?"

I glanced at my watch and stood. "I'll take the first shower, if that's okay. I have to get to the office. Call me if you need anything."

"Not until you finish those berries."

"I've had enough." In my terms, three spoonfuls had been two too many.

"Don't be a baby."

I didn't sit, but I did force another spoonful.

"To call you, I'll need your number."

I held out my hand. "Give me your phone."

She handed it over.

I added myself as a contact and sent myself a text, so I'd have her number as well.

She followed me to the sink with her plate and bowl.

I felt that same electric shock as her arm brushed against mine, and I pulled away. Distance from temptation is what I needed.

She was rinsing the dishes when I looked back before exiting the kitchen. Her ass from this perspective was perfect, too perfect.

"Don't use all the hot water," she called as I mounted the stairs.

∼

BRITTNEY

HE'D GIVEN IN PRETTY QUICKLY FOR A MAN WHO CLAIMED HE didn't eat fruit. Whatever his problem was, I intended to fix it. Good nutrition was the bedrock of good health. Everybody knew that. Even if the seeds were hard to get out from between your teeth.

Cleaning the dishes, I mulled over my plan for the day. Dr. Fosback was first on my to-do list. Getting on his schedule quickly was imperative, and Dr. Fosback had always been good to work for. With some coaxing I might even get a few extra days out of him.

Back upstairs, I took my turn in the bathroom once Zack had finished.

Last night I hadn't realized how quaintly cute it was with the pink tile and vintage world-map wallpaper above that. The free-standing linen cabinet, dressing chair, and antique brass fixtures gave the room real character, like the grand old lady this house had once been.

I pulled out a cleaning wipe and removed my mascara—Dr. Fosback didn't allow hygienists to wear makeup—allergy avoidance, he'd once explained. Stepping into the tub, I pulled the curtain, adjusted the water, and smiled to myself—Zack liked my cooking.

MY FAVORITE PARKING SPOT IN THE FAR CORNER BEHIND DR. Fosback's practice was empty when I arrived. I checked my ponytail in the mirror. It didn't look tight enough, so I redid it—professional job, professional appearance.

Inside, Martha was at reception, just as she'd always been. "Brittney, it's so great to see you. How have you been?'

"Good, thanks."

"I couldn't believe it yesterday when Darren said you were coming back. I thought you'd left us for good."

She had worked with Dr. Fosback forever and was the only one who got away with calling him by his first name.

"I've had enough of San Jose. Is he in yet?"

"Yeah, you know the way."

I let myself in past waiting and found Dr. Fosback all the way in the back.

"Brittney Spear, look at you, pretty as ever." He greeted me with the same firm handshake he always had.

"It's Clark now," I corrected him.

"Married? Good for you."

"Not anymore, but I'm keeping the name. It was difficult always getting mistaken for the pop princess."

The marriage assumption was a common one. I hadn't gotten married, or divorced, but nobody here needed to know the real reason for my name change. Anonymity meant safety.

"Sorry to hear that. Anyway, I wasn't expecting you so soon."

"I left as soon as we got off the phone."

His brow dropped slightly. "Well, when I said I could fit you in a few days a week, I didn't mean this week. I was thinking more when Sandy goes out on maternity."

I forced as much of a smile as I could muster. "Oh. Well then... In the meantime, I'm available to fill in if any of the girls needs to take a day off."

This was bad news for my bank account, and it wasn't the sense I'd gotten from him on the phone yesterday.

"Sure thing. Why don't you get the paperwork started with Martha, and we'll be in touch as soon as anything opens up."

"It's great to see you again, Doctor," I said as I backed toward reception.

He nodded. "You too, Brittney." He went back to the patient record he'd been reviewing.

I found Martha out front and took the spare seat. "Dr. Fosback said to do paperwork with you."

She pulled a file folder from under some others. "I made this up yesterday. Did you bring your hygienist license?"

"Sure." I retrieved the folded paper from my purse and handed it over.

She read the name, and then eyed my ring finger before taking the paper back to the copier.

The first form in the folder was an I-9 for me to fill out, followed by a W-4. I handed over my driver's license.

Martha copied my ID. "Name change, I see," she said, glancing up.

"It didn't work out." I didn't say any more. She could work out the implication without me having to lie.

"Good for you. Better to cut your losses soon if it isn't going to work in the long run. I learned that the hard way."

I nodded.

"The government needs a second form of ID these days as well."

I mentally kicked myself for leaving everything behind. "My papers are with the things being shipped. Can it wait a few days?"

"Sure, bring it in when your things arrive. You'll need your marriage license too for the name change." She handed me an employment application.

. "Do I really need to do this one?" I took the application and didn't correct her about the marriage license. I had the Arkansas court order for my name change coming.

"Yeah, you never know. You might have been convicted of a felony or something since you last worked here." She laughed.

"Goodness, no," I said.

I worked through the forms slowly and tried not to show my concern. I pulled up the address and phone number for Dr. Call's practice on my phone as I filled out the employment history. It was a complication I hadn't anticipated. I hadn't broached the subject of my suspension with Dr. Fosback on the phone yesterday. I hadn't thought it would come up. I was moving back into town, and I'd had to leave Dr. Call's practice—it should be as simple as that. My hand shook as I wrote *moving* in the column labeled *reason for leaving*. I did the same for the Pink Pig entry.

As I continued through the form, my phone vibrated with an incoming call.

"Do you need to take that?" she asked.

Seeing Benji's name on the screen made for an easy decision. "Nah. It can wait." I sent the call to voicemail, then turned it off. I had no desire to be interrupted again by Benji, and that's exactly what he would do—call three times in a row before giving up.

"Dr. Fosback mentioned that Sandy would be going on maternity leave soon," I said.

Martha looked up. "She should be taking it easy, if you ask me. Girls these days seem to want to work right up until the end, without any thought of the baby. Becoming a mother is a job in itself."

"I agree. Sooner is better. She should think about the baby. Is it a boy or a girl?"

"Twins, one of each, I think. You're a twin, aren't you?"

I knew the situation well. "That's right. Mom said we were hell on wheels for a few years."

"Don't tell her that. She's nervous enough as it is."

I laughed. "Got it. Growing up a twin was a great experience. You can tell her that."

"I will. At least she'll have an easier delivery. My first was nine pounds twelve ounces."

I didn't want to get into the difficult delivery discussion she'd had with me more than once. "When is she due to go out?"

Martha checked her calendar. "In about two."

"Two weeks? She is getting close."

"No, dear. Two months."

I couldn't keep my shoulders from slumping. That wasn't the news I'd expected.

Back in my car, I leaned my head against the steering wheel and tried not to cry. I had to be strong for Samantha and power through this rough patch. Two months, though, was more than a rough patch. I pulled out my ponytail, started the car, and turned it toward home. My grandmother's dark house was now my home, my only place to call home.

The low fuel light came on, and I turned into the gas station two blocks down. A twenty and two fives stared back at me from my wallet. I marched one of the small bills into the mini-mart and handed it to the cashier. "Five on three please."

She nodded without a word, and I pumped the tiny amount of fuel into my tank.

Two months would be an eternity to go without hygienist pay. Hopefully the Rusty Bucket would come through with lots of hours.

After the short drive back to Zack's house, I let myself in with the key he'd provided and pulled a Pepsi from the fridge. I'd have to add diet to my shopping list for next time.

It took a moment to locate the number for LA's department of water and power, but the nice lady there was happy to take my credit card number for the turn-on deposit. She told me to expect technicians for the water and electric by the end of the day. Unfortunately, without any time frame, I was stuck here until they came.

That meant no visit to the Rusty Bucket this afternoon to talk to Max about getting my old job back. But first things first, I needed the utilities turned on as quickly as possible.

I hadn't shopped for lunch fixings, so I set about frying eggs and toasting English muffins for an early lunch.

After eating, I started pulling things out of the pantry and putting them on the table to restock in a proper order. The box of protein bars fell over and knocked my purse to the floor.

I knelt, and the second thing I picked up was my pink penance envelope—the one with the reminder of the worst stage of my life, the reminder to be a better person in the future and not let others down. I replaced it in my purse without opening it to read again.

One by one, I replaced the pantry items in a sensible order.

When I turned, the pink envelope still peeked out of my purse. I pushed it to the bottom. Things were shitty enough. I didn't need to torture myself that way today.

CHAPTER 8

Zack

With every ding and ratchet upward of the red numerals, I moved farther from where I wanted to be.

The elevator door opened, and I straightened my mandatory tie.

Wendy checked her watch as I approached.

"Let me guess. Stanton again? Did you give him my message?" I asked.

I'd instructed her last night to tell him I didn't want to discuss irrelevant items going forward.

"Yes, yes, and he assured me these were important."

"Yeah, right."

It was getting late in London, at least by Stanton's standards, but I still went to fetch coffee for Wendy and me. "Decaf?"

"Regular," she responded.

Returning, I put the mocha down on the coaster she used to protect the elegant mahogany of her desk—the perk of being an executive's PA.

She pulled out a sweetener packet from her drawer. She

insisted on Stevia, which wasn't stocked at the coffee machine. "Thank you."

"If Brittney Spear calls at any time, put her right through, or hunt me down if I'm out and about."

"The singer?"

"No, just Spear—no *S* on the end."

"Brittney, huh?" Her eyebrow arched with an unasked question.

"It's just in case she calls, but she probably won't. She moved back to town, and I promised her brother, I'd help her if she needed it."

"Right." She stirred her coffee with a smirk. "Hunt you down. I'll definitely do that."

I had just dispensed with London and Rome when Wendy popped her head in. "Harold is here to see you."

"Sure," I responded.

Harold Synderman, our company CFO, let himself in and closed the door. "I guess it's my turn now."

"I guess." We'd previously discussed my father's view that we Benson children should be rotated through several departments in the company to *broaden* our exposure.

Harold understood that his role in this was to provide a position and training at the appointed time, whether he needed us or not.

He unbuttoned his coat and sat. "I know finance is not anybody's first choice."

"I'm not sure it's the right time."

Harold thought the rotations were a good idea, and he seemed to view it as his place to encourage the reluctant among us to see the light. But I wasn't in the mood to discuss it this morning. Many people in the company would relent quickly in an argument with me, but not Harold. He was confident enough in his position and his relationship with my father that the family name didn't sway him. For that, I was grateful—on occasion. It allowed me to bounce ideas off him with a rigorous testing of my position, but not this morning.

"You know the opportunity Lloyd is providing for you is one of a kind." He lowered his voice. "The experience will be valuable. On top of that, London is an exciting city."

"Like I said, the timing might not be right. I'll need to give it some thought."

He rose. "Well, you do that. Decisions like this are important, but you know he'll expect an answer soon." He buttoned his coat.

"I know."

After he left, I turned toward the window to think. I took out my keys and fingered the attached coin he'd given me.

Dad wanted me—no, expected me—to take the London assignment, then come back here to take on his next lesson. Such was my family obligation. Obligation with a capital O.

Harold had been right; the management training aspect of it was invaluable.

I turned back to my desk and got busy on tomorrow's customer presentation. Deciding later meant exactly that, *later*.

As the day progressed, the occasional call from a US-based sales guy brought my desk phone to life, but my cell stayed silent.

I double-checked that it was on and charged.

Wishing didn't make things happen.

BRITTNEY

MY PHONE RANG AS I BEGAN COLLECTING MY BAGS OF CLOTHES IN the room upstairs at Zack's place. The screen said Darth Vader, and I had no idea who that was. I sent it to voicemail, but it rang again, and I gave in.

"Hello?"

"Wanna have lunch?" Zack asked.

The mere sound of his voice lightened my mood. He must have

named himself Darth Vader when he'd put in his contact information this morning.

"Sorry, I already made myself something, and I have to wait for the DWP guys anyway to get the water and power back on. They wouldn't give me anything more definite than sometime today."

"Oh…then dinner."

"I can take care of myself, you know."

"If you're going to be snotty about it, forget it." He hung up on me.

He was right. I needed to control my urge to talk back. Today he was the one friendly face in town, and I'd just been bitchy to him.

I returned his call. "I'm sorry. I'd love to have dinner with you."

"Great. I'll get off early. How does Cardinelli's sound to you?"

"Way too expensive. I can't afford that. Taco Bell is even stretching it on my budget these days."

"Forget that. I'm paying, and no complaints. I'll be back around five."

"I can't let you do that. Taco Bell, and I'm paying my share."

He chuckled. "You argue with me one more time, and I'm gonna have to take you over my knee."

He had no idea what that threat did to me. I couldn't count the number of times I'd envisioned his hand on my bare bottom, and if I had to go over his knee to get it, fine.

I swallowed. "I'll be good, but just this once."

"What are you doing to stay busy this afternoon?"

"Just doing my nails and watching a few soaps." I hung up before he had a chance to say anything.

The phone rang again, as if on cue.

"Can't you be serious for a change?"

"Well, you deserve it. You called me snotty."

We both hung on the line in silence, daring the other to say something.

I broke down first. "I'm actually going to take my things over to the house while I wait for the DWP guys to show up."

"I'd be careful about that, if I were you."

"Why? It's my house now."

"I'm just worried for you."

The sentiment warmed me. I'd always wished he'd care about me, and worry was close enough for today.

"I can handle a few bags of clothes."

"It's not the bags I'm worried about."

"What then?"

"The spiders," he said in a low tone.

I shivered at the word.

He knew I'd had severe arachnophobia ever since the bite I got in the fourth grade. It had been a black widow—a female, the kind that ate her mate after sex. Although I'd survived it, the experience had left me jumping at the sight of a spider, regardless of the type. There was no such thing as a *good* spider. I didn't trust any of them.

"You're just saying that," I shot back with false confidence.

"Take your chances, if you want. Or wait for me to get home and help you."

He was trying to scare me needlessly. That had to be it.

"Thanks. I'll manage."

"Also, the back kitchen door doesn't lock. That's how the kids got in, so I wouldn't take anything over you're not willing to lose."

Great. Now I had another thing to pay for. "Who do I call to get that fixed?"

"Nobody. I'll handle it for you."

We hung up after he admonished me again to be careful.

He didn't run my life. Nobody did.

With a purse and two bags in hand, I headed next door. I wasn't going to be scared out of making progress, but the bags I brought didn't have anything I needed for work.

I opened the door to my new *old* house with the key I'd retrieved from the planter yesterday. In the afternoon light, it looked dirtier than it had last night. Dust hung in the air, high-lighted by the streams of light sneaking around curtains that were not quite closed. The onion-like odor of the pepper spray lingered, and my airway tightened with the memory of not being able to breathe last night.

I put the bags of clothes outside on the porch and returned to open the curtains. The situation looked way worse with more light.

Cleanup would have to come first.

Three hours, three buckets of water carried from Zack's house, and four rolls of paper towels later, I was done for the day. I'd wiped down the walls and floor upstairs—which had taken the brunt of the pepper spray—worked on the stairs, and swept lightly downstairs.

Every stitch of furniture in the house needed heavy-duty cleaning. Grams hadn't been up to it in her later years, and wouldn't hear of letting a stranger in the house to touch her things.

I put away four bags of clothes upstairs and re-purposed the bags to hold the miscellaneous trash that had been left around, mostly fast-food wrappers, beer cans, and the like. A receipt from a Burger King bag showed it hadn't taken the local kids long to start occupying the house after Grams died.

The pantry still had miscellaneous spices and canned foods. I added the few things that were obviously too old to the trash bags. The safe was on the floor of the pantry where it had always been. Gramps had said this was the last place a thief would never think to look. The pepper spray can found a new home next to the safe. I was probably safer without it in my purse.

The bathrooms and toilets were a disgusting hazmat situation, and not getting any better until the water was back on. The rugs were going to need a good vacuuming, and probably a proper cleaning when I could afford it. I was sure they had looked quite nice in their prime, but today they were terrible. The furniture was old, really old, but solid and in good condition.

The surprise had been the two hypodermics I found in the

corner behind the loveseat. They had to have been from after Grams died, so at least they weren't from any of my victims.

Just the thought of that made me cringe. The nightmares had only recently stopped, and I hoped this wouldn't bring them back.

I went to the front door to answer a knock.

Two guys in brown LADWP shirts were at the door. "Miss Clark?"

"Yup." I went out to greet them and get things started.

They each had a white DWP truck on the street.

I went with Jerald, the electric guy, first, and turning on the juice to the house was done in ten minutes. I thanked him and approached Ernesto, the water guy, who wore a worried expression.

He was messing around on the front lawn, looking into what must have been the water meter box.

"Something's wrong," he said.

"Like what?"

He twisted a long-handled rod. "I have to keep you shut off until you fix the leak."

"What leak?"

"No idea. You'll have to have your plumber figure that out, but your pipes aren't filling up like they should. I had the water running full blast for a good five minutes. You're not running any sprinklers that I can see, so you have some monster leak in the house. I can't turn you on until you get it fixed. Those are the rules."

I kicked the dirt. "Damn," I said. It took all my strength not to swear up a storm.

"Look, it's just the rules."

"Sorry. I didn't mean you. It's just the damned situation."

He slid the concrete cover back over the box. "When your plumber fixes the problem, call the installation number, and I'll be right back here in a flash."

"Thanks." I didn't have a plumber, and if I did, I couldn't afford to pay him.

He picked up his things and left, probably anxious to get away from the angry lady.

I trudged back up the steps and into the house. I flipped on the light switch inside the door.

Nothing.

Fuck.

I tried lights on the stairs, and in the kitchen—still nothing.

Why did everything have to go wrong? Now with bills from an electrician, as well as a plumber, and with no hygienist job, I was in even worse shape than I'd been in San Jose.

Double fuck.

I locked up and went back next door to get cleaned up. I wasn't going to dinner with Zack with this layer of dirt on me and my clothes. I sniffed the shoulder of my shirt—or this BO.

After cleaning up and dressing in clean clothes, I looked semi-presentable. I decided on a little mascara tonight.

CHAPTER 9

Zack

The weekly advertising review was running long. I checked my watch: ten till five. "Hey guys. We're cutting this short. That's all for today."

With the exception of Stan, who hadn't gotten a chance to present yet, I didn't see any disappointment around the table.

"Stan, we'll start with you next week."

He perked up and nodded.

The group gathered their papers, and the room emptied quickly.

"You're done early," Wendy noted as I returned.

I parked the papers on my desk, grabbed my coat and briefcase, and locked up. "Have a dinner meeting I have to get to."

Wendy flipped her calendar back and forth. "Sorry, I must have missed it."

I smiled. "I forgot to put it on the schedule."

She cocked an eyebrow. "Give her my regards."

I walked away without answering and waved over my shoulder.

She didn't miss a thing.

THE DRIVE HOME HAD BEEN SLOWER THAN NORMAL WITH ALL THE traffic on the roads that I normally missed. Pulling up, I parked out front instead of turning into the driveway alongside the house, which led to the garage in back. I wandered past the front room into the kitchen and found Brittney at the table, head in her hands.

"Hey, Sunshine. Ready for dinner?"

She closed her eyes and mumbled, "The house is all screwed up."

I set my briefcase down. "Come on, we're burning daylight here. I'm buying you a good meal, and you can tell me all about it. I'm a great house fixer and an even better listener."

That got a hint of a smile out of her. "But it's so bad."

"What did I tell you about causing trouble earlier? No moping allowed in this house." I rounded the table, grabbed her arm, and pulled her up.

"Hey," she complained.

"No moping, no complaining. Dinner first. After that, I'll go over and look at the house with you, and we'll make a plan."

She huffed. "But I can't afford to fix it."

"What did I just say about complaining? You can tell me all about it over dinner." I motioned to the front. "Your chariot awaits."

She stopped her mumbling, and I followed her to the front. I locked up before descending the steps.

"Which car is yours?"

"The blue one." The car still had its original Acapulco blue paint. "I call her the Snake."

She walked toward it, and her mouth dropped open as she went to the back to check out the name plate.

"You drive a Shelby?"

"They don't make 'em like this anymore."

That was an understatement. A '67 Shelby GT500 was the pinnacle of the early Mustangs, the ultimate big-block muscle car from that era—all engine and little refinement. This wasn't a sissy car with leather seats, cup holders, a million-watt stereo, and a moonroof. It was a car that took off in a squealing cloud of tire smoke if you had a heavy foot. And, I had upgraded it to Super Snake specs.

"Does Doug know you have this?" she asked.

"I got it after he left. It'll be a surprise next time he's back."

She put her hand on the roof and looked inside. "He'd kill for a car like this."

She had that right, any car nut would.

I had debated getting a Cobra roadster, but chose the GT500 with a roof and real roll bar as being more practical.

"He'll be jealous when he hears you got to ride in it before him." The car was ten-percent practical and ninety percent chick-magnet. Make that ninety-nine percent chick magnet.

Piss Boy was walking down the other side of the street, his eyes glued on either my car or my date, I couldn't tell which.

"I still need that letter if you want your phone back," I shouted.

He gave me the finger, looked away, and kept walking.

"What's that about?" Brittney asked.

"Tell you at dinner."

She tilted her head and frowned, no happier about delayed gratification than she had been growing up.

I opened the door for her. "Climb in."

I hurried around and got in myself, taking a quick glance at Piss Boy up ahead.

He looked back in our direction again, walking slowly away.

"I can't figure out how to work this seatbelt," Brittney complained.

"Here, like this." I showed her how to fasten the twin shoulder belts that went with this car—another racing heritage setup.

Since the engine was warm, the car started easily. The big V-8 roared to life and settled into a rough, burbling idle. I pulled out and headed north.

Piss Boy threw us another middle-finger salute as we passed him.

"Are you going to tell me what his problem is?"

She hadn't changed; waiting didn't suit her.

I shifted into third. "He was one of a group of kids I rousted from your house two nights ago. I took all their phones and told them they would only get them back when they brought me apology letters for breaking into your house."

Brittney laughed. "Let me guess. He's too proud?"

"More like too stupid. Anyway, I still have his phone, waiting for the punk to wise up."

She watched the road silently as we wended our way north. "Thank you."

"For what?"

"Guarding the house for me."

"The least I could do for the neighborhood. Next thing you know they'd be too drunk one night and break into my house by mistake."

I was only half joking. Letting them get away with partying in an abandoned house would only escalate to worse things later.

CHAPTER 10

Brittney

Zack pulled to the curb in front of the restaurant: Cardinelli's in Westwood.

The young valet opened the door for me.

Zack traded him the keys for a stub.

"You sure you trust him with your car? He looks a little young," I noted.

I guessed him to still be in high school.

"Tony will be careful. He knows what will happen if he dings any of the cars, and mine in particular."

"You must eat here often."

Zack guided me toward the door with a hand at the small of my back. It scorched my skin through the fabric.

My reaction to the touch surprised me.

He must've felt the heat too, as he quickly removed his hand. "Often enough."

I slowed my walk, yearning for that touch again, but he didn't provide it. I followed the couple ahead of us toward the entrance.

"This seems a little fancy. Are you sure I'm dressed well enough?"

The man ahead wore an expensive suit, and his date wore an equally elegant dress. Make that his wife, judging by the wedding band and monster diamond on her finger.

"Trust me," he said. "Your beauty will put the rest of the women in here to shame."

A blush rose in my cheeks, and I gave him a light punch to the shoulder. "Stop that. You're embarrassing me."

"The truth, the whole truth, and nothing but the truth."

My blush rose to three alarms, but I managed to hold my tongue.

"You remember Bill Covington from Brentmoor?"

It only took a second to come back to me. The Benson boys and the Covingtons had often hung out together. "Yeah, vaguely."

"He's a part owner of this place. He and Marco Cardinelli started it after school."

Naturally the rich families owned restaurants to dabble in. "Does that mean you get a discount?"

"No, but I do get a good table."

The well-dressed couple ahead of us gave the hostess their name and were told they would have to wait.

"Mr. Benson," the hostess said as we approached the stand.

Zack's status as a VIP customer was evident when she picked up menus and ushered us in without even bothering to look at her reservation list.

Mr. Expensive Suit checked his watch with a scowl.

The ceilings were high, lending the room a spacious atmosphere. White tablecloths and waiters in matching vests and trousers set this apart from any place I could afford to frequent.

As he'd predicted, the hostess stopped at a table by the window with a view up the hill. The perks of being rich.

Zack pulled my chair out for me—we were going first-class tonight—almost as if I were a girlfriend.

"Nice place."

"You deserve it, Brit."

I basked in the warmth of his smile and opened the menu. The writing was in Italian, naturally, but it was close enough to Spanish that it was possible to pick out what I wanted.

Our waiter, Vinny, arrived with bread and an olive oil-vinegar dipping plate.

Zack put down the wine menu. "Prosecco okay?"

"Sure," I said. When in Rome and all.

Zack ordered a bottle for us and bruschetta to start.

I watched his lips as he spoke, wondering what they tasted like, and what they felt like. The impure thoughts made my pulse race.

Zack set his menu down and looked at me oddly. "The house. You were going to tell me about the house."

I must have missed the question. Just the thought of the problems threatened to give me a headache. "I spent the afternoon cleaning, and I pretty much got the pepper spray cleaned off everything. Then the DWP guys showed up, and the electric guy turned on the power, but none of the lights I tried worked."

"Did you check the fuses?"

"I wouldn't even know where to start."

"No matter. I do."

Vinny interrupted us with the prosecco bottle, which he uncorked with a loud pop.

I perused the menu again while Zack approved the wine. I settled on the *ravioli alla lucana* for dinner.

Zack lifted his glass. "To getting into your new house."

I clinked my glass to his and sipped. The sentiment was nice, if a little out of reach.

Zack set his glass down. "It's probably the fuses. I can check for you when we get back. Mine have blown on occasion. These old houses weren't built with very hefty circuits."

"Thanks, but that's just the beginning." I broke off a piece of bread.

"How so?" he asked.

I dipped my bread in the oil and vinegar plate. "The water guy wouldn't turn the water on. He said there was a big leak somewhere."

Zack took some bread as well. "Did you see a leak, or hear anything?"

I had to finish chewing. "No, but I wasn't inside when he was doing it. I went through the house when I closed up and didn't see any water, but I didn't check upstairs either."

"A water leak is not good. You wouldn't want standing water on those nice floors. That's for sure something we should look at when we get back."

A knot formed in my gut at the thought that my Grams's nice house might be getting damaged as we sat here. "Is it something we should go back and check on right now?"

He waved his piece of bread. "No. It's a question of days, not minutes. We can check when we get back." He dipped his bread in the oil plate.

"But he said I have to have a plumber fix it."

He sipped his glass of bubbly. "I'm your plumber."

"But I can't—"

"We got this," he said, interrupting me. "Let's catch up over a nice meal and worry about the plumbing when we get back. What you can't do…" He pointed his finger at me. "…is obsess about it. You know I'm right."

I let out a breath. "I guess."

Vinny reappeared and took our orders.

After the waiter left, Zack leaned back in his chair. "So catch me up. What have you been up to?"

I wasn't really sure where to start, the question was so open-ended. "Nothing much. I've been up in San Jose for a few years."

He leaned forward. "And?"

"Not much, just tending bar and doing hygienist work during the day. That is, when I can get the days, the hours."

He spun his glass a bit. "Is that a problem? Getting work?"

"It was with the practice I joined. Our dentist, Dr. Call, didn't... Well, she hired enough hygienists that none of us ever got very many days. We were always trading off with one another, so I averaged two days a week, sometimes three, when what I really wanted was a full four."

"That sucks."

My feelings exactly.

"Is that why you're back down here?" he asked.

I debated giving the full answer, but chickened out. Rattling the words around in my head, they sounded pathetic, even to me. "Yeah. I want to get back to working with Dr. Fosback here in LA."

"That sounds like a good plan. That practice will give you the hours you want, right?"

"Yeah, I think. Sooner or later." I shrank down in my seat.

His eyes widened a bit, apparently sensing the deception in my answer. "You checked with them before coming back, right?"

At least my answer could be truthful. "Yeah, I called them."

"You said you had to go to his office today. How did that go? When do you start?"

Vinnie came back to the table with our salads—Caesar for him, house for me—sparing me an immediate answer.

"Doug tells me your little sister is going to business school."

Mercifully he'd changed the line of questioning.

"You two keeping in touch?" I asked, although I knew the answer.

"Yeah, we keep up." He forked a bite of salad into his mouth.

I did the same.

We were like a couple of prizefighters circling each other, cautiously looking for an opening. He was trying to get up to speed on my history, and I was trying desperately to withhold it.

"He told me you broke up with a guy that was an idiot," he said, peering over his wine glass at me.

There it was, a question about Benji. "My ex an idiot? That's the nice way to put it." Actually he was much worse.

"He's still hassling you, then?" Zack asked before taking another bite of the salad.

"What do you mean?" I asked, feigning ignorance. With a little luck I could get out of this without a full data dump.

"Doug said he was turning into a stalker." Zack took a sip of his prosecco, not taking his eyes off of me for a moment.

I regretted having opened up to Doug about that now. "A little. He's a creep."

If I'd given Doug the whole story, Benji would probably be in pieces in a landfill by now.

"You could've called me, you know."

That was the suggestion Doug had made when I told him about it.

"You were too far away." I looked down, avoiding his eyes.

"Using Dad's jet, it's only an hour. You should've called."

I looked up and appraised him.

He looked as if he meant what he'd said. He would've protected me in a heartbeat.

"One visit is all it would've taken," he said. "You should have called."

"I guess." I took another bite of salad to keep from having to say any more.

"I bet it'll be good to get back to your hygienist job right away. Doug told me how hard it's been for you to put Samantha through Wharton."

He seemed to have gotten much more detail about our lives from Doug than I'd guessed.

Vinny arrived with our dinner plates.

Mine smelled and looked as scrumptious as the menu description. The first bite was even better than the aroma.

"Like it?"

"Delicious, absolutely delicious."

I didn't have the words I needed to describe how good this

was. I should have known Zack wouldn't choose anything but the best.

"Marco—that's Bill's partner here—really does a good job."

I decided the best defense was a good offense. "You haven't told me what you've been doing."

"Same old, same old. I'm working in marketing now." He didn't elaborate further.

∾

ZACK

"DO YOU HAVE A PICTURE OF THIS JERK?" I ASKED.

"Why?" Brittney eyed me skeptically.

I put my fork down. "Do you?"

She took another bite of ravioli and shrugged.

I held my hand out. "Just give me your phone."

She cocked her head. "Yes, I have a picture. Why? Are you going to smack the picture or something?"

I kept my hand out. "I want to be able to recognize him if he shows up. That's why."

She seemed to deem that reasonable enough and handed her phone over after scrolling through pictures.

The guy didn't look like much, but at least now I knew who to pound if he came by. "Thanks." I put the phone down and slid it to her. "What's his name?"

She frowned. "Ex."

I waited, but didn't get anything more out of her.

She swallowed the wine she'd sipped. "Thank you." She licked her lips.

That simple gesture had me wondering how they would taste, and how they would feel, if the time ever came.

I shook off the thought. "For what?"

"For being concerned. I'm used to looking out for myself."

"I'll protect you," I offered. It sounded lame after I said it. "I promised Doug," I added, which didn't sound any better.

"I have pepper spray, if I need it."

I laughed. "And we saw how well that went for you."

"I didn't do very well, did I?"

"Nope. You should take that out of your purse before you hurt yourself."

She giggled. "I already did."

I grinned. Seeing her giggle was a treat. She needed to do it more often, and somehow that task was going to fall to me.

"What are you smirking about?" she asked.

"Nothing."

"Really? You're going to try that on me?"

"I was grinning, not smirking, and it was because I enjoy seeing you happy for a change. It's a good look on you."

She blushed. "Oh."

The blush was also a good look on her, and another thing I would have to encourage. She dug back into her food.

To change the subject, I asked about Samantha's situation and how things were going for her.

Brittney was very proud of her sister. That came through clearly.

I ate as Brittney talked, and admired the pale blue of her eyes, the way they sparkled when she was enthusiastic or giddy. I watched her lips as she spoke and couldn't help but want to touch them with mine—explore them, or have them explore me.

Before long, the meal had come to an end, and it had been quite enjoyable. Brittney had grown into a beautiful woman. She just needed to control her impulse to argue, although she was adorable when she got worked up.

Vinny took our plates and brought the dessert menu.

I had it memorized.

She looked it over briefly. "It all looks like too much for me, and you've already spent so much this evening."

"Nonsense. No amount is too much for you." It sounded sappy, but it was the way I felt.

She shook her head. "These are too fancy for me."

"I've got simple ice cream at home," I offered.

"I don't need anything."

"I'll be insulted if you refuse my dessert invitation."

"Okay then. I'd love a simple bowl of ice cream."

I settled the bill and helped her to the door. When my hand touched the small of her back, I felt another jolt up my arm. I pulled it away and opened the restaurant door for her.

The gesture earned me a sultry *Thank you.*

I walked beside her out toward the valet stand.

She stopped. "Just a sec."

I looked back to find her looking down into her purse.

She tripped and came flying my way.

I stepped toward her and grabbed her to prevent a face plant.

"Careful." My arms came around her and she ended up against me, chest to chest.

She grasped me and steadied herself, looking up, her chest hot and soft against mine. "Sorry."

I kept her close. "Don't be."

Those were the only words that came to me. The sudden warmth of her body obliterated rational thought for a moment. Time stood still as I stared back into those eyes, the pale blue eyes that drew me in, that begged me to pull her closer yet, to fist her hair and pull her mouth to mine. I lifted a lock of her hair to my nose and breathed in the scent. "Vanilla?"

"Like it?"

I nodded, relishing the feel of her tits against me. My cock pushed against my zipper, taking more than a casual interest in her.

"You can borrow it if you want," she said, her fingers stroking my chest lightly.

I let her go and she stepped back, just far enough away that I longed to feel her body heat again, yet close enough that I could still detect the vanilla.

I turned back toward the street and was surprised when she took my hand in hers. I didn't resist as I should have. This was dangerously close to PDA.

Tony raced off to retrieve my car. He didn't need the chit to know which one was mine.

Remember Rule Number One, I mentally chanted to myself.

I pulled my hand away to retrieve cash from my wallet to tip Tony. I could have waited until he got back. I should have waited, but it was too late. The moment had passed.

Why was I conflicted? I should have been relieved to avoid the temptation—she was becoming my Kryptonite. Actually, that's what she'd always been. Without Doug to remind me of the rules, I was becoming weak. I was becoming a pathetic excuse of a friend. Doug deserved better from me.

Tony brought the car up, breaking the awkwardness.

I opened the door for Brittney.

She smiled at me as she scooted in—a smile that seemed to say more than merely thank you. Had she felt it too?

I climbed in the driver's side, buckled in, and we were off. Motoring toward my street, I reviewed my to-do list. Fix her fuse-box issue, turn off the water to her leaky faucet or whatever, fix the back door deadbolt, and she would become my neighbor instead of my guest. *Roommate* was too dangerous a word. It implied cohabitating, sharing the television, the kitchen, and let's not forget the bathroom. It implied glimpses of her in a towel, or hearing her through the wall as she undressed, picturing the scene in my mind. It implied a treacherous closeness that could involve accidental touching. Touching that threatened to erode my discipline.

It also would mean marshaling the self-control to keep from knocking on her door in the middle of the night to join her in bed. In the end, those urges would tear me apart. Just having her in the seat next to me was difficult. A whiff of the vanilla in her hair drifted my way and brought back the feel of her against me, along with the desire to feel that again, without the clothes separating us.

I shook my head in an effort to rid myself of the thoughts, the temptations.

"What's wrong?" she asked, her voice a reminder of her closeness.

I clenched my teeth. "Nothing."

She wasn't the problem. I was.

Being a neighbor was better, safer, a more controlled situation, one with less temptation.

I would still be able to see into her kitchen from mine in the morning. I could wave through the glass. I could invite her over to share Hot Pockets, maybe even fruit, if she insisted. That would be the ticket—fresh blueberries and a Hot Pocket for breakfast across from Brittney, the perfect start to the day. I could stomach berries for her company, and the table between us would provide enough distance for safety.

I stopped at a red light.

"What are you brooding about?" she asked.

"I'm not brooding."

"You haven't said a word since we left the restaurant. That's brooding."

"You haven't either," I reminded her.

"I was waiting for you," she complained.

"And I was trying not to talk your ear off."

She just stared at me. "Bullshit."

"Okay. I was thinking about fixing your house." At least my answer was partly truthful.

"Oh… Do you think it will be hard?"

"I doubt it, but we won't know till we look. If it's just a fuse or two, Home Depot is open until ten, and we'll get the lights on for you this evening."

She played with her hair. "That sounds good."

I looked over, and her smile had turned down for some reason. "What's wrong?"

"How much do fuses cost?"

"I don't know. Maybe a few bucks a piece."

The answer seemed to relieve her.

"Don't worry about the money. I'll take care of it."

She turned toward me. "No, I'll pay. I can't accept any charity."

I pulled the car quickly to the curb. "We're going to settle this right now. I'm paying to fix your house so it's safe, and that's that."

She huffed. "I pay my own bills."

"You aren't this time. I told you what's happening. I'm taking care of it, end of discussion."

She glared at me. "I'm paying you back."

"No. You're Doug's sister, and I'm keeping you safe. I'm taking care of it, I told you."

"That's the problem. You only see me as Doug's sister. But I'm me, and I get to make my own decisions. I'm paying you back."

She had hit the nail on the head. She was Doug's sister, and that changed everything. All the rules were different. And it wasn't something that could be undone.

"Fine. If you want to pay me back, you can make me breakfast every morning."

"Make you breakfast? No way." Her temper was getting the better of her now.

"What, you don't know how?"

"Of course I do. And a lot better than you too."

"Since when did you become so obstinate? That's the deal. Take it or leave it. Unless you want to fix the house yourself."

"Who put you in charge?"

"I did."

"You're impossible."

"I'm practical." I moved my hand to the shift lever, ready to leave. "So, do we have a deal?"

"I guess." Her hands clenched. "You're bossy, you know that?"

I pulled back into traffic before answering. "And you're being irrational." I could live with the bossy description if it meant I could keep her safe.

"Why, because I'm a girl?" she spat.

I knew enough not to respond to such a loaded question. "Because you're getting mad at me for trying to do something nice for you."

"I still say you're bossy."

I let it go. No matter what, she was going to insist on having the last word.

CHAPTER 11

BRITTNEY

THE ENGINE ROARED AS WE PULLED AWAY FROM THE CURB TO resume the trip back to my new home.

Make him breakfast, my ass. And me irrational?

The first chance I got, we were going to see how much hot sauce he could stomach in his eggs. Or maybe salt and pepper on his berries. He'd be begging to do his own breakfast again.

How had the ride back from the restaurant become such a study in contradictions?

First there had been my stumble into him as we walked to the car. I'd been tempted to kiss him when he caught me and held me in his arms. I'd never felt so mesmerized by a man's embrace. I hadn't known what to do, and like a dummy, I'd waited for him to make the first move. The way he'd sniffed my hair had been a ten Richter-scale shock to my libido—a move straight out of a movie, or at least a movie I wanted to be in. My breasts ached to be pressed up to his hard chest again.

But then I'd said something lame about letting him borrow my shampoo, and the moment had passed.

I should have offered to let him wash my hair. No, I should have asked him to join me in the shower so I could wash his hair, or he could watch me wash mine, or something. Anything about getting in the shower together would have been better than what I'd said.

Or maybe I should have just kissed him, or closed my eyes and moved closer, offering my lips. I could have rubbed up against his crotch—that might have gotten the message across.

Fuck it, I was so confused. All I knew was I'd blown it somehow, and we'd ended up arguing about paying to fix up the house.

Now I was a fucking breakfast cook.

"Now what are *you* brooding about?" he asked.

"Just worried about getting things fixed at the house." I couldn't possibly be straight with him about my daydreaming.

He turned onto our street: Snakewood. "Don't worry, I'm sure it's minor."

Now this was home; it was where I belonged. Belonging next to him just seemed right.

He pulled into his drive and drove toward the garage. The door rolled up after he pressed a remote, and the car slid in. It was quiet for a second after he turned off the rumbling motor.

"And I'm not bossy. I just want what's right."

I gave up on arguing with him, for tonight at least. It wouldn't have gotten me anywhere. "Yeah, right." I pulled the door handle.

"Stop. Stay there."

Mr. Bossy was back. He got out and jogged around the car to open the door for me.

I hadn't realized I'd broken one of his rules, but the gesture was cute.

"A gentleman opens the door for a lady," he explained as he pulled the door open.

"I'm not always a lady," I replied.

"You are in my book—except when you argue."

I stifled the comeback that started up my throat and let the compliment he meant it to be flow over me.

We walked in silence back to the street and up to my house.

Something was wrong with me tonight. I couldn't manage to go more than a few minutes without saying something that ended in a fight.

We ascended the stairs to the porch, and I let us in.

He tried the light switch, resulting in the same disappointing lack of response I'd gotten earlier. He tried each of the switches we came across without any success.

"Time to check the fuse panel." He led me out the back door. "I need to fix that deadbolt for you tonight as well."

Until he mentioned it, I hadn't noticed that it had a handle, but the mechanism had been taken out.

We went around to the back wall, and he opened a metal panel.

He turned on the flashlight of his phone and looked around inside it. "I'll need my ohm-meter to check the main fuses, but all the branch ones look fine."

"Is that good or bad?"

"Don't know yet. Let's look around for that water leak."

We went back inside and after checking all the rooms found nothing indicating a leak.

"That only leaves the basement," he said as we finished in the last bathroom upstairs.

"I didn't see any stairs. Are you sure there's a basement?" I'd been everywhere in the house, and I should have seen them if there were any.

"You get to it from the back," he told me as he ushered me toward the kitchen.

Outside, he pulled up a slanted storm-cellar door, like out of an old movie. "They built these in the old style. You couldn't reach them from inside the house."

I made my way down the creaky stairs after him and heard the splash of water. I quickly stepped back up onto the step. In the light of his flashlight it was now obvious where the DWP guy's water had gone. An inch of water covered the floor.

He walked through the area, shining his light up toward the floor above us and across to the walls. "Fucking punks."

"What?"

"Go back outside." Bossy was back again.

I climbed the stairs to the backyard and waited.

He slammed the cellar door closed after coming back up. "Fucking thieves." He kicked the door threshold. "I'm such a fucking idiot." He kicked it again, harder.

I backed up. He was one pissed-off dude—scary pissed off. "What? What is it?"

He kicked at the wood again. "Fucking copper thieves."

He wasn't making any sense as he kicked it again.

"Copper?" I pulled at his arm to get him away from the door before he broke his foot.

"Yeah, fucking copper. It's expensive, and since the construction sites started adding security, they've been hitting abandoned houses. They yank out wiring and piping and sell it for scrap."

"And my house?"

He took a deep breath and blew it out slowly. "They ripped out a bunch of water piping and wiring from under the house. I'm sorry, but it's going to take a lot more than one evening of work to make your house livable again."

I almost fainted. I stumbled to the back steps and sat. "This can't be happening," I moaned into my hands as the tears started. "I can't afford this." I felt the warmth of a shoulder against mine as Zack sat next to me.

He laced his arm behind me and pulled me toward him. "I've got you, Brit. You're staying with me. You're my roommate until we can get this fixed up." His words soothed me.

"But I told you I can't afford to have work like this done."

"I can, and I'm going to fix it for you."

"But—"

"Stop, dammit," he said, releasing his hold on me and standing. "What is wrong with you, woman? I'm not having this argument again."

He walked two paces and turned. "You sit here and feel sorry for yourself all you want. When you're ready to face the situation and get on with fixing your life, you can come in and join me for dessert. You just have to agree to stop complaining. We all have choices to make, so make yours." He walked off.

My life had completely imploded, and all he could think about was his stomach? The man was impossible.

Slowly, my tears dried, and I shivered as the cool evening air chilled me. I was trapped with nowhere to go. I stood and hesitated before starting my inevitable walk to his door in the failing light. I could sit on the steps all night and freeze, go inside my house with no lights, no water, and hazmat traps for toilets, or join him for ice cream and chocolate sauce in a house with working toilets and a bed with clean sheets. Some choice.

I went back through my house, locked it, and took the sidewalk to his front door.

Watching the kid in the hoodie on the other side of the street, I completely missed the raised crack in the concrete sidewalk and tripped, falling forward.

My palms stung, but it was my right knee that took the brunt of the fall and hurt like a mother. I grabbed it as I struggled back to my feet.

My hand came back with a spot of blood.

CHAPTER 12

BRITTNEY

I LIMPED UP THE STAIRS TO ZACH'S DOOR AND LET MYSELF IN. I found him in the kitchen.

"What did you decide?" he asked as he turned to open the freezer.

I swallowed as if my pride had clogged my throat. "I'd like to stay with you."

He pulled out a gallon of vanilla ice cream and a squeeze bottle of Hershey's chocolate syrup. "And?" he asked, facing the cabinets.

The cobwebs of my brain were not giving up whatever it was I'd forgotten.

He collected bowls from the lower shelf. "And?" he repeated.

Replaying his words in my mind, it dawned on me what he was fishing for. I gave in.

"*And* I'll stop complaining."

There, I'd said it.

With his back still to me, he scooped ice cream into the bowls. He added spoons and turned to bring them to the table.

He looked at me and quickly put them back down. "What happened?" He pulled a paper towel off the spool and rushed to press it to my knee. "Sit." He ushered me to a chair.

I steadied myself with the table as I sat.

He lifted my leg on to the other chair and put my hand over the paper towel. "Hold this in place." He rushed off and returned with a first aid kit. "Did you fall?"

"Duh."

He wetted cotton gauze with alcohol. "Where?" He pulled the paper towel away and dabbed at the wound through the rip in my jeans. "This may sting."

I cringed. Sting was an understatement. "Out front on your stupid sidewalk."

He took scissors to the leg of my jeans and started cutting. "My sidewalk?"

"Hey. These are almost new."

He kept cutting. "Not anymore. What are you going to do? Mend them?"

"Ripped jeans are in. Don't you know that?"

"Now you can turn them into cutoffs." He cleared away the bottom half of my jeans leg and cleaned the wound with stinging, alcohol-soaked gauze. "I'm going to use a styptic pencil on this."

He held up two fingers in front of me. "How many?"

"Duh, two."

"Did you hit your head?"

"What's with the twenty questions?"

"Did you?"

"No," I said emphatically.

The styptic whatever made my wound hurt even worse.

"Why'd you fall? We have street lights."

"I was worried about this kid across the street. So I guess I wasn't looking."

He fussed over me for a few more minutes before putting away his supplies and offering me Advil.

I swallowed the pills. "Thanks."

"In the meantime, you're not going out at night by yourself."

"You can't say that."

"I just did. I'll keep you safe, and you can watch where you're putting your feet without having to worry about the local kids. This isn't the greatest neighborhood."

I took a breath. I wasn't going to win this one. "I don't mean to argue with you. I just want this string of bad luck to be over."

"So you'll stop complaining when I offer to help?"

I nodded.

"Good. Working on the future is always preferable to dwelling on the past."

That was easy for him to say. With his money, his future was always guaranteed to be bright. He brought over the Hershey's syrup and drizzled some on his bowl before offering it to me.

I took it and added some to my ice cream, but not as much as he had.

He sat and prepared to dig in.

"Stop," I almost shouted.

His spoon froze in place, and his head jerked up. "What?"

I stood and went to the fridge. "If I'm living here, and cooking for you..." I pulled the strawberry container from its shelf. "You're going to eat healthy, and that means fruit." I found a knife and sliced a few of the berries over his bowl. "There. Now it's ready."

He feigned a scowl, but a smirk grew from behind it. "If I have to."

I'd won a round for a change. I added berries to my bowl as well and re-took my seat.

He lifted his spoon of ice cream toward me. "To living together."

I filled my spoon and raised it to his toast. "With fruit at every meal."

It wasn't what I would have pictured years ago when I dreamed of being with Zack, but I was living with him for real now. There was no going back. I glanced up to see him smiling at me.

As much as he'd complained, he wanted me here, and that was the most comforting thing I could have asked for.

The thought rattled around my brain, sending an odd warmth through me. I took another spoonful and decided this was the best dessert I'd had in quite a while, and it was all due to the man I sat across from. He'd vowed to take care of me. It wasn't something I'd ever sought out, but from Zack, it seemed to fit naturally. Accepting help from him was the right thing to do.

"Thank you," I said.

"For what?"

"For caring."

His brow creased, and he went back to eating. Compliments were obviously not his thing.

I looked around the kitchen. If I had to live here with him and cook for a while, this was my kitchen, and I was reorganizing it.

Take that, Mr. Control Freak.

He rose suddenly. "I have to fix that lock on your back door."

"Can I help?"

"No, I got it."

"To proud to accept help from a girl?"

He took a deep breath, and his expression said I'd almost pushed too far.

"Sure," he huffed. "If you're up to it."

I followed him as he picked up a Home Depot box, a screw-driver, and a hammer.

Once on my back porch, he handed me his phone. "You can hold the light."

"I want to do more to help."

He handed me the box and took back the phone. "Okay, you do it, and I'll hold the light."

How hard could it be?

I struggled to get the pieces out. If getting the lock set free of the molded plastic was any indication, this was not going to end well.

"Want some help?"

"I'll get it."

He handed me a knife.

Once I used that, the plastic gave way and yielded several parts. "Thanks."

He showed me where to unscrew the old parts from the door, and how to insert the new ones with the new screws from the package.

My mind went places it shouldn't have when he told me to put the male part into the female part, but once I got past that, the rest of the installation went quickly.

"Now, try the keys before you shut the door."

I did, and they both worked. I closed and locked the door with a sense of accomplishment.

The project had only required the screwdriver and the knife.

I picked up the packaging and the old parts to take back. "What's the hammer for?"

He held up the tool. "Wolf spiders hunt at night."

ZACK

SOMEHOW DOUG'S SWEET SISTER HAD BECOME AN ARGUMENTATIVE little monster. The bad part was I found it refreshing, and even alluring.

She wasn't afraid to talk back to me. I'd pressed her buttons, and she'd come right back for more, completely unlike any previous women in my life—except for my sisters, of course. They had, on occasion, relished giving me shit about one thing or another.

But outside of family members, my family name had always set the dynamic off kilter. I towered over all the women I dated, and I could karate chop a board in half, but that wasn't it. The physical differences didn't intimidate them so much as turn them on. It was the money and position that set us apart. Until now, I hadn't found a woman who had the self-confidence to take me on.

My sisters had conflicting ways of looking at it. Serena had always said I was such a good catch that none of them wanted to risk losing me. Her way of explaining it certainly massaged my ego, but it didn't always ring true.

Kelly, on the other hand, thought I attracted deferential women. She hadn't said it in so many words, but she'd implied that maybe that was the kind of woman I was attracted to as well. Of the two, I preferred Serena's analysis.

Did I choose women who were deferential to me? I didn't think so, but Kelly's question deserved serious consideration—not tonight, but sometime.

Brittney had brought this all suddenly into contrast. Perhaps it's because we'd grown up together in a way, with all the time Doug and I had spent together with her hanging around in the background. Could that have her seeing me as a stand-in for a brother? That would be awkward. I got a hard-on just thinking about her, and that didn't fit the brother prototype.

Back upstairs at my house after dessert, Brittney had busied herself in the guestroom, and I pulled out my laptop to email Doug. He was an Osprey pilot stationed at Marine Corps Air Station Futenma in Okinawa, and emails worked better than texts for communicating. He deserved to know Brittney was safe.

Doug-

I thought you should know that Brittney came back to LA. It turns out the house she inherited from your grandmother is right next to the one I'm rehabbing (who knew). The house is a mess and uninhabitable until it gets fixed up (the copper thieves hit it). She's staying with me in the meantime, and I'm taking care of getting the house ship-shape for her, so no need to worry. I'll keep her safe for you.

Keep the safety on, and the shiny side up.

-ZB

I promised to keep Brittney safe, and that was paramount, but I also had to worry how I would keep myself safe from her. My cock stood at attention as I closed my eyes and saw that body again, the one I'd wanted to touch and to hold for the longest time, the one that drew me in with every glance.

Now that she was mere feet away, this was going to be sheer torture, but I'd brought it on myself. I could have sent her to room with my sister Serena maybe, but that wouldn't have worked, because she'd be over here trying to fix the house by herself and probably fucking it up—or even worse, getting hurt in the process.

No, I was doing the right thing, the only thing that made sense. I had to get her house up to snuff, and make sure it was done right. If I let it get screwed up somehow, Doug would hold me accountable, and he'd shoot me if anything bad happened to his twin sister.

I blew off the idea of resuming floor work tonight because it was too noisy. Everything related to this house would have to take a backseat to working next door. I got up to brush my teeth and turn in for an early night.

When I opened the door, she was there at the sink, peering into the mirror. "Am I in your way?" She wore a night shirt barely long enough to cover her ass.

"Not at all. I'll wait till you're done." I retreated to the hallway and closed the door.

She opened it right back up. "Come in. You forget Doug and I had to share a bathroom growing up. It's no big deal."

This house was suddenly a lot smaller. In my haste to do the remodel, this was the only functioning bathroom, outside of the half bath downstairs. I hadn't contemplated guests.

I followed her back into the bathroom, which had seemed larger yesterday. I added toothpaste to my brush and started on my teeth. In the mirror, I caught sight of her nipples poking against the thin fabric of her shirt and almost lost my mind. I closed my eyes as I continued brushing. I willed my cock to ignore the sight I'd taken in—unsuccessfully. I rinsed quickly and escaped to my room. Mind over matter was one thing, but mind over hormones was a completely different ballgame, and I was currently losing.

A while later, I heard her finish up, and I snuck back into the bathroom.

Once back in my room, I heard a knock against the wall between our rooms.

"Good night, Zack, and thank you," she called through the wall.

"Good night, Sunshine."

For the longest time, I lay awake in bed. All I could think about was Brittney. Brittney at dinner, Brittney in the car, Brittney over ice cream, and Brittney with pokey nipples in that night shirt. That led to imagining Brittney without the shirt. What would her tits look like? What would they feel like? What would she feel like wrapped around me. What would she taste like? Would she whimper, or yelp, or scream? How would she look when she came? How good would it feel to fuck her brains out?

She was going to be the death of me.

Remember Rule Number One, I mentally reminded myself. *She's Doug's sister, for Christ's sake. Hands off the sister. Hands fucking off the sister. No fucking the sister. No imagining fucking the sister either.*

Doug's sexy sister.

And she was more than sexy. She was smart, dedicated, and compassionate, not to mention tough.

I knew from Doug how she was almost single-handedly putting Samantha through school. Everything she'd done, she'd done for family.

Those were values I could relate to and admire. In that respect, we were cut from the same cloth.

Then I came back to sexy and those pokey nipples under the night shirt. Those legs, and those wonderful tits.

Doug's incredibly sexy sister.

Tomorrow I had to get busy fixing her house to get her the hell out from under my roof, before she ended up under me and I did something we would both regret.

∿

Brittney

I COULDN'T GET TO SLEEP. THOUGHTS OF THE DAMAGE TO MY house kept intruding. Then the fucked-up situation with Dr. Fosback, which meant I wouldn't have anything beyond bar work for a while, depressed me. Managing Samantha's tuition was looking harder by the minute. Pretty soon, I was going to have to come clean with her that I just couldn't make it work, even with no rent to pay.

But until then, I would put off destroying my sister's dreams and just work harder at finding a way to make them come true. That strategy had worked before. Each time I'd managed to pull a rabbit out of the hat at the last moment and make it work for her. She deserved every ounce of effort I had before I gave up, and that's exactly what she was going to get.

I might be able to get another credit card, or increase the limits on my current ones. There had to be alternatives. There always were.

I put those thoughts out of my head, rolled over, and thought about Zack. Annoying, bossy Zack had brought a smile to my face and calmed my inner fears. Just spelling his name in my head had finally soothed me enough to slip off into the refuge of sleep.

CHAPTER 13

BRITTNEY

THURSDAY MORNING THE SOUND OF THE TOILET FLUSHING WOKE me. Light curled around the edges of the shades.

Fuck, I was late. I had to have breakfast ready for him. It was part of my job now, and I never failed at my jobs. I slid out of bed, found my sweatpants, and pulled them on. Shoving my feet in my slippers, I rushed down to the kitchen.

I located an old box of pancake mix in the rearranged pantry. I didn't bother checking the expiration date. It would do for this morning. The back of the box called for milk and eggs, and I had those, so we were off to the races.

I mixed up the batter, added blueberries, heated a skillet on the stove, and in short order had a stack of mostly presentable pancakes warming in the oven.

Mango slices on the plates, OJ in the glasses, and I was ready, but something was missing—napkins. I searched and couldn't find any. Paper towels would have to do till I got back to the store.

My phone rang. Pulling it from my pocket, I was greeted by Samantha's cheery face on the screen.

She didn't even wait for me to say hello before she started her harangue. "Why didn't you tell me you moved to Grams's house?"

I sat. "I haven't had a chance to call you yet. And it was your idea anyway."

"And were you gonna tell me you're living with Zack?"

It was as if she was spying on me.

"I'm not *living* with him," I corrected. Technically, I guess she was right, but she'd made it sound like the *other* kind of living with a guy.

The sound of Zack's footsteps coming down the stairs filled the small kitchen. Without any carpets and minimal furniture downstairs, sounds carried.

Zack appeared at the kitchen doorway. "I have to get an early start on work. I'll see you this afternoon."

"I can hear him," Samantha said through the phone.

"No, you don't. Not without your breakfast," I told Zack, a hand on my hip.

My sister was instantly in my ear. "You tell him, girl."

"Call you back later," I told her. Not waiting for an answer, I hit the end call button and laid the phone down.

"Sorry, I don't have time," Zack said.

"Bullshit." I walked over and tugged him toward the table. "Remember our deal? My job is to make your breakfast. Your job is to eat it."

His eyes locked with mine for a moment—a test of wills.

"And smile," I added. I didn't blink.

He huffed loudly and sat, handing me another victory. "Now who's being demanding?"

"It was your idea, as I recall." I went to the oven and retrieved the plate of pancakes. "I did my part. Now you do yours."

His eyes softened, and a smile appeared that actually looked real.

I split the stack of pancakes between our plates and took a seat across from him.

Without another word, he dug into the food. "I really have to go," he said between mouthfuls.

The pace at which he was devouring it and the hint of a grin every time he looked up told me all I needed to know. He might be grumbling, but the complaints were fake.

"Tell me what we need to get," I asked him.

"Pardon?"

"To fix the house. I can go get materials, but I have no idea what we need."

He thought for a second. "I think we should start with the plumbing."

That was certainly a sentiment I could agree with—working toilets were top of the list.

"Why don't you call me when you get to Home Depot, and I'll help you figure out what to buy. It's a little complicated for me to put into a list right now. Like I said, I gotta get in to work."

I held out my hand. "I'll need some money." I wasn't about to be bashful about this.

He sat up, fished his wallet out of his back pocket, and set some bills on the table. Five Benjamins. Who the hell has a wallet full of hundred-dollar bills? That certainly put a point on the contrast between us. He got hundred-dollar bills out of the ATM when the rest of us settled for a twenty or two.

I gathered up the money. "Thank you. I'll need some for food too."

He released another bill onto the table. "Will that do?"

I scooped it up. "For a start."

He speared some more mango. "Like I said, I'm paying."

In a few minutes he was finished with his breakfast and stood.

"And your OJ," I reminded him, pointing to the half full glass.

"Demanding, aren't we?"

I pasted on my best smile. "It's my job to cook for you, remember?"

After finishing the glass, he waved his goodbye and was out

the door in a flash, apparently worried I might make him eat another despicable fruit if he dallied for even a moment.

I cleaned up and loaded the dishwasher before dialing Samantha back.

She answered quickly. "So give me the skinny, and don't leave out any of the dirty details."

"It's pretty simple, really. Sometime after Grams died, the house got sort of trashed."

"What do you mean *sort of trashed*?" she demanded.

I took a breath. "They ripped out some of the wiring and plumbing. The place was pretty filthy on the inside too. Local kids have been using it as an after-school hangout and party place."

"That sucks."

"It took me a few trash bags just to gather up all the fast food wrappers and shit that they'd left lying around."

"How'd they get in?" she asked.

"They broke in through the back and took out the deadbolt so they could come and go as they pleased."

"That's all well and good, but I want to know what the deal is with Zack."

Of course she did. Gossip was her fuel. She couldn't pass the tabloids on the checkout aisle without buying one. Samantha had always been up on which movie star was breaking up with or dating somebody new, on pretty much a daily basis.

"Who told you? I just got here." It had been two nights ago, why quibble?

"I had to find out from Doug. He got an email from Zack. Somehow I got left out of the loop here, and I'm your sister, for God's sake. When you move in with a guy, I should be the first to know, not the last."

"I didn't *move in* with him."

Not exactly true, and I felt a pang of guilt that I hadn't called yesterday like I should have. Dinner with Zack and finding out about the damage to the house had thrown me.

"So tell me about Zack," she prompted again.

"Nothing to tell. He's just letting me stay at his place while we fix up Grams's house—our house—and make it livable."

"I heard that."

"What?"

"You said we," she threw back at me.

"Yeah, so? He's going to help me fix things."

"And his place, is it a penthouse? How far can you see?"

"It's the house next door—another old Victorian that hasn't been torn down and replaced yet."

"That sounds cozy. So have you…" She let the naughty implication hang in the air.

"No way," I said firmly.

Not that I hadn't thought about it, but I'd just gotten back to town. I wasn't a first-date girl. Holy shit. Was I calling dinner a date?

Her voice brought me back to the present. "I don't believe you."

"Believe what you want. He's just letting me crash here," I shot back.

"Have it your way. I wouldn't mind living with Zack. He's a hunk, and Zachary is a really strong name." The visual of Samantha coming on to Zack made me squirm.

I squeezed my legs together. I hadn't peed before making breakfast because Zack had been in the bathroom—naked probably. "Don't you have schoolwork to concentrate on or something?"

"Well, if you want to know, I think getting away from Benji was the right thing to do. But you can't always run from your problems."

"I'm not running. Moving into Grams's house saves money in the long run. It just made sense."

"Maybe I can come out at Christmas and see what you've done with the place."

"Maybe," I answered with as much conviction as I could muster. The way the finances were stacking up, it wasn't going to be even remotely possible. Assuming I got this semester paid for, the next tuition bill would be due right around Christmas. "Look, Sam, I gotta go."

We hung up, and I went upstairs. I should have skipped the coffee.

I'd moved to get my pants down too fast. I sat without bothering to look.

"Shit."

He'd left the toilet seat up, and I ended up on the dirty rim before I knew it. *Yuck.*

I wiped myself off, put the seat down, and swore at him under my breath.

Guys.

CHAPTER 14

Zack

THE ELEVATOR DOOR OPENED ON THE FAMILIAR TOP FLOOR OF OUR building.

Wendy was at her desk as usual. "You look chipper." She smirked. "How was your dinner?"

"Just fine, thank you. What do we have this morning?"

She shot me one of her tell-me-more looks. "And?"

Wendy was uncharacteristically curious this morning.

"Nothing to tell."

"Right." Her disbelief was obvious. "Stanton is having a bigger fit than normal today, and your dad stopped by." She handed me a few message slips. "These you can take care of later."

I walked into my office, turned on my computer, and sat down to take a look out the window while it powered up. Stanton could wait. The view was different this morning—more colorful, I decided after a moment. The wind had probably done a job on the smog.

Breakfast had been an interesting experience. Breakfast that didn't start in a wrapper and finish in a microwave was a new concept, at least recently. Brittney was determined to make me change my diet, and I was going to have fun resisting. I didn't care for the mango, but otherwise, fresh had its advantages.

I closed my eyes, and the scene came back to me. The pouty lips and the cute snarl as she told me to finish my OJ. And those eyes. Eyes that could convey fire. I wondered what they looked like when she came. Did they go wide and wondrous or slam shut?

Turning back to my desk, the monitor had come alive, and I logged in. Checking my watch, I pulled up the emails Stanton had sent overnight before picking up the phone to dial London.

The call was routine, with nothing very important to discuss, as it turned out.

Just as I was ready to hang up, he added, "I also wanted to go over the preparation for your visit next week."

My planned trip to London had completely slipped my mind. Brittney's arrival had crowded out other less-important items, and this was one.

"If you send me your presentation, we could go over it," Stanton offered.

I hadn't actually started working on it. "Maybe later. I'm a little busy this morning."

"We only have tomorrow left," he complained.

"That's all we need. We can go over it tomorrow." I didn't need him telling me what to do and how to prioritize things.

"But if we need to make changes..."

"Tell you what, if I need to go over anything today, I'll call you at home. Otherwise we'll talk tomorrow morning."

He got off the line with only a minor grumble. My call to Rome followed, which as always, went rather smoothly by comparison.

After finishing with the European calls, I noticed a return email from Doug and opened the message.

Zack-

Great to hear you're taking care of Brit. I know that can be pretty much a full-time job. Sorry to hear about the condition of the house - that sucks big time.

I need you to keep a close eye on Brit because she can get herself into trouble pretty easily. She has a tendency to fall for the wrong kind of guy. Her latest mistake was some asshole she hooked up with after I left - a real piece of work to hear Sam tell it. Brit was afraid to tell me all the details about how bad he was. Probably afraid I'd break the guy's legs when I rotate back to the US.

So do me a favor. Keep a close eye on her and check out anybody she dates. I don't want her getting involved with another loser. I've got enough blood on my hands already.

Thanks,

Doug

I composed a quick reply.

Doug-

I got it covered. She's full of sass, but I'll keep her under control somehow. No getting involved with any losers—I'm on board with that. I've got your back.

-ZB

Like it or not, I was Brittney's official guardian now—and I did like it. I owed it to Doug to keep her under control. Her ex sounded worse than she'd let on.

It was later than normal when I rounded up the coffees and returned to Wendy's desk with her mocha.

"Are you going to tell me, or am I going to have to call Serena?"

Her threat to call my sister was a serious one—an intervention I didn't need right now.

I took the guest chair on the side of her desk. "Brittney is my friend Doug's sister."

Her silent stare demanded I continue.

"She moved back from San Jose, and she's staying with me while I fix her house up."

Her head cocked slightly. "Staying with you?"

"Till I get her house fixed." I stood. "Could you please ask Kaden to come see me?"

She lifted her phone, and I took my coffee into the office. That was as much as I was willing to share this morning, and it was pretty much all there was to tell anyway.

I pulled up the customer-visit summaries Stanton had sent a few weeks ago and printed them out.

Kaden Peralta showed up a few minutes later. "Yeah, boss?"

He was the perennially eager type.

"Is your passport up to date?"

Only the briefest look of confusion crossed his face before it was replaced with a grin. "Sure. Where are we going?"

"How do you feel about London?" I asked this only as a courtesy. I was sending him regardless.

"I like London. I mean, I haven't been, but I'd like to go someday."

The exposure would be good for him.

I turned, pulled the sheets from the printer, and offered them to him. "Have a seat."

He accepted the papers and started to scan them.

"I was supposed to make these customer visits next week, but something has come up, and I need you to fill in for me."

"Sure thing. You're not coming along?"

"No, this is a solo assignment."

"Okay." Just the slightest quiver in his voice indicated nervousness.

"You'll do fine. Go over these and give Stanton in London a call later this morning with any questions you have. And plan on reviewing your slides with him first thing tomorrow morning. Wendy can give you copies of the correspondence, and ask her to book you a flight for Monday."

He looked at me expectantly, but I didn't have any more for him.

I sat back. "Well, go ahead. You need the slides ready by tomorrow morning."

He left with a spring in his step. I could hear the excitement in his voice as he talked with Wendy about flights.

I was still responding to emails when Brittney's call arrived. I closed my eyes, and the mere sound of her voice lifted my mood.

"I'm here at Home Depot. Now, what do I need to get?" she asked.

"Thank you for breakfast," I said first. I hadn't told her over the table this morning the way I should have.

"Thank you for the roof over my head. We're even."

"Let me give you a list of things from plumbing." I then proceeded to list the pipe and the dozens of fittings and supplies we would need to start rebuilding the piping in her house.

"I don't know if this will all fit in my car."

"The pipe is in ten-foot sections, so it'll have to hang out the window. That's what everybody does. The guys there will be happy to help you."

I had no doubt of that. The guys would fall all over themselves to help a pretty girl like her.

∽

BRITTNEY

"I THINK I'VE GOT IT ALL," I TOLD ZACK AFTER I WROTE DOWN the items he'd listed for me.

"Don't forget grade L," he reiterated. He'd said twice that the pipe needed to be grade L, not grade M.

After we hung up, I found Marvin in plumbing who was happy to help me, the clueless woman, find the dozens of fittings Zack had given me, as well as the proper grade of pipe.

"Grade L is the thicker, better one," he told me, something Zack hadn't explained.

I had a shopping cart full of stuff, including the torch, solder, and flux to make the joints.

"I'll bring the pipe up front for you, but first you should get a few items your boyfriend didn't list."

"Go ahead." I didn't correct the boyfriend comment.

He walked back up the aisle. "You'll need one of these flame protectors, and just in case, get two plant sprayer bottles from the garden center."

"What for?"

"You'll be soldering up against the wood of the house. This mat keeps it from catching fire, and the squirt bottles are just in case."

This suddenly sounded a lot more dangerous, like burn-my-house-down dangerous.

I took the black pad and wheeled my way to the garden center for squirt bottles. I got three.

With a dozen lengths of pipe hanging out the window, I drove home carefully, unloaded, and followed that with a trip to the supermarket.

With my chores done, I grabbed an apple and a paper towel, and started the drive to the Rusty Bucket to meet with Max. After finishing the apple, I wrapped the core in the paper towel and dialed my sister back.

Samantha didn't pick up, so I left a quick message.

After parking, I realized I'd forgotten to let Lillian know I'd arrived safely. I couldn't decide if I wanted anyone to have Grams's address, so I settled on a simple text.

ME: In LA safe and sound – talk tomorrow – thanks for everything

When I stepped through the familiar door, the Rusty Bucket was getting ready to open for lunch. I didn't recognize any of the servers readying the place as I made my way to the back. Since I seemed to know where I was going, none of them paid me any heed. I found Max in his office with Maria, so far the only one I recognized from before. I waited in the hallway.

He turned from his desk, and his eyes lit up. "Brittney Spear, as I live and breathe. You're a sight for sore eyes." He got up and gave me a quick hug. "Maria, I'll get with you later."

As she left, Maria shot me a scowl, clearly unhappy that Max was prioritizing me above her. She'd started just before I left, and had never been particularly friendly.

I'd need to apologize to her later and not start off on the wrong foot. It was my fault for not standing farther down the hall, out of sight.

"Come on in," he bellowed.

Max Stover was a bear of a man size-wise, but a real pussycat with the employees. On occasion, when an argument between pool players got heated, Max would read them the riot act, and I'd never seen anyone foolish enough to take him on when he did that.

"I'm back in town, and I was hoping you might be able to fit me into the schedule a little bit."

He stroked his chin before answering. "You in town for long?"

Given my sudden departure last time, his reticence wasn't surprising.

"Yeah, Grams left her house to me and Sam, and I'm moving in, permanent-like."

He returned to his chair. "Take a load off." He motioned for me to sit as well, which I did. "We've got a full crew right now."

My heart stopped with his words.

"But for you, I'm sure I can free up a few shifts, if you're okay with days."

My heart restarted. "Thanks. I'll take whatever you've got. Days is fine." I would have preferred nights because the day crowd was sparse and didn't tip as well as evening customers, but beggars couldn't be choosers. "A lot of new faces out there."

Max chuckled. "Yeah, turnover in this business always sucks.

Almost everyone from your old days is gone. Now it's return-to-Max time. Maria there and Celeste both came back about a month ago, and now you. Go figure. Next thing you know, Lisa will be knocking on my door."

I knew better than that, and Max probably did too. Lisa had given birth to triplets, and I doubted she had the time.

He opened a drawer, pulled out forms, and handed them over. They were the familiar I-9 and W-4, but thankfully no application.

"Sorry you have to fill these out again, but the government is really a stickler these days on paperwork."

"No problem." I had the forms filled out in a few minutes, and after he photocopied my ID, I was ready to rejoin the workforce.

Max cocked his head as he viewed the copy. "Married?" He'd caught the name change.

I settled on a truthful statement. "Not now."

He checked his schedule. "You can start with lunch next Thursday. I'll figure out more after that. Drop the forms off with Maria. She's helping out with the paperwork."

I gave him my best smile. I'd hoped for something sooner, but at least it was a start. "Thanks, Max."

"Grab yourself a shirt on the way out. You know where they are."

"Will do, and thanks again." I excused myself and took two black shirts with *The Rusty Bucket* emblazoned on them from the stack on my way.

Maria accepted the papers from me once I found her.

"We need two forms of ID."

I handed over the copy of my driver's license. "My papers are being shipped down from San Jose. I'll bring them by in a few days."

She didn't look happy. "We need two. I can't file the form without it."

Max walked by. "Problem?"

"She doesn't have two forms of ID," Maria answered. She was being a pain in the ass.

I looked meekly toward Max. "It's in my stuff being shipped."

Max shrugged. "A week or two doesn't matter." He turned to Maria. "Get her signed up, and we'll fill that in later."

Maria forced a half-smile. "Welcome back. Be sure to read this." She handed me Max's little blue pamphlet of employee rules. "And the shirt limit is two."

I separated the shirts to show her what I had. "Only two."

She hadn't been overly friendly the short time I'd known her before I left, but now I could move her from the unsure column to the bitchy one.

A quick glance inside the pamphlet showed it hadn't changed.

Once outside, I fist pumped the air—my first success. I was back on the payroll at one place at least. Now I had to get my house livable and find some more work until Dr. Fosback came through for me.

The depth of my plight had just been made clear by Maria. The Bucket and Dr. Fosback were willing to let me slide on the two-ID requirement, at least for a while. But trying to land another gig was clearly out of the question until Lillian sent my desk stuff.

The drive back home was quick in the light mid-day traffic.

Zack had given me the code to open his garage, and I found the extension cords exactly where he'd said they'd be. I ran the electric cord over the fence to my house so I could continue cleaning up the inside with his vacuum.

I hadn't gotten very far when Samantha called. "Now I want to hear the real skinny on you and the Zack man. And let me remind you, Zachary is a super-duper name. Lots of good qualities, but you already know that."

That was as good a vote of confidence as Samantha ever gave.

I didn't start by asking if *opinionated* and *bossy* were qualities on her list.

"I told you already. Our house isn't ready to be lived in yet." I needed to stop referring to the house as Grams's; it was now mine and Samantha's.

"And you're making him meals?"

"Well, I need to pitch in a little."

"And the sleeping arrangements?" she asked.

"I'm in a separate room. Now, where is all this coming from anyway? Zack and I have been friends forever."

"Uh-huh. I remember how he used to look at you when you weren't looking, and it wasn't a friend look."

That couldn't be true. "Get outta here. There was never anything going on, and you know it."

"And the very first thing you do when you get back to LA is look up Zack and play house with him?"

"It wasn't like that at all."

"Then tell me how it is."

"You're impossible. If you must know, when I got to the house, the lights wouldn't come on. I was checking upstairs, and I heard a noise and a voice. Well, it turned out it was Zack. I pepper-sprayed him, and he turned it on me."

I had to work hard to keep from laughing at this part.

"You pepper-sprayed each other?"

"Kinda stupid, huh? But yes. His house is right next door, and he thought I was a prowler or something. Anyway, that's how I bumped into him, and I'm staying at his house while he helps me get our place fixed."

"So you're really not jumping his bones?"

"No way."

"And he isn't trying to date you?"

"No, we went to dinner is all."

"You liar, that's a date."

"It was not."

"Did you pay?"

I didn't answer the incriminating question.

"See? It was a date. I'll stop giving you a hard time once you admit it. I'm happy for you. He's a great guy."

Zack was a great guy, and by her standards, it had been a date, even if he hadn't meant it to be.

"I gotta go," I told her.

"I'm rooting for you, Brit. You need to stop falling for jerks like Benji and go after one of the good ones like Zack—someone who'll treat you right."

She had a point that Zack was one of the good ones—one of the really good ones, just not for me.

After we hung up, I went back to running the vacuum.

Had I always fallen for turds? Benji was in that category for sure. Better than Sully, but only by a little. He was definitely not a keeper in anybody's book. Why couldn't I have seen it earlier with either of them? With Sully, I'd thought him also being a twin would give us something special in common. I couldn't have been more wrong.

I didn't like the implication that I had a defect in my guy radar. Either that, or I wanted to be unhappy, which didn't make any sense.

Did I do this to myself on purpose? Was I twisted?

I shook off the thought, but only after I realized I was going over the same section of carpet with the vacuum again and again.

CHAPTER 15

ZACK

IT WAS HALF PAST FOUR WHEN KAYDEN KNOCKED AT MY OPEN office door. "I've got the first pass of the presentations ready to review."

I wasn't in the mood. "I don't need to review them. Go over them with Stanton in the morning. That should be good enough."

He cocked his head. "You sure? It'll only take a minute."

I'd always reviewed his presentations—until today.

Getting a head start on fixing Brittany's house was higher up on my agenda than a marketing presentation. "I've got confidence in you, Kayden."

He beamed ear to ear as he left.

I gathered my things, turned off my computer, and locked my office.

"You're leaving early," Wendy said, stating the obvious.

"I've got important things to get done tonight."

Done was a bit of an overstatement. All I expected to do was get started. I backed toward the elevator.

"Don't let her keep you up late," Wendy called after me, trying to get under my skin.

I stopped and pointed a finger at her. I made a zip-your-lips-closed motion across my mouth. I didn't need the gossip mill getting hold of this.

She mimicked the motion herself and gave me a thumbs up to go with her knowing smile.

Right. Don't let her keep me up late.

The drive home was annoying in the traffic, which was heavier than I was accustomed to because of the time of day. My legs were jittery with frustration when I pulled into the garage. Brittany had left the door open.

I picked up my briefcase, closed my valuable car in the garage, and bounded up the back steps of my house. Inside I found the kitchen empty, and I called Brittney's name up the stairs. No response came back. She had to be next door.

I grabbed a Coke from the fridge before heading upstairs to change.

The door to her room was open, so I glanced in. Just the sight of her things on hangers comforted me. Somehow I'd had a fear that I might come upstairs and find her gone, similar to the way she'd disappeared those many years ago. No notice, no visit, no explanation—*poof* and she was gone, without even a call afterward.

I'd never understood it back then, and I didn't want a repeat. Someday when she was ready, I'd ask her to explain things to me, and hope she would be willing.

Doug had clammed up when I tried to get it out of him. He'd said it was something for her to explain when she was ready, if she ever was. He'd insisted I drop it and never ask again. Whatever it had been, must have been traumatic.

After putting on working clothes, I made my way over to her house. The front door was open, and inside the change was dramatic. A lot of effort had obviously gone into cleaning the place. It was no longer a filthy, dusty, abandoned, teenager hangout.

"Brit?" I called.

A vacuum was running upstairs, so I followed the sound to find my Brittany.

Her back was to me as she ran the machine back and forth over the floor and carpet runner.

"Brit," I said as I tapped on her shoulder.

She jumped with a start and turned around. "Don't you know better than to sneak up on someone like that?" she shouted over the noise of the vacuum.

She switched the noisemaker off and scowled at me.

I raised my hands in mock surrender. "I wasn't sneaking. It's not my fault you didn't hear me."

Her face softened.

"You made a lot of progress today. The downstairs looks great."

"It's a start. This place was a mess."

"I got off early so we could get started on fixing your plumbing. Let's take a look at what you brought back from the store."

She started for the stairs, and I followed. "I put it all out back."

When we reached the backyard, I found all the things she'd purchased arranged in nice neat stacks. I pulled open the cellar doors.

She pulled an apple from a paper bag and held it out to me. "You can start on this."

I didn't take it. "I don't eat apples."

"Why not? Everybody eats apples."

"The skin gets caught in my teeth."

She pushed it at me again. "Don't be a baby. I cook, you eat."

"This isn't cooking."

She gave me an I-can't-believe-you-just-said-that look.

I gave in, accepted the apple, and bit into it. "Undo that extension cord you have for the vacuum. We're gonna need it down here."

"Can't I keep cleaning while you do this stuff?"

"It will go a lot faster if we have two pairs of hands."

"But the spiders…"

"Do you want running water or not?"

I brought a set of work lights from next door while she got the extension cord from the house. In a few minutes, we had light on the situation in the basement.

The damage was worse than I'd realized. The thieves had made a complete mess of the place, and I might not have had her get enough materials to finish the job.

She helped by retrieving the parts I needed one by one, and also by holding things in place as I rebuilt the water system underneath the house. A few hours later, we called it quits for the night, having made good progress.

~

BRITTNEY

BY THE TIME WE CALLED OFF THE PLUMBING PROJECT FOR THE night, my stomach had been objecting for over an hour.

"What's on the menu for dinner?" Zack asked.

Luckily I'd thought ahead and spared us a microwaved monstrosity of some sort. "Mushroom chicken bake."

It had been the simplest thing I could think of on short notice that didn't need looking after—two chicken breasts, some rice, and a can of cream of mushroom soup over the whole thing. It was waiting for us in the oven.

"If you cooked it, I'm sure it will be good."

Compliments on my cooking were a welcome change.

After washing up, I served the piping hot concoction to my equally hot plumber, friend, neighbor, housemate, roommate, or whatever he was. Samantha was right, he was one hot package of a man.

"Better let it cool."

I settled on housemate as being the closest to accurate, but roommate sounded enticing.

I added pear slices to the plates for a serving of fruit.

He wasn't willing to wait for the meal to cool, and resorted to blowing on it one forkful at a time to start eating.

I followed suit. "So how was your day today?"

Only after the words escaped did I realize how much I sounded like a housewife asking about her husband's day at work.

His eyes narrowed slightly as he continued chewing.

"Never mind," I added.

He swallowed and thought for a moment. "A boring day at the office. Except that I forgot I was scheduled to fly to London on Monday."

"You're leaving?"

The thought of being alone without my house ready to live in scared me for some reason. I'd always been independent, but relying on Zack felt suddenly natural. I raised a bite of chicken to hide behind and blew on it. I hoped the steam from the food hid my disappointment.

"No. I canceled." He took another bite of dinner.

I let out a relieved breath.

He swallowed and added, "I'm sending another guy instead. He needs the experience. It'll be good for him."

I bet he was a good manager, but I realized we'd only talked about my life in San Jose, and I didn't know enough about what he did at the family company.

"I'd rather stay here," he added with a slight upturn of the corners of his mouth that had me hoping to be the reason he wanted to stay. His eyes locked with mine.

My phone rang. I ignored it.

"Aren't you going to get that?" he asked, his eyes still boring into mine.

Breaking the moment wasn't what I wanted.

He cocked his head as his question lingered in the air. His eyes left mine, and the moment dissolved.

I pulled the phone out of my pocket. It was Lillian. "Hi, Lil, were you able to get into the apartment okay?"

"Yeah, and we have your clothes. Where should we send them?" she asked.

"You can send them to a friend of mine." I gave her Zack's address for the boxes.

Zack took another bite and watched me.

"About the couch..." she said.

"Yeah?'

"Randy thinks it's a little big for our place, but we would like the desk, the table, and the chairs, if that's okay?"

"Sure, anything and everything you want."

"You sure you don't want any of it?" she asked.

"Absolutely."

I couldn't afford to get it here, and there was already plenty of furniture in the house. Grams's stuff was better than the particle-board crap I'd accumulated up north.

"About the desk. You said you wanted me to mail the stuff in it, but it's empty."

My stomach knotted at the words. I needed my birth certificate and name change papers for work. "What do you mean empty?"

"Exactly that. Not even a paper clip. And..." She hesitated ominously. "The manager mentioned that Benji had already been by."

"That little slimeball," I hissed.

"The manager said he had a key."

I swore under my breath.

Benji had given me back the key to my place, but had probably made a copy, and I'd been too stupid and too poor to have the lock changed.

I thanked her for the heads up and for sending my things.

Now Benji had fucked me again. He had my birth certificate,

all my papers, my tax returns, my name change paperwork, everything.

"Randy will put the stuff in at UPS this weekend," Lillian said, breaking the silence.

"Thanks, Lil, that's a great help," I said before we hung up.

Zack's eyes were dangerously cold.

∼

ZACK

SHE PUT THE PHONE DOWN WITH A DEJECTED LOOK. IT HADN'T been good news from the bit I'd heard on this end.

"Problem?" I asked.

"Just Lillian, a friend from San Jose. She's sending the rest of my things."

Brittney wasn't going to offer the answers willingly.

"I got that part, but who's the slimeball?"

She twirled her fork in the food before answering. "My ex. He's a creeper." She didn't meet my eyes.

"So what did he do now?"

The call had clearly upset her.

"How long have you been working on this house?"

"Don't try to change the subject, Sunshine."

She played with her food as she conjured up an answer. "He came by my old apartment." After a moment she decided to add, "He must have kept a key. He got into the place and took some stuff, from what Lillian could tell."

"Tell me his name. I'll pay him a visit and get your stuff back."

I knew how to handle creeps like this.

Her eyes went wide. "No way. Promise me you won't."

I gave in for the moment. "For now… We need to get your house ready first, I guess."

"Yeah, the house comes first. But thanks for offering."

Her smile said she'd gotten the message that I could fix this for her. It might take her time to come to grips with it, however.

We both went back to eating our late dinner.

After a moment I tried again. "I still want to know his name."

She sipped her water. "Tell me what marketing is like." She was intent on getting away from the subject.

"Nothing much to tell, really."

She kept up the questioning about my job through the rest of dinner. Every time I diverted back to her history or the creep, she returned the conversation to my work.

"And the London trip?" she asked.

"Customer visits. We have two big contracts pending, and the local sales guys can only take it so far. In the end, the customer wants to meet with someone from headquarters. They know we have more leeway to negotiate than the field sales guy. So we visit, give them the final little price cut, and everybody's happy. They get to report to their bosses that they called us in and got a better deal, a win-win."

"Why not let your London salesman give them the better deal? Then no one has to make the trip."

"Because a sales guy will fold like a wet noodle and give almost every customer the lowest price in record time. It would make their job easier, but it would be a price race to the bottom. This way the customer has to work at it to get a lower price, so it's more satisfying for them. And more profitable for us."

"Too much psychology for me. I'll stick to cleaning teeth," she replied.

"At least my customers are happy to see me."

She giggled. "True enough. Mine aren't happy till they're on the way out the door."

I pushed my plate forward.

"You're not done till you finish your pears," she told me with a scowl.

Busted. I'd hoped to get away with the single slice I'd eaten first. It was okay, but not worth repeating.

"I'm watching," she said.

She was cute in this argumentative mode.

"Not without some topping," I told her.

She marched to the fridge and brought back the chocolate syrup.

"That'll do." I took the bottle from her and squirted a bit on. I made a face as I chewed the next piece and swallowed.

"If you keep acting like a baby, I'll feed you stewed prunes tomorrow."

"Prunes are for old people." I forked up the rest of the pears and chocolate. It was actually quite good, not that I would admit it to her.

I scraped up the last bit of chocolate sauce and licked the fork. "Satisfied?"

"That wasn't so hard, now was it?"

I didn't want to lie, so I kept quiet. I forced a frown to answer her.

CHAPTER 16

BRITTNEY

HE FINALLY FINISHED HIS FRUIT, ALBEIT WITH CHOCOLATE SAUCE, and took both our plates to the sink. I followed with the glasses. As he rinsed the silverware, he stretched his shoulders with a grunt.

I set the glasses on the counter and took a chance. I put my hands on his shoulders and kneaded.

"Stiff?" His muscles were tight knots under my fingers.

"Oh, that feels good." The sigh that accompanied his words told the story.

"It should. I'm a trained medical professional."

I continued while he finished rinsing and loaded the dishes into the dishwasher.

He braced against the counter, his back to me. "Keep it up."

I did for a minute, but this position wouldn't do. "Get on the couch."

I pointed into the old dining room he'd outfitted with a couch and a TV, a typical guy move—television over all else.

I followed him there, and he plopped face down on the sofa.

I straddled his back and started at his shoulders, working my way slowly down his back, rubbing and kneading over his clothes. I was afraid if I worked on his bare skin, I wouldn't stop at stripping off his shirt.

The groans kept coming as I moved from spot to spot, over his broad shoulders toward his lower back and the tight ass right in front of me. The man was all muscle—tight and knotted muscle, but slowly loosening under my touch.

"Ohhh, keep that up," he groaned as I leaned into my work.

"Is this helping?"

"You have no idea."

I scooted lower, over his thighs, to work his lower back.

He lifted up and gathered his shirt at his armpits.

Suddenly faced with touching skin, I hesitated.

"Don't stop," he mumbled into the couch cushion.

I took a breath to steel myself and started again at his lower back, working my way up. I didn't know if he felt it, but the warmth of his skin under my hands was way above body temperature. Closing my eyes worked better to control my feelings as I alternated kneading with my fingers and grinding the heel of my hand or my knuckles into the tight knots.

Little grunts escaped him when I leaned in especially hard.

"Keep it up," he urged.

Slowly I could feel progress. Denying what I wanted was silly, so I opened my eyes and watched my hand work over his skin. My temperature edged up too. If I closed my eyes now, I'd just be imagining other areas I wanted to get my hands on.

He surprised me by struggling out of his shirt when I got back up to his shoulders.

I leaned forward and worked my way out his arms to his deltoids, then back to his shoulders and down his back again. I leaned hard on his lower back, mightily tempted to travel even lower. As I worked my fingers back up to his shoulders, I leaned over. With my breasts brushing his back, I whispered into his ear. "Enjoying this?" The light pine scent of his hair tickled my nostrils.

"You bet."

I straightened up and instantly missed the contact of my chest with his back.

"Your turn," he announced and started to wiggle out from under me.

I couldn't have kept him pinned there if I'd wanted to. I scrambled off, straightened my shirt, and then lay down when he stood. I went face down into the cushions, and he straddled my thighs, anchoring me in place with his weight.

He started on my lower back and worked his way up slowly. He was much gentler with me than I'd been with him.

"You can press harder. I won't break." Heat spread through me with the feel of his touch. This was even better than the reverse.

He pressed harder, but was still careful not to hurt me.

"Is that all you got, big guy?"

The challenge got him to really press in—almost, but not quite, too hard. He pulled the hem of my shirt, and I lifted myself, letting it ride up to my shoulders and off my arms.

The chill of the room made the heat of his touch even more enticing against my skin. I reached back and unhooked my bra.

He worked up and down with rhythmic kneading.

I slowly melted into the cushions under the combination of pain, relief, and excitement from his touch. I moaned, encouraging him. Closing my eyes, I envisioned myself turning over and enjoying a front rub of a gentler, more sensual kind.

"Had enough?" he asked.

"Not nearly." I was willing to be selfish right now as I luxuriated under his strong hands, just imagining all the things I'd like them to be doing a little later.

He kept it up a few more wonderful minutes before climbing off. "All done. Time for dessert." He reached for his shirt and pulled it back on, hiding what I wanted to watch.

I located my bra straps and re-hooked myself before sitting up.

He glanced at me, then quickly away as he ventured back into the kitchen.

I sat up, found my shirt, and followed him without putting it on.

Opening the freezer he asked, "Ice cream again?"

I put my shirt down and pulled bowls from the cupboard. "Only if we add fruit."

His eyes raked the length of me, and I didn't miss them stopping at my chest.

I brought the bowls to the table.

"Put your shirt back on," he said.

"I'm hot." The goosebumps on my skin said otherwise, but the heat in my core agreed.

He took my shirt from the counter and threw it in my direction.

"You're being bossy again."

He stayed turned toward the wall, avoiding looking at me the way I could tell he wanted to. "And you're being obstinate. Now behave yourself and get dressed before I spank you."

I huffed. "If it makes you happy." I pulled the shirt on.

"It's what's right."

He didn't say it was what made him happy, and the distinction was clear.

ZACK

UNBELIEVABLE.

The girl was trying to drive me insane. Walking into the kitchen in only her bra and claiming to be too hot? I turned away as she finally pulled her shirt back on. I blinked hard, but I couldn't get the sight out of my brain—her wonderful tits overflowing the cups of her bra, and red lace no less? That sight was going to haunt me all night.

Un-fucking-believable.

The feel of her skin under my fingers had been hot and soft, just as I'd imagined and dreamed of last night.

I sliced the strawberries slowly onto a plate, trying to regain my composure. "I've got the berries if you can get the chocolate sauce out of the fridge."

"Are we putting chocolate on everything?" she asked.

"Everything but pizza."

"You're twisted."

"That's what my sisters say." I put the knife in the sink, brought the strawberry slices to the table, and slid some into each bowl before sitting.

She sat and passed me the Hershey's sauce without adding any to her bowl.

"Sure you don't want any?"

"I'm good."

"That you are. Really good," I said before I caught myself. "I meant a good masseuse." I stretched my shoulders. "That helped a lot."

Her mouth turned up in a smile hot enough to melt my ice cream. "You too. Thanks. You can give me a rubdown any time."

I looked quickly down at my bowl and took a spoonful. When I looked back up, she was eyeing me over her spoon.

"What's the deal with this ex of yours?" I asked. "What did he take?"

The question wiped the smile off her face.

"Why does it matter?"

I put my spoon down and reached across to hold her hand. She looked up, but didn't pull away.

"Because it's a problem for you, and I want to help."

She didn't open up.

"You're my roommate, and I care." I let go of her hand. "So tell me, what's his problem?" I spooned another bite of ice cream. "I'll promise to eat my fruit."

Her shoulders relaxed. "He's just a creep."

I swallowed. "You said that."

"Lillian said my desk was empty. He took everything."

"Anything valuable?"

"And she said according to the manager, he had a key."

I tried again. "What did he take?"

She shook her head. "I thought I was going crazy. Every once in a while something would be off just a little, not quite where it normally was, and I couldn't remember moving it—like my clock. I always had it pointed at the couch."

This implication was ominous. "You think he was sneaking into your place?"

"I don't know for sure, but it would explain things." She spooned a bite of ice cream into her mouth.

I waited.

"I kept papers in my desk. Bills, my tax returns, pay stubs, stuff like that, and my birth certificate." She stopped. A second later, her fist slammed down on the table. "Fuck. Everything was in there. I shouldn't have left so quickly. I just got my clothes, and I forgot about everything else. I can't sign up for work without a second form of ID."

A dejected look came over her.

"What's his name?"

"No. I can't have you get involved."

"I can help."

Her gaze locked with mine. "No."

I gave up for now. Doug would know the name. She didn't need to tell me.

"What else did he do? Did he ever hurt you?"

She shook her head again. "No, not like that." She was holding back, but twenty questions wasn't going to pry it out of her tonight. It would come in time, perhaps when she trusted me more.

I ate the last of my strawberry slices. "Look, I finished my fruit, like I promised."

That garnered a faint smile from her before her eyes settled on her bowl. Her face twisted into a scowl, and her mind seemed to drift off somewhere dark.

"Sunshine?"

"Yeah?" she answered weakly before looking up.

"I'm here for you. Anything you need."

This time she was the one who reached her hand across, and I took it. "Thanks, Zack. That means a lot."

"Anything you want, it's yours."

"Really?"

"Anything," I repeated.

"Can I save that wish for later?" she asked as she squeezed my hand.

"Absolutely." I squeezed her hand back. "But there's one thing I won't do for you."

She released my hand, stood, and picked up both our bowls. "What's that?"

"I won't eat a pomegranate." Some people loved the seeds, but I couldn't see the allure. I hated the things.

She laughed and took our bowls to the sink. "Okay, I can work around that, but everything else is fair game, is that right?"

"Sure." I joined her at the sink and started the dishwasher after we finished loading it.

"Maybe I'll have you give me a foot rub," she mused as I turned off the light and we started for the stairs, "in the bathtub."

I didn't dare go for that bait, and immediately regretted not setting some limits on my promise.

CHAPTER 17

Brittney

Friday morning I woke more rested than I'd been in quite a while, with lingering memories of a dream. A dream of me and Zack by the pool.

It hadn't just been the backrub that relaxed me, because truth be told, it was the backrub that had gotten me excited—excited for the possibilities in the future.

I'd had my hands on Zack, and he'd had his hands on me, hand to bare skin. He certainly hadn't been touching me where I yearned for it, but progress was progress—baby steps.

In my dream, he'd offered to rub sunscreen on my back, and when he finished that, he'd asked me to turn over and done my stomach and shoulders as well. The good part had been when he'd moved down to my legs and up my thighs, right up to my bikini bottoms, inside my thighs, oh so tantalizingly close to where I yearned for him to touch me. Then I'd awoken, and realized how far from reality the dream had taken me.

Zack was already in the shower when I got up, so I went down-stairs to start breakfast. My previous shopping trip had only been a few items, so the choices were limited for this morning's meal. I chopped up the tomato and onion before grating cheese for omelet filling. I would've preferred more ingredients, but this would get us started.

I heard him coming down the stairs before I saw him as I started to cook.

"Morning, Sunshine," he said with a rich voice that lifted my spirits.

"I hope you like omelets."

"Does it really matter? The deal was you cook, and I eat."

"Of course it matters. I want to make things you like."

"Then yes, omelets are just fine—unless you're putting fruit in mine."

I shook my head. "No, the fruit's on the side." I loaded the omelets onto the plates and carried them to the table.

He stared at the kiwi like it would jump up and bite him. "This isn't fruit."

"It's not pomegranate, so you can eat it."

"Apples and oranges are fruit. This is something else. It's got fur."

"Stop being a pussy and eat it."

The grumbles continued, and he took the tiniest slice of the green delight.

I got up, strolled around behind his chair, and started to knead his shoulders. "Eat it, and you get another backrub tonight."

He sliced off another even smaller piece of kiwi and mumbled, "Why can't we stick to real American fruit instead of this imported shit? You said you were going to feed me things I liked."

I slapped the top of his head lightly. "I asked what you liked, but fruit is part of the bargain. And what country do you think this comes from, anyway?" I went back to working his shoulders.

He snorted. "New Zealand. Where else, with a name like that?" He poked at what remained of the kiwi but didn't cut into it.

"These are from here in California, so shut up and eat it."

He huffed and cut off another piece, followed by a bigger piece and then the last. "Only 'cuz you promised a backrub."

I finished his shoulders with another few tight squeezes and backed away. "Thanks."

He got up and carried his plate to the sink.

"What can I do while you're at work to move things along?"

"You mean next door?"

I nodded.

He ran fingers through his hair. "Nothing until I get back. We have to finish soldering those pipes before you can call DWP again."

"What about the electric?" I asked.

"What about it? Trust me, you want running water first."

"But can't I do anything on the wiring? There has to be something I can do instead of sitting around."

He took a deep breath in and out. "Okay, follow me."

I followed him to the other room.

He rummaged through a tool bag and handed me a green instrument with wires attached. "This is a multimeter. Turn it to twenty here on the scale to turn it on."

I nodded. "Got it."

"Down at Home Depot, tell the guy in electrical that you need to set up a circuit trace with this."

"Circuit trace," I repeated.

"He'll give you a little box with batteries and two leads with alligator clips. Go under the house and attach those clips one by one to the white and black wires of each of the cut-off wires under the house. Then you go upstairs and plug the multimeter into each of the electrical outlets in the house and write down the results. We need a map of what's connected to what."

I nodded. "Got it, a map." I thought I understood well enough. And I appreciated being useful in putting my house back together.

"A map. That's your job." He checked his watch. "I gotta go." For a second he stared at me, and it felt like he might make a move to hug me before he left. But the moment passed, and he turned to go.

"See ya," I said as he retreated upstairs.

I began on the dishes, and in a flash he'd collected his bag from upstairs and was out the door. The house was quiet when I shut off the water and closed the dishwasher. I missed him already.

Upstairs, as I stepped into the tub for my shower, I remembered last night.

He'd promised me a wish. I could have anything. "*Anything you want, it's yours,*" he'd said.

A foot rub in the bathtub—naked.

That had gotten to him, and it wasn't such a bad idea for a wish after all.

I soaped up, and when my hands ran over my shoulders, I closed my eyes, remembering last night.

I kept my eyes closed, my hands kneading my shoulders. Everything melted away, and I imagined being face down on the couch, his hands on my bare skin, leaving trails of sparks with every movement. Why hadn't I rolled over to face him and asked for more? Because I'm a dumbshit, that's why.

The warm water rolled down me, and I added more soap.

The door squeaked open.

I shrieked from fright.

"It's just me," Zack said.

My hands instinctively went to cover myself. "Shit, you scared me." I could make out his form at the door through the shower curtain, which wasn't much protection.

"I forgot to tell you something. Before you do anything, unscrew all the fuses in the fuse box—all of them."

I regained my breath. "Uh, okay."

"Sorry. Didn't mean to scare you, but I forgot about the fuses, and I didn't want you to get hurt. Oh, and I left money for you downstairs."

He didn't want me to get hurt—the words resonated in my brain for a few seconds.

"Zack..."

I considered my next move, my next request. If this were a romance novel, I'd ask him to soap up my back or maybe join me —*definitely throw open the shower curtain and ask him to join me.* I lowered my hands to my sides. If I could make out his form through the curtain, certainly he could see what I'd done.

"Yeah?" he answered.

I chickened out. What if he said no? This wasn't a book, and I wasn't brave.

"Thanks."

When he closed the door, I could have kicked myself. That had been the perfect opportunity to find out how last night's dream might have played out, and I'd let it get away.

I was glad he cared enough to come back and tell me about the fuses so I didn't end up a crispy critter under the house after touching a live wire. That's why he'd come back, of course—not to see me naked in the shower and take up where we'd left off last night.

He'd left so easily, he obviously wasn't as eager to see me naked as I was to undress for him.

I took the soap, closed my eyes, and let my hands run over my breasts. What would his hands on me have felt like?

Heavenly was the answer that came to me as I let my imagination run a little too wild.

Next time, I wouldn't be such a chickenshit.

ZACK

DRIVING IN, I COULDN'T GET THE IMAGE OF NAKED BRITTNEY OUT of my head. Sure, there'd been a shower curtain between us, but her form was easy to see. Although she'd initially covered herself, once she dropped her hands, it had been difficult to leave. She obviously thought the curtain was more opaque than it was.

I'd wanted to pull the curtain aside and show her the way I felt, but common sense had prevailed. My imagination was playing tricks on me, tricks on us. She hadn't meant anything by it.

Fuck it. That had to be it. Then there was Doug—he'd kill me for even imagining Brittney was interested in me. That was a whole other can of worms, and an even bigger reason to get my imagination under control.

As I parked and shut down the engine, I made a mental note to Google ways to curb this imagination of mine. There had to be exercises for it—ones that didn't involve cold showers. I hated cold showers.

Upstairs, Wendy handed me the normal urgent message from Stanton, and two others that had come up late yesterday after I'd left.

I laid them on my desk and fired up my computer.

"What's your poison this morning?" I asked as I picked up her coffee mug on my way to the machine.

"Caffeine is good this morning. The more the better." That wasn't an unusual request for a Friday.

When I returned with the two steaming mugs, Wendy nodded toward my door. "Your dad is waiting," she whispered.

After entering, I closed the door.

Dad didn't often stop by first thing.

"Morning," I offered.

He didn't wait for me to get seated. "I got a complaint early this morning from Mario that you were blowing off next week's customer visits in London."

Stanton could be such an ass.

Mario Shepard was his boss, the worldwide VP of sales, and he'd obviously complained to him to get my decision on next week's meetings overturned. The sales guys were all wimps, afraid to take me on directly. Logic wasn't always their strong suit, but I responded better to that than common bitching.

"I didn't blow them off. I'm just sending Kaden Peralta in my place."

He shifted in his seat. "Why the change?"

The twenty questions had started, but that was better than the alternative of being directly countermanded, which was always a possibility with Dad.

"He needs the experience. It'll be good for him."

He stroked the end of his goatee. "But as I hear it, the customers are expecting to see the marketing VP, not a flunky." *Flunky* wasn't a term in my father's vocabulary. It had obviously come from the sales team.

I took a breath. "He's not a flunky, and he'll have full authority to negotiate the deals."

"You trust him?" he asked.

"Yes. Do you trust me to make the call?"

That backed him off a bit. "Of course. It's just unlike you to avoid a meeting with customers. I'm surprised is all."

"I'm busy next week, and Peralta needs the experience, so it's a good solution."

He leaned forward. The tick in his jaw was the one he got when he'd found a thread he wanted to pull on until he unraveled a mystery. "Busy?"

"I need to help a friend."

"Go on," he urged. "It sounds important."

It was important to me, but on a personal level that I didn't care to discuss.

"It is."

He stroked his goatee for a moment, seeming to mull whether to take another run at me.

"I'll tell Mario to move the meetings out three weeks," he announced, "so you have the time you need here first. And when you go to London, take young Peralta with you. I agree that it's good for these guys to get overseas customer experience."

With that, Dad had devised a solution to the problem meant to keep us all happy, or at least equally unhappy—no losers in the deal. He had a knack for that kind of thing. It actually was a tack I should have considered yesterday with Stanton, but hadn't.

"Works for me. Should I talk to Mario about it?"

"Nah, his office is on my way back. I'll let him know what you proposed, and I'm sure he'll like it. And don't worry about young Stanton. If Mario likes it, he won't be an obstacle."

That Stanton wouldn't bitch if it came from his boss was a given. It was interesting that Dad was trying to give me credit for the compromise he'd cooked up—one I should have thought of myself yesterday. Perhaps that was the lesson he was teaching me today. With Dad there was almost always a lesson, if we were smart enough to notice it.

He leaned on his cane, got up, and made his way to the door before turning back toward me. "Your friend, who is she?"

His powers of deduction hadn't slowed one bit. He'd guessed my issue without even asking.

"Brittney. Doug Spear's sister."

His eyes lit up for a second. "Good man that Spear boy. Joined the Marines, didn't he?"

Dad had been a Marine himself, and anyone who joined the corps had his instant respect.

"Yup, deployed to Okinawa right now."

"Good for him. One more thing…"

I waited for the other shoe to drop.

"Why don't you bring her along this weekend? I'd like to meet her again. It's been a long time."

The Habitat day had slipped my mind somehow. A house-building day with Habitat for Humanity was a family ritual multiple times a year. It *had* been a long time since Brittney had left town, and none of us had seen her since then.

"I will. I think she'd enjoy it."

Brittney had seemed enthusiastic last night when we were working together to redo her plumbing, not to mention her desire to keep the project moving forward today, and I hoped that would carry over to our Habitat construction event. Nothing like a day in the sun, cutting wood, banging nails, and watching a house come together in record time with dozens of busy bodies working on the project.

Dad nodded and turned for the door.

Bringing Brittney to the Habitat project would mean a delay in getting her house fixed, but it couldn't be avoided. The barbecues and these construction weekends were the only times I really got to see the rest of the family now that we were all grown and out of the house. Family attendance at these events was virtually one hundred percent, and I hadn't missed one in years.

And there was always Katie Knowlton's apple pie.

Bill Covington's sister had married Nick Knowlton from high school. Nick had gotten into a fight with Bill's brother Patrick back in those days. Patrick had gotten his nose rearranged, but in the end it was Nick who got kicked out of school. Years later, Nick dating his sister had been hard for Bill to swallow early on, but now that they were married, all was good.

I followed after Dad and stopped at Wendy's desk. "We need to cancel Kaden's bookings for the London trip. Have him stop in, and I'll explain it to him."

"He was really looking forward to it."

"Just a timing change. Let me explain it to him." To keep morale up, it needed to seem like our idea rather than a complaint from Stanton.

CHAPTER 18

BRITTNEY

THIS ELECTRICAL WORK WAS HARDER THAN IT LOOKED, BUT I WAS making real progress. And keeping busy was a damn sight better than sitting around waiting for Zack to get back.

It had taken me three trips to the store to get what I needed. The first to get the box Zack had told me about so I could trace the wiring. A second to get a ladder, and a third to get a tool called a wire stripper so I could actually clamp onto the ends of the wires—he'd forgotten to mention that part.

I'd also had to make a dozen trips from the cellar to upstairs already, and I wasn't even half done.

The thieves had made a complete mess of everything, and I was cursing them for the millionth time when my phone rang. I pulled the noisy device from my pocket.

Zack's name lit up the screen. "How's it going?" he asked.

"It's going." I set the wire stripper I'd been using on the shelf of the ladder and moved down to the bottom rung where I felt more comfortable.

"You sound tired. You don't have to finish it all today, you know."

I wasn't about to let this beat me. "I'm getting there." I checked the time on the phone. "I'll call it a day in a little while. I still need to go grocery shopping before dinner. What would you like?"

"Let's do steak on the grill out back. Does that work for you?"

"It's a plan. What cut do you like?"

"Let's go with filet."

I would have chosen filet mignon as well. "You got it."

"See you tonight, Sunshine."

I sighed. I could listen to that nickname all day long.

It dropped right in front of me.

"Shit," I yelled.

I freaked and fell backwards off the ladder.

My phone clattered to the ground.

The spider was a monster—at least it looked that way to me. Probably one of those wolf spiders Zack had mentioned.

I got up, never taking my eyes off the beast as he continued lowering toward the floor. I shifted sideways, and with a quick movement retrieved my phone.

"Brit? Brit? You okay? What happened?" Zack was saying into the phone.

My heart pounded. "A fucking spider."

"Step on him and show him who's boss."

I could barely breathe. "I can't. He's still in the air."

"Wave your hand above him and break the thread, then step on him when he hits the ground."

Easy for him to say.

"No way. You get him. I'm done for today. I'm not getting anywhere near that thing." I didn't add that I knew some spiders could jump—I'd seen it on *Animal Planet*—and I wasn't going to be his next meal if I let him get to the ground.

"Suit yourself, but sooner or later you've got to learn to whack your own spiders."

I walked the long way around the beast toward the exit. "Later sounds good."

We hung up after he tried two more times to talk me into doing battle with the creature. Now I was going to need a flyswatter as well before I ventured down here again—something I could use at a safe distance. How far could they jump? I didn't remember.

I needed time anyway to clean up and go shopping for dinner, so I brushed off and locked up the house. I closed the cellar doors on Wolfie, the wolf spider.

The store was only a short drive away, and when the last item in my basket passed over the scanner and beeped, I inserted my Visa card in the reader.

The cashier was loading my items into a paper bag when the card reader beeped at me three times with the message *DECLINED.* The cashier's frown meant he knew what three beeps meant—another deadbeat customer.

He stopped filling my bag. "Perhaps another card."

That wasn't an option. I knew I didn't have enough on the MasterCard. I'd maxed it out with the first portion of Samantha's tuition. The Visa had been the one with headroom. Something was drastically wrong in Cardville. I checked my wallet for cash as I replaced the card. The total on the register was more than I had.

"I'll have to cut this down a little," I admitted with the heat of embarrassment burning my cheeks.

He reloaded the items in my basket, and I left the checkout line for the back of the store.

Checking my choices, it became clear I couldn't afford the steaks. I took them back to the meat section and substituted them for a package of two small pork chops. Then I put the steak sauce back on the shelf, along with the pineapple. My mental calculation said I'd make it out with a dollar to spare.

For my second attempt at checking out, I chose a different line, and I still had two dollar bills to my name when I walked to the parking lot.

Once I was in the safety and privacy of my car, I pulled my phone out and dialed the 800 number on the back of my Visa card.

After keying in my account number and zip code, the mechanical lady proceeded to tell me the bad news according to Visa's computer.

A cold stone formed in my stomach with the balance the mechanical voice read out, and I could hardly breathe after she announced I had no remaining credit.

This can't be happening.

I punched zero a dozen times to get transferred to a talking human, not that there was much humanity in the way they treated me. Every month I paid them a king's ransom in interest, and now they'd just cut me off.

"Your call is important to us. Please stay on the line for the next available agent," the mechanical lady said.

The hold music started, and the same bullshit line about how important my call was got repeated every three or four minutes.

I pulled an apple from the shopping bag. The apple was gone before I finally heard the line ring to some support desk somewhere in the world.

"Thank you for holding. May I have the account number you are calling about?" the actual human lady on the phone said.

I read the long number off my card for the second time and gave her my name, billing address, and mother's maiden name. I expected her to ask me my birth weight and sixth grade English teacher's name as well.

"How may I help you?" she finally asked.

I took a calming breath. "I got declined in the store just now, and I'm trying to figure out what's going on."

"First I'll need to verify one more piece of information. Can you please give me your four-digit PIN code."

I gave her the four numbers.

"Very good. That's a match. It's just a precaution to keep unauthorized individuals from accessing your information."

"Thanks, I know," I responded.

"Let me see. Just a moment please. There are quite a few transactions and notes here."

"Yes. I see the declined transaction this afternoon. Miss Clark, it seems you've simply exhausted the limit on this card. If you'd like, you can give me your checking account information and we can make a payment today that will free up some room."

I huffed. "That can't be. There was several thousand left on my last bill."

"Just one sec," she said again. "Yes, that's correct, but all the purchases you made on the new card we sent have used up your available balance."

I hadn't used this card except once for gas. "What purchases? And what new card?"

"You called and ordered another card with the name Benjamin Sykes, and we overnighted it."

My blood started to boil. "I did no such thing," I said loudly. I'd cut up Benji's old card a long time ago, and no way was he getting another one.

"Miss, calm down."

"You're telling me to calm down? He's not authorized to have a card."

"Miss Clark, as we just went through, only authorized users with the proper PIN code can access the account. And a replacement card is no exception."

"When?" I spat.

"Two days ago. On Wednesday."

I slammed my hand against the wheel. "And the purchases?" Now my hand hurt as much as my head.

"They were yesterday and today. Two at Best Buy, two at Target, one at Game Stop, and one at Walmart, from what we have processed so far."

"I didn't authorize those purchases, so we have to reverse the transactions."

She sighed over the line. "Miss, I'd like to help you, but if you gave him the PIN code, that authorized him to get a replacement card and make those purchases. You'll have to take it up with him."

The tears started to flow. I sobbed. "But he stole it. I didn't give it to him."

"Miss, if you have a police report, that would be something we could start with. You can mail it to the dispute address on the website."

"I don't have a report." I shook my head. "We need to shut down the account then."

"What I can do for you is invalidate the current cards and issue new ones to you, but you will still have to pay down the balance to be able to use them. You're currently two hundred and thirty-one dollars over your limit."

It might as well have been a thousand dollars. I didn't have that kind of money.

I told her to go ahead and mail me a new card at my new address here.

"One more thing, miss," she said.

This whole conversation had exhausted me. "Yes?"

"I would suggest changing your PIN to start with."

I should have thought of that.

"If there's nothing else, I'll transfer you so you can do that. The computer will ask you to key it in twice, and then it'll be done."

"Thank you," I said.

This wasn't her fault. That asshole Benji had gotten into my desk and was still fucking with my life even though he was more than three hundred miles away.

Fucking Benji.

She transferred me, and I went through the process, cutting Benji out of my credit card life. Again.

I never should have given him a card in the first place, but I'd fixed that by taking it back and cutting it up, or so I'd thought.

Two fucking dollars in my wallet and no credit cards—I couldn't be more broke if I tried.

With my vision blurred by tears, I didn't dare drive yet. I laid my head against the steering wheel and let them flow.

CHAPTER 19

ZACK

HOURS LATER I WAS STILL SMILING ABOUT MY PHONE CALL WITH Brittney. Once I'd confirmed she wasn't hurt, I'd found it pretty amusing to think of her hightailing it out of the cellar because of a spider. I stood and stretched my shoulders, which were still sore from all the overhead work under her house yesterday. I smiled as I contemplated another rubdown.

I finished what was left of my afternoon coffee and wandered out to Wendy's desk.

"Let's call off the social media review." It was scheduled for later this afternoon, and any excuse to skip it was good enough for me.

She looked up. "Spider problem, or girl problem?"

"Wendy, were you listening?"

She tilted her head. "The door was open, and you were pretty loud." She smirked and lifted her pen to her chin. "Would you like me to call a pest guy for you?"

I turned. "No thanks. Just cancel the social media meeting."

"Lucky girl," she said under her breath as I closed the door behind me.

Was I that obvious?

I got busy with the purchase requisitions I needed to finish before I could call it a day. I'd put these off yesterday, but another day's delay wasn't called for.

An hour and a half later, after three minor emergencies and an interminable stack of purchase reqs, I was ready to leave. I still had a half dozen customer deal sheets to go over, but those could wait, so I stuffed them in my briefcase for weekend review and locked up.

"Give her my regards," Wendy said as I turned the key.

"I will."

"Do I get to meet her?" she asked as I started for the elevator.

"If you come to the Habitat project on Sunday," I told her as I stopped and turned around.

"I'll pass on that." She laughed. "I'd probably nail my foot to the floor."

"You're always welcome." I waved and turned back toward the elevator.

The ride home was uneventful, but that didn't keep me from getting more and more tense as I got closer. I'd been looking forward to getting back home to see Brittney since the moment I left this morning. That girl did something to me I couldn't explain, but something I was quite happy for.

Turning into my driveway, I found the garage open behind the house. I pulled the car up to the tennis ball I'd hung from a string, turned off the engine, and set the brake. The space was short by modern standards—long enough to get the Shelby in there, but not by a lot.

I bounded up the stairs to the back porch and entered through the kitchen. The room was empty, with no sign that Brittney had started dinner yet.

I should have called and given her warning.

Opening the fridge, I pulled out two cans of beer before changing my mind and opting for a bottle of wine.

I found her on the couch in the old dining room I'd set up for TV. "Hey there. Like to start with some wine?" I held out the glass for her.

She looked up with red, watery eyes.

I set the two glasses down on the coffee table and sat beside her. "What's wrong, Sunshine?"

"Everything."

Her answer didn't give me a lot to work with. I sat back, forced past my inhibitions, and put my arm around her. "Tell me."

She didn't resist my touch. "I couldn't get you the steaks for tonight. I'm sorry." She sobbed.

My arm around behind her felt more natural than I'd expected. Exciting, but natural.

~

BRITTNEY

ZACH'S ARM FELT SO WARM AND COMFORTING, EXACTLY WHAT I needed right now.

"No worries, Brit. I should've left more money this morning."

"It's not your fault. It's mine." I sobbed again. "I've let Samantha down."

That was the true end result of this.

His fingers traced a circle on my shoulder as he kept me close and waited for more of an explanation. "I'm here for you."

I blinked back more tears as I realized the meaning of his words. He truly was the one I could count on, and he always had been. Until I left.

"If you're not ready yet, it's okay."

How could anyone be so understanding?

"There are things I didn't tell you." I hesitated, not knowing really where to start, and how to explain everything.

"I've got all night."

I sniffed. "This afternoon at the grocery store, my card got declined. And when I called the company, they said I was over my limit. But I shouldn't have been. Remember I got a call from Lillian saying some stuff was taken from my apartment in San Jose?"

"Yeah."

"Well, it was my ex, like I told you, and he's been busy with the stuff he took."

He stiffened, and the fingers that had been tracing circles on my skin stilled.

"He called the credit card company, and they issued him a card for my account." I sobbed. "And he used it again and again until my account was at the limit."

"Sunshine, I can help." His fingers resumed their gentle movement on my shoulder, a calming touch.

I snuggled closer. "It's all my fault."

"It's not your fault."

"Yes, it is. I shouldn't have left that stuff. I wasn't thinking."

"I told you, it's not your fault."

I couldn't accept that. "I'm failing Sam because I was stupid. And now she's not going to be able to finish. And she has interviews lined up. I've screwed it all up."

"Say that one more time, and I'm gonna have to spank you," he said firmly.

I pulled away. "I'm not a kid anymore."

"Then stop acting like one." He let me go as his gaze held mine. "It's not your fault."

"Of course you wouldn't understand," I spat. "You've got all the money in the world. What would you know about being broke?"

"I know a lot about making mistakes. I've made my fair share. You have to stop blaming yourself."

"I'm the one who screwed up. It's my fault."

In a flash he grabbed my arm and yanked me over.

I ended up over his knee.

"You really want to get yourself spanked?"

"Hey." I struggled, but it was no use against his strength. "Let me go."

"It's not your fault that your stupid ex-boyfriend—what's his name?"

I squirmed to no avail. "Benji."

"So, you're telling me it's your fault Benji is a thief?"

"Well, no."

"Benji's an asshole and a thief. Your life's in the shitter. All that means is it's time for you to pull up your big girl panties and get to work fixing it."

I struggled again and pushed at his leg, but he still held me down. "Are you going to let me up?"

"Are you going to behave and stop blaming yourself?"

"But I'm flat broke. I can't afford Sam's tuition. Fuck, I couldn't even afford tonight's dinner. I don't have a job, and without the papers from my desk I can't get one. I need a second ID. And the house I thought I had isn't even livable. Everything is so fucked up."

He sighed. "That wasn't the question."

"What was the question again?"

"Are you gonna behave yourself, stop dwelling on the past, and start moving forward?"

I didn't really see a choice. "Sure."

He started to tickle me.

I couldn't keep from laughing. "Hey, stop that. You said you'd let me up." I squirmed.

He relented and let me go.

I retreated to the other end of the couch. "You…you..."

I couldn't form a sentence. It was then that I realized just how easily he'd taken me from a downer pity party to laughing. I stopped complaining and folded my arms.

He shifted to face me. "I can help you, but only if you're willing to help yourself."

I couldn't figure out where he was going with this. "I can't accept your money."

"Clean out your ears, girl. I said I would help you. I didn't say I was giving you money."

"Big help you are. Money is what I need right now."

"Bullshit. The only thing you need is self-confidence." He stood and held out his hand. "Come with me." His tone was a demand, not an offer.

He hadn't heard a thing I'd said about my maxed-out credit cards and no job. That was the very definition of needing money before anything else. Sometimes the rich were so clueless about the real world.

At the risk of getting spanked, I sat still. "Where?"

"Sunshine, can't you stop arguing for once and just come along? I'm gonna show you that you have a lot more options than you think you do. A lot more of everything…except confidence, that is." He held out his hand.

I huffed, but stood anyway. It was a better idea to play along with him than argue while he was in this delusional state.

When I didn't take his hand, he turned and walked into the kitchen toward the back door.

I followed. "Where are we going?" I asked again.

He stopped and turned to face me. "Pick a piece of fruit. I'll eat it if it'll get you to be quiet for a moment and just come with me. I have something to show you."

I almost stomped my foot in frustration, but caught myself. I pulled an apple from the grocery bag still sitting on the counter and tossed it to him.

He caught it, took a bite, and opened the back door.

I followed him down the steps, through the backyard gate to my house, and up the back steps. We entered through the kitchen.

He put down the half-eaten apple and turned on the light in his phone.

I did the same and followed him into the dining room.

He shone the light on a small framed sketch on the wall. "What do you see?"

This was by far the stupidest question tonight. "It's probably something one of us did in art class for school."

I could see a smile appear on his face in the dim light. "You know what I see? I see money."

"No way."

"And this. What do you see?" He shifted to a small landscape painting on the opposite wall. Another stupid question.

"A painting." It wasn't large and didn't even look that good.

"So many people don't recognize value when they see it. The artist is Andrew Wyeth."

"Doesn't ring a bell," I told him.

He smiled again. "It's not a very large one, but it would probably fetch fifty to a hundred K at auction."

I stepped back, not sure I'd heard him correctly. "Fifty grand? As in dollars?" The number stunned me.

"That's right. Your grandmother collected really nice things. Right now they all look like shit because everything is so filthy. But clean them up and you've got a lot of valuable art in this house, and very nice antiques as well. What you called the kid's sketch…" He motioned to the other wall. "A small Picasso probably worth about five K, but you could unload it for three in a day at any one of the galleries around here."

I had to steady myself against a chair. Right now I'd kill for a few thousand dollars. "I had no idea."

"Do we agree now that things are not as dire as you thought?"

"I guess."

He switched off his phone's light, pocketed the device, and took me in his arms.

The comfort of his embrace was what I'd wanted earlier. At least I had it now, and it was better than I could've imagined. His body heat filtered through the clothing and into my heart.

"Sunshine," he said, pulling me tight.

I nestled my head into his shoulder, and his protective arms around me soothed away my worry. "Yeah?" I muttered.

He whispered in my ear. "I'll listen to all your troubles. I want you to tell me everything. Don't hold back; I'm here to listen—but only so long as you agree to not blame yourself. Got it?"

I nodded into his shoulder. "You're being bossy again."

"It's for your own good. You have to get it off your chest." He lifted my chin up with a finger. "Let me help you."

I looked up into his warm eyes and nodded. "Okay."

He let me go, took my hand, and led me back toward the door.

Immediately I wanted to be in his arms again, have him rub my back and let my fears melt away.

"But first you can cook that dinner you promised me," he said as he walked ahead of me.

I had to rush to keep up, he was in such a hurry. "Are pork chops okay? I couldn't afford the filet."

He opened the back door and ushered me through. "Any meal with you will be wonderful."

"Don't forget the rest of your apple," I reminded him.

"I still hate apples." He grimaced, but went back and rescued the apple before locking the door behind us. He took a loud bite for my benefit.

"Don't give me that look. You're the one who offered to eat it."

He shook his head and started down the steps. He'd gone from being bratty to saying the nicest things, and I liked this side of him better. I had to figure out where the switch was to get him to be like this more often.

Back at his house, he lit the grill on the back porch and started the meat.

Inside I prepared the Rice-A-Roni I'd gotten to go with it. While the mushrooms sautéed on the stove, I sliced up two pears for our fruit.

He located candles in a cupboard, lit them, and brought the wine from the other room.

When the food was finished, I sat down to candles, wine, fresh-cooked dinner, and Zack across from me. It wasn't as fancy as the dinner he'd taken me to at Cardinelli's, but it struck me as even more romantic. Maybe it was because we were alone, or maybe it was the look in his eyes as he took bites of the food I'd prepared and smiled at me. I knew we were just two people rooming together in a house and sharing dinner chores, but it felt more intimate than that.

He hadn't said a word beyond "*Bon appétit.*"

When I finished cutting another piece of meat, I looked up to catch him smiling. The look was something beyond friendly.

"What?" I asked as I put my fork down to wipe my face with my napkin. "Did I spill?"

"No, it's nothing," he answered. "I was just admiring your smile."

Heat rose in my cheeks. "Stop it. You're trying to embarrass me."

"No, it was a sincere compliment, but if you want, I'll think of something nasty to say instead." His words only increased my self-consciousness.

"You're weird, but compliment away if you must. I'm just not used to hearing any."

I didn't dare admit how good it felt.

"You obviously don't hang around with the right kind of people," he said.

Maybe not. Whatever it was, he made me happy. This afternoon I'd been staring into the abyss, and this evening he'd brought me back from the edge to the equivalent of a sunny meadow. I had no way to know for sure, but I had faith that with Zack's help, my tomorrows would improve.

"Benji was a complete shit," I blurted.

Zack looked up. "Well sure, with a name like that anybody would be. I feel sorry for the guy already."

"Yeah, that's what Sam told me too. She knew he was a loser as soon as she heard his name."

"I'm with her. I've never met the guy, and I already don't like him."

"Trust me. If you met him, there's no way your impression would improve."

"You mentioned you left in a hurry..."

The statement was simple, but my answer couldn't be.

"Things sort of came to a head all of a sudden on Tuesday."

He scooped up a bite of rice and continued to eat, waiting for me to put my thoughts together.

"He came to my work and started to make a scene in the reception area. It got so bad he scared off some patients. That's when Dr. Call decided she'd had enough, and the only way she could get rid of him was to get rid of me, so she let me go."

Zack's brow furrowed. "You mean to say the little shithead got you fired?" The anger in his voice was obvious.

"Technically Dr. Call suspended me," I corrected. "But he cost me my job." I took a sip of water before continuing. "The real kicker was when I got home."

Zack stopped chewing and looked on expectantly.

"He'd gone to town on my door and the wall outside my apartment with a can of spray paint."

"He tagged you?"

I nodded in disgust. "Yeah, and I got evicted from my apartment."

"That sure qualifies as a shitty day. Now I'm gonna kill him for sure."

I cut another piece of meat, because the statement spoke for itself. "That's why I was in such a hurry to get away from there and come down here."

He reached his hand across the table.

I reached the rest of the way to take it, and the sparks ignited as soon as I did.

"I'm sorry that happened to you. You deserve better."

The emotion in his eyes warmed me through and through.

CHAPTER 20

Zack

On Saturday, we'd made progress on her house, but between missing fittings that required trips to the store and difficulty reaching some of the connections, I hadn't gotten it finished.

I could have worked later into the night, but I'd lacked the motivation. I told myself I was going slow to be careful, but could it have been that I didn't want Brittney to leave my house and move into hers?

Today was Sunday, Habitat day, and we'd gotten up early.

I forced down the kiwi she made me eat for the second day in a row. I'd requested oranges instead, but it fell on deaf ears.

She packed a ton of fruit for the day after I told her the size of the group we'd be lunching with. She hefted the grocery bag, and I hurried her out the door.

"It pays to be early to these things," I told her as I locked the door behind us.

"Why is that?"

"Then we get our pick of jobs. This being your first weekend at one of these, I want us doing the right kind of thing."

"Why does that matter?" she asked.

"It matters to me. I don't want you up on the roof."

I was responsible for her safety today, and not that we had many accidents at these things, but I didn't need to hear from Doug later that I shouldn't have let her handle something dangerous—like a hammer.

"Think I can't handle it?"

"That's not the point," I shot back as I opened the garage.

"And what is the point?"

I popped the trunk while searching for a way out of this argument. "I don't want to explain to your brother that you fell off the roof avoiding a spider."

We packed up the trunk with the food she'd gotten, along with the extra shirts, hats, and sunscreen I'd brought out.

Her brow furrowed as she contemplated my answer. "Spiders?"

"They like to sun themselves on roofs."

"I don't believe you. You said they were in the basement. I saw one there."

I cocked my head. "That doesn't keep them from wanting to sun on the roof. If you want, I'll catch one for you. They make good barbecue."

"Get outta here."

"Just sayin'."

"Okay. No roof work."

I opened the door for her, and she slid in.

She buckled up, and I jogged around.

The engine started like a charm. I backed out onto the street and turned north.

"Why did you choose this car? You could've gotten yourself something nice, like a Ferrari," she said.

I glanced over and caught her grin.

She was goading me.

"Newer is not always better. I guess I just like some of the older classics. The new cars are all automatic this and automatic that, electronic this, electronic that, with a ton of extras—power seats, fancy turbochargers, GPS, and heated cup holders.

"This car, however…" I patted the steering wheel. "…is simple. Nothing but pure, unadulterated horsepower. In its day, it was the ultimate car for turning gasoline into noise, tire smoke, and speed. A simple machine with a simple mission—going fast as fuck."

She considered for a moment before stating, "You seem to like old things."

"I appreciate the classics. My house, and yours for that matter, were built by craftsmen. They have character. This car is the same. It's one-hundred-percent character. It doesn't pretend to be something it's not. It's about noise, fury, and speed."

"A man's car," she said.

I wasn't about to argue with that. "I'm not apologizing. If you're saying it's not a sissy car, I'll agree."

I turned onto the freeway onramp, and as we came to the merge, I saw a truck coming up fast in the right lane. I downshifted, popped the clutch, and with a squeal of the tires, we were up to speed and in front of him in seconds. It was a pity we didn't have an autobahn here to let me open it up.

Glancing over, I caught Brittney gripping the door, but also grinning ear to ear. She liked speed too.

I put it in fourth, and we settled down for the long drive over the hill.

"I wasn't interested in cars growing up, like you guys were, but this car is certainly growing on me," she offered. "When can I drive it?"

"The tenth of never," I answered. I'd never let anybody drive this car. "You don't even know how to drive a stick."

"Yes, I do. My first Corolla was a stick."

"Trust me, this is nothing like a Corolla."

She crossed her arms. "This is nothing but a stupid old Mustang with fancy paint and a snake on the carpet." She rubbed her foot on the cobra stitched into the floor mats.

My blood boiled momentarily, but that's exactly what she wanted. "For your information, this is a real GT500 upgraded to a Super Snake, with the old engine swapped out for a racing 427—the same engine that won the twenty-four hours of Le Mans for Ford and took the crown away from Ferrari." I clenched my hands on the wheel and loosened them, reminding myself to calm down.

"When do I get to drive it?"

"Like I said, the tenth of never."

This wasn't the car to learn on. Just like you didn't learn to ride a horse by jumping on a thoroughbred.

She changed the subject. "Where exactly are we going?"

"Over the hill to the valley. Habitat is building a house in Van Nuys."

We motored on and were over the hill and down into the San Fernando Valley relatively quickly in the light Sunday-morning traffic.

I'd checked the address before leaving and navigated off the freeway and through several turns until we arrived at the right street. The build site was obvious, with dozens of people milling around out front. I had to park down at the far end of the block. I jumped out, and Brittney wisely stayed in her seat until I opened the door for her.

"More people than I expected," she noted.

"I hope we got here early enough." I led her through the crowd to a table where they were handing out gloves and hardhats. Bill Covington and his wife, Lauren, were behind the table. Lauren had their son strapped to her in a front baby carrier.

Bill looked up from the paper he was consulting. "Hey, Zack, glad you could make it." His eyes flashed to Brittney with just a hint of recognition. "And your friend," he added.

I shook Bill's hand. "You might remember Brittney Spear from Brentmoor." I urged her forward.

Bill pointed at her. "Yeah, I thought I recognized you." He put his arm around his wife and baby. "This is my wife, Lauren."

Lauren offered her hand. "You wouldn't by any chance be related to—"

Brittney cut her off. "No such luck, and I can't sing worth a damn."

"It's a pleasure, Brittney. Any friend of Zack's is a friend of ours."

"How old is he?" Brittney maneuvered to get a better look at the baby.

"This is Wendell, ten months."

Brittney cooed to the little guy. "He's cute."

"Named after Bill's father," Lauren added.

I glanced over the crowd. "Dad around?" I asked Bill.

Bill, who was busy greeting the next person in line, pointed to the back. "At the plan table, I think."

"Glad to have you with us. Just don't forget to keep your sunscreen up to date," Lauren warned Brittney with a smile.

I picked up two hard hats and dragged Brittney away from Lauren and the baby.

"Got it—sunscreen," Brittney said as we left.

Dad was easy to spot at the plan table in the middle of what would soon become a house.

"Good morning," he called as we approached. "Zachary, I see you convinced her to join us."

"Couldn't possibly keep me away," Brittney responded.

"I don't know if you remember me," Dad said.

Brittney put on one of her winning smiles. "I couldn't possibly forget you, Mr. Benson."

"Lloyd, please. We're all family here," he said. He opened his arms for a quick hug, which she accepted.

"Tell your brother *Semper Fi* for me next time you talk to him," Dad said.

Brittney nodded. "Sure thing."

"Dad, you got something nice and easy for us for her first weekend?" I asked.

He picked up his clipboard and scanned it. "Want to start with electrical drilling?"

I didn't like the sound of that. "How about electrical boxes? Is that available?"

"Dennis is already down for that, but I'm sure you can convince him to give it up for the right price."

No price would be too high this morning.

"Glad to have you with us. Don't forget to keep your sunscreen freshened up," Dad warned Brittney as I pulled her toward my older brother.

"Yep. Sunscreen," she answered.

Dad pointed to his head. "Hard hats too," he reminded us.

I gave Brittney one of the yellow plastic hats and donned the other myself.

Dennis looked up as we approached. "Dad said you were bringing a girl today, but I had no idea it would be anybody as pretty as Doug's sister here. Brittney, isn't it?"

She blushed. "Thanks. Flattery is gladly accepted. You should teach your brother that trick."

I ignored the dig. "Hey, Dennis, since this is Brittney's first time, can we swap with you and take the electrical boxes?"

"What do you have to swap? I'm not doing roofing again."

"Electrical pass-throughs," I answered.

"And follow you two around all day?" He stroked his chin for a second, obviously giving me a hard time. "I guess, but just because it's her."

"Thanks, Dennis," I told him.

"I'm doing it for her and Doug, not for you," he said.

He was always busting my balls.

He handed me the electrical plan sheet. "You'll need this."

"And the tape measure," I told him.

Dennis unclipped a tape measure from his belt and handed it to Brittney.

"Try to keep up," I told him as I took Brittney to the supplies in back.

I located the cardboard boxes with the blue single- and double-gang electrical boxes and handed the one with the triples to my helper. After grabbing a hammer and a pencil, we were ready to start.

"We'll start at the front door and work our way around. Just follow me."

She followed me to the front of the house, where I checked the plan for the door swing and switch position. I held out my hand. "Tape measure."

She gave it to me.

I pulled it out and locked it with enough tape to measure forty-four inches.

"Okay. This is what we do: At each of these locations on the plan, we're going to nail in one of these blue boxes for the switches and outlets. For switches, we measure forty-four inches up from the floor and mark it with a pencil. Then we nail the box there so the bottom lines up with the mark. For outlets, the measurement is twelve inches, except in the kitchen and bathroom. We'll figure those out later. Got it?"

"Twelve and forty-four. Got it. But which size box goes where?"

I pointed on the plan sheet. "This is a single-gang box, this denotes a double, and this here is a triple. So, what size do we put here beside the front door?"

She checked the paper. "A three?"

I nodded. "You're a natural. So make your mark."

I picked a triple out of our supplies while she measured. Lining up with the mark on the stud, I banged in the nails attached to the box, and we had one complete.

"One down, and a hundred to go." It wasn't that many, but it would feel like it soon enough.

We were more than halfway through when Phil Patterson came by.

"My God, I thought I recognized you," Phil said as he got a look at Brittney's face. He pointed to himself. "Phil Patterson. We went to Brentmoor together. It's Brittney, isn't it? Brittney Spear?"

"It's Clark now, Phil. But yeah, good to see you too."

It almost got by me—almost. She said her name was now Clark.

Had she gotten married?

She wasn't wearing a ring.

There was definitely something I didn't know. Why hadn't she told me?

"Zack, I need four singles for the attic space. Can you spare 'em?" Phil asked.

"Huh?" I was still processing Brittney's married name.

"I need singles for up in the attic," he repeated.

I offered him the one I was holding. "Sure. Whatever."

Phil took the boxes and left.

Brittney tapped me on the shoulder. "This one's ready. The plan says a single."

I picked another single from the box and started to bang the nails into the stud when I missed and hit the box instead. The box cracked. I pulled the nail and threw the broken plastic to the side.

"Careful. Do you want to switch for a while?" Brittney asked.

"No, I got it. I just think I'm ready for lunch."

We made our way around the room, more slowly now, and still stayed ahead of Dennis drilling holes in the studs for the wires to pass through.

It wouldn't be long before Dad sounded the lunch horn.

Married? What the hell is with that?

CHAPTER 21

BRITTNEY

I RECOGNIZED ZACK'S SISTER, SERENA, AS SHE WALKED UP.

After a quick hello, she asked, "Hey Zack can I borrow Brittney?"

Zack shrugged and checked his watch.. "Sure."

Serena tapped me on the shoulder. "How about you join me for the sandwich run?"

I stood. "Sure."

"And no forgetting my meatball again, Serena," Lloyd called as we walked by him.

After we were out of earshot, Serena said, "I'm trying to get him to eat healthier, but it's not working. He insists on having a meatball sub even though he knows it's bad for him."

"Men can be like that."

"Don't I know it." She pushed the button on her key fob, and the Escalade ahead of us unlocked.

We got in and started down the street.

"Subway is just around the corner. I called in the order early, so it should be ready for us." She smiled in my direction. "I'm really glad you could join us, Brittney."

"Me too. This is a lot of fun. You guys do it often?"

She turned left at the stop sign. "Not quite every month but pretty regularly. Sometimes a weekend is called off because of rain in the winter."

"That sounds like quite a lot."

"The community's been so good to us. This is our way of giving back a little. And, it's always good to get out in the sunshine and do a little honest work instead of sitting behind a desk. The most important thing, I think, is that it gets us together as a family."

I appreciated the sentiment—family was important. It was the one thing we could always rely on.

The Subway was just a few blocks away, as she'd said. It took a large bag to hold all the sandwiches she'd ordered, and another bag for the chips. We loaded ourselves and our stash back into her car.

We stopped at another stop sign, and she looked over. "When did you get back to town?"

"Just this week."

After turning on the street she asked, "Where are you staying?"

"With Zack," I said, not wanting to elaborate.

"That's good. He's a good guy."

Of course his sister couldn't say much else. I would always say the same about Doug.

Zack was waiting on the sidewalk in front of the construction site when we parked and got out.

A loud horn blast startled me.

I looked behind me to find Zack's father in the middle of the project holding an air horn above his head. He gave it another long honk.

Serena opened the back to retrieve the bags. "That means lunch."

Zack took my hand. "Now you get to meet the rest of the crew."

"Crew?" I asked.

"Yeah, a mixture of Bensons and Covingtons. We're pretty much all out here every time we have one of these things, at least those of us who are in town."

"I need to get the fruit from the car," I reminded him. He probably hoped I would forget.

"Right. Almost forgot," Zack said.

"Go ahead, I got these," Serena told us.

I pulled Zack down the street toward his car. The sun was high in the sky, so we retrieved the hats as well as the bag of fruit.

"We may not need all this," he said. "I'm sure Katie brought fruit with her too."

"Katie?" I asked. I thought I'd seen Katie Covington wandering around earlier. "Katie Covington?"

Zack handed me the bag. "Yes, but it's Knowlton now."

"You mean Knowlton as in Nick?"

"Yeah, she married him over her brother's objections. But now Nick's one of us, just a part of the family—a nice guy once you get past the rough exterior he puts up. And, he's a professor now at UCLA."

That floored me, because the Nick Knowlton I'd known in high school had been all about motorcycles and skipping class, not exactly the type to become a university professor.

"Are we talking about the same Nick?" I asked as we walked back toward the house.

"The same. See that bike over there?" He pointed at the Harley across the street. "He and Katie rode up on that."

When we reached them, Zack introduced me to the group, and I waved around the circle. The Covingtons were Bill, Lauren, Katie, and her husband, Nick. The Benson crew included Zack's father, his brothers Dennis and Josh, and his sister Serena. His brother Vincent lived in Boston now, and his other sister Kelly was in Europe today. Phil Patterson, who'd introduced himself earlier, and a Winston somebody rounded out the group.

With a cap that read Patterson Construction, Phil was the only pro among us.

I'd seen many of them at one point or another years ago, but they were all so grown up now.

When Serena set down the bags, everybody was in a hurry grabbing for their favorite sandwiches. I noticed Serena pull one of the meatball subs and hide it behind her back. Zack snatched the other one.

Frustrated after looking through the sandwiches that remained, Lloyd glared at Serena. "I warned you," he said with a pointed finger.

She produced the sandwich from behind her back. "I was just messing with you, Dad."

He wagged his finger again. "Do that one more time, young lady, and you'll regret it."

I doubted that his bite was as bad as his bark. It was easy to see he loved his children.

Everyone dug into the subs and chips.

Serena had ordered more sandwiches than people, which came in handy when most of the guys, including Zack, checked the bags and grabbed a second. Physical labor like this amped up the appetite.

Lauren, who was sitting to my right, leaned over and nodded toward Zack. "You two could get a little away time up at the cabin, if you like."

Zack was talking with Phil and not paying attention.

"Cabin?" I asked.

"Bill and I have a cabin in the mountains. We don't get much free time to go up, so it's available to family and friends. Very romantic." She winked. She seemed to have me and Zack pegged as a couple.

"Thanks for the offer," I said, not venturing to correct her impression of our situation.

When the sandwiches were mostly devoured, I brought out my bag and offered fresh fruit around.

Everyone except Zack was a taker. "I'll wait for Katie's fruit, thanks," he told me.

Katie turned and brought out two boxes from behind her. "I brought two today, both apple."

"Now that's my kind of fruit," Zack said as Katie opened the boxes to reveal gorgeous pies.

She'd also brought paper plates and plastic forks.

I shoved an orange at Zack. "No, you don't. Not until you finish this."

"You tell him, girl," Serena said.

A comment I didn't need.

Zack scowled, but started to peel the orange. "You know you can walk home, if you like."

The group became quiet.

"Just kidding," he said, realizing his comment hadn't gone over well. "Thanks, Sunshine." He smiled, and the group's banter resumed as they attacked the apple pies.

Her baby had been fussing a bit when Lauren stood. "It's his lunchtime too." She took her chair over by the fence.

"He's a cutie," Serena said softly to me.

I glanced over to where Lauren was starting to nurse her son. "Sure is." I couldn't help but smile.

After Zack finished his orange, he and I shared a large piece of pie.

"Thank you," I whispered into his ear between bites.

He shrugged.

"Who's turn is it for clean up?" Lloyd asked the group.

Serena raised her hand. "I think it's me."

"I nominate the new girl to help," Zack said.

He was probably getting me back for insisting on the orange.

I stood. "Sure, I'll help you, Serena."

The group slowly dispersed, and Serena and I were left alone with the aftermath.

Mr. Benson sounded his horn, and the other volunteers started getting back to the business of house building.

"I'm really glad you two got together," she said as we were picking up.

Before I could correct her, she continued, "He's had a crush on you since the seventh grade—a crush like you wouldn't believe. My room was next to his at home, and the walls aren't as sound-proof as they should be. I heard him say your name in his sleep more than once—not that I would ever tell him, but it's the truth. That's half the reason I think it never worked out with any of the other girls."

I couldn't believe what I was hearing.

She smiled again. "Secretly, I think he was always waiting for it to work out with you."

This was a revelation. A surprise to top all surprises.

I contemplated an answer but didn't have one. "We're not—"

She interrupted me. "I get that you're not super serious yet. I just think it's good you got together. He deserves someone like you. I always thought you two would make a good couple." She tied the top to the garbage bag she'd filled. "And I was right. You're cute together."

"We're not seeing each other," I said, setting her straight.

She giggled. "Okay. If that's the way you want to play it, I'll go along. My brothers can be pretty secretive, not wanting people to know who they're going out with."

She didn't get it, but I'd said enough already. I didn't correct her again.

As we carried the full garbage bags to the dumpster by the street, her words haunted me. *"He's had a crush on you since seventh grade."* Earth to Serena, that can't possibly have been the situation.

I knew the truth. I was just his best friend's sister, so maybe it had looked from the outside like he was coming over to our house to see me.

I tossed my bag over the edge. "Doug was his best friend."

"Guys can be so transparent sometimes. He likes Doug, but even if Doug really pissed him off, he was never going to stop going by to see you."

The implication was eye-opening. I still had a chance with Zack.

Still wasn't the right word. *Now*, I had a chance with Zack. I hadn't been imagining what I felt between us.

"Today is the happiest he's looked in a month," Serena added as we walked back to the construction site. She winked.

That wink hinted at the possibilities I had with Zack. That wink meant that as his sister, she knew things—things other girls wouldn't know. Sibling bonds allowed truths that otherwise got distorted or hidden. I knew that well enough myself, with Doug and Samantha.

"I'm glad he got over that best friend's sister crap. Guys can be so stupid about shit like that—the bro code, you know, hands off your best friend's sister, that kind of shit. Doesn't make any sense to me. You like him, he likes you, you're adults. Where's the harm? Doug should be proud you've got a boyfriend as cool as his best friend. Well, that's just me. Anyway, I'm glad he got over that shit and finally got smart enough to get together with you."

She went to the back of the house, and I went inside to work with Zack.

He looked my direction as I walked up, but then averted his eyes without a smile.

The bro code? Could that be the problem?

CHAPTER 22

BRITTNEY

ALL AFTERNOON ZACK HADN'T SAID MORE THAN TWO WORDS THAT didn't relate to the stupid electrical boxes, followed by the plates we hammered on the studs at the height of the pass-through holes.

The drive back over the hill from the valley had been equally quiet. Now we were almost home, and I wasn't sure what to do.

I didn't know where to start to make it better. "I'm sorry I embarrassed you."

He looked straight ahead. "What?"

"The orange. I didn't mean to embarrass you in front of your family and friends."

"Forget it" was his only reply.

I needed more than that, but he wasn't opening up. I waited, but still got nothing. I continued to watch him, looking for the slightest glance in my direction, the slightest opening.

We drove in silence for another few miles.

"I'm sorry," I said.

He looked over this time. There was something unreadable in his eyes. "I said it's not a problem."

"Then what is it?"

He took a long, deep breath. "Do you have anything important to tell me?"

I did not see that coming. "No."

He took the off-ramp toward our neighborhood. "Then why are we talking?"

"Because I want to apologize."

"You did."

I crossed my arms, looked straight ahead, and managed to restrain myself from stomping my feet. I felt like hitting him, he was being so obstinate. "What is your problem?"

"I don't have a problem. I just don't like being lied to."

I jerked my head to look at him. I hadn't lied to him, and I couldn't think of what would have given him that idea. "I haven't lied to you."

He turned right onto Snakewood. "Right. Your last name isn't Spear anymore, it's Clark, and you're running away from this Benji character. Did you forget to mention he's your husband?" He pulled into the driveway around the house.

"I'm not married, and he's not my husband," I shouted as he stopped the car.

"Right, ex-husband then."

"You wouldn't understand." I unbuckled and bolted from the car. I started toward the back gate between the houses.

He shut down the engine and got out. "Where are you going?"

I turned around and yelled back. "I'm going to get the art out of the house before someone steals it."

"Do you want help?" he called.

I walked through the gate and slammed it shut, letting that be my answer. Call me a liar, will you? I'd been called a lot of things, but never that. I may not have explained everything, but I hadn't lied.

I stomped up the stairs and unlocked the back kitchen door.

"Stop running away," Zack said from behind me.

I ignored him and went inside.

Out of habit I flipped the light switch, and of course nothing happened. No electricity. For a moment I'd forgotten how fucked up things were.

I took the Picasso gently down from the wall and placed it on the table before going into the other room to get the more expensive painting.

That's when I saw it.

A brick in the middle of the floor amid broken glass from the front window.

I couldn't breathe. I leaned over, hands on my knees, trying to compose myself. Everything in my life was falling apart. The tears started and I crumpled to the floor.

CHAPTER 23

ZACK

BRITTNEY WAS IN ONE PISS-POOR MOOD. SHE'D SLAMMED THE GATE in the fence between our properties so hard it rattled. A few more jolts like that to the old wood, and it would fall apart.

I followed her into her house, but she wasn't in the kitchen. It wasn't until I looked through the doorway toward the front of the house that I saw her kneeling on the floor, sobbing.

I rushed to her and knelt beside her, putting my arm around her shoulder. Shattered glass sparkled over the floor, and a brick lay in the middle of the mess.

"Are you okay?"

She shook her head and continued to sob. "Why is everything going wrong?"

I cradled her in my arms. "I'll take care of this, Sunshine."

Her sobbing slowed. She sniffed and wiped her nose with her sleeve. "I don't deserve this."

"Of course you don't," I assured her. "Let's get you back to the other house." I got to my feet and pulled her up.

She wiped under an eye. "Okay."

I pulled her toward the kitchen.

"But the pictures."

"I'll come back and collect them."

She stopped arguing and came down the back stairs with me. She shivered lightly as I held her and we made our way back through the gate and up the back steps into my house.

I deposited her on one of the kitchen chairs. "Stay here while I get the pictures."

She opened her mouth as if to protest, but closed it and nodded instead.

Good girl.

Back in the other house, I carefully removed the precious artwork from the walls, piece by piece, and placed each on the table or leaning against the chairs. It took three trips to bring them all to my place, and then I made a trip back to see what I could do about the broken front window.

The brick had two rubber bands around it, and when I turned it over, I found a note secured to the projectile. It was written in red ink.

I WANT WHAT'S MINE - LEAVE IT UNDER THE FLOWER POT AND THAT WILL BE THE END OF IT

I folded the note and stuffed it in my wallet.

Only a small section of multi-pane window had been broken out, and that would be easy to replace. For a temporary fix, I returned to the kitchen for the roll of duct tape I'd left there earlier. A few strips over the opening, and I had it closed off enough to keep the insects out.

"You're going to get yours, you little fucker," I said after the last piece of tape was in place.

That little Piss Boy was one asshole I was going to teach a lesson he would never forget. The fucking pain in the ass was going to learn the hard way not to mess with me or my friends.

And no fucking way was I putting his phone under the flower pot —not in a million years. I had a better idea.

Walking back to check on Brittney, I smiled as I envisioned him opening the surprise I had planned for him. Adding surveillance cameras to the house was also going on my to-do list, to catch the little weasel on tape in case he tried another stunt like this. There was no telling how stupid he was, no guarantee he'd learn his lesson quickly.

The deadbolt on my kitchen door locked with a pleasing click as I closed it behind me. I set one last picture down in the other room and returned to Brittney.

Her eyes were moist, and she still trembled. "Thank you."

I held her eyes with mine. "Have I ever lied to you?"

She shook her head.

"You have to believe me. You're safe here with me. I'm going to fix this."

She blinked back a tear, and the slightest hint of a smile appeared.

I took the other chair. "Now, I need an honest answer to a few simple questions, Ms. Clark."

She looked up with teary eyes.

"Are you going to do what I ask you to do?"

She gave me a shrug and a nod.

"Yes?"

She sighed. "What choice do I have?"

It seemed like the best I was going to get this evening.

Pushing out the chair, I rose. "None. To start with, don't go over there without me."

She drew in a breath and bit her bottom lip, but the argument I expected didn't come.

I took her hand and pulled her up. "Go sit down, and I'll get the wine." I pointed her toward the couch. "White or red?" I asked.

"Jack," she replied.

"You're getting wine. You don't need anything stronger right now."

She shook her head. "Easy for you to say."

I walked after her. "Come here, Sunshine." I opened my arms and took her into a hug.

She still shook. "Zack, I'm scared." She gripped me tightly.

I rubbed her back and kissed the top of her head. "I won't let anything happen to you. Now sit down while I get the wine. And then you can explain what's going on."

She didn't let go of me.

I ran my fingers through her hair. "Please," I added.

She did as I asked and slumped at the end of the couch.

"The question stands, white or red?"

"White, if I have to, but I really want Jack."

I poured us each a large glass of sauvignon blanc and returned to her.

I offered her the glass. "And I said no."

She accepted the wine. "Can't you be a little less…bossy?" She threw back a large gulp of the wine.

I sipped mine. "Can't you be a little less…argumentative?"

"I guess," she answered.

I shifted the glass to my other hand so I could pull her up next to me. "To less bossy and less argumentative." I offered my glass to hers.

She clinked with me. "Sure."

I took another sip. "I think you have something to explain."

She took another large gulp. "I guess. But I didn't lie to you."

"I'm sorry I said that. I was a little angry that you hadn't told me you'd gotten married. It's sort of a big deal. And telling Doug to keep it from me—that was just mean."

I didn't tell her how much it hurt to know she hadn't wanted to include me in that part of her life.

"That's because I didn't get married," she shot back.

"I'm listening."

She drained the rest of her glass and handed it to me.

I put it on the coffee table.

"I'll take a refill," she said.

"Not yet. Not till we finish here."

She took in a breath through gritted teeth. "But I want—"

I interrupted her with a finger to her lips. "Calm down, Sunshine. Less argumentative, remember?"

A grimace appeared. "But…"

I raised a finger. "Come here." I moved my hand from her shoulder to her neck and pulled her face to within inches of mine. "I'm here for you."

I pulled her the rest of the way.

She closed her eyes.

I brushed her lips with mine, not daring for more of a kiss, lest I get carried away.

She sighed.

"Tell me everything." I moved just a few inches away. "Slowly," I added.

Her eyes opened, tinged with wetness.

I moved back, away from the danger of being that close.

She took a breath and ran her fingers through her hair. "You don't know the story of why I left, do you?"

"I wasn't around, but Doug said you broke up with that guy Todd."

"That was the story he was supposed to tell you."

This was getting ominous. The secret she'd withheld wasn't a small one.

I took another small sip and waited for the other shoe to drop.

"I left because I testified against a guy, and it wasn't safe here."

"Go on," I urged.

"Todd's brother, Rick, had the bright idea to rip off this house. It turns out the house belonged to a drug dealer—Delgado was his name. Anyway, somehow he figured out who did it, and he killed Rick. I saw it, but for the longest time I refused to say anything to the cops."

"You were scared. That's understandable."

"It was six months later when Detective Swenson convinced me to testify. The trial was moved to Bakersfield, so nobody around here knew about it. It was only a two-day trip and then back here."

She took another deep breath. "A few weeks after the trial was over, Todd won this trip to Mexico—four days in Acapulco, some kind of contest prize. I didn't want to go. You know, Montezuma's revenge and all, but he wasn't going to let it go to waste, so he went alone." She sniffed. "He never came back."

"You mean…"

"He checked into the hotel and never checked out. *Missing* is what the Mexican police said."

I pulled her closer. "I'm sorry for you."

"When I went to the police here, they said the contest company didn't exist. I left that night. I just packed a bag and drove. Delgado killed him, and he meant to kill me too. He would have if I'd gone on the Mexico trip."

"Is that why the name change?"

"I ended up in Arkansas, changed my name to Clark while I was there, and eventually moved to San Jose. I didn't ever intend to come back here. Most people don't know my name was ever Spear. If I meet somebody who knew before, they assume I got married, and I'm not going to say no and explain—that kind of defeats the purpose. I can't have my old name talked about."

I put the glass down. "Until stupid Benji wrecked things."

She nodded. "Fucking Benji. If it hadn't been for him, I'd still be safe in San Jose with my old job."

I leaned in to kiss her temple. "But then you wouldn't have come back into my life."

Her smile grew. "There is that."

"What happened to Delgado?"

"He got twenty-five to life for Rick's murder, so he's still locked up."

I reached for my glass again and took another swallow. "I'm sorry I thought you lied to me."

"I'm sorry I didn't tell you. I should have said something before. Can I have my Jack now?"

I rose from the couch and took both our glasses. "Pick something relaxing to watch on TV. I'm ordering pizza for dinner."

"I can cook," she offered.

"No. You relax. I got this."

"But we need some fruit."

I located the pizza shop number on my phone. "I'll make it Hawaiian then. Pineapple will be our fruit tonight."

"But that's not enough."

I hit dial on the phone and pointed my free finger at her. "No arguments, remember?"

She looked ready to throw back another comment, but restrained herself and picked up the remote.

I listened to ringing on the phone. "You can feed me two kiwis in the morning to make up for it."

After ordering, I settled into the couch again.

"Sorry about the window. That brick was meant as a message for me."

Her head cocked to the side. "What do you mean?"

"Turns out there was a love note on the brick from the neighborhood juvenile delinquent. Piss Boy, I call him."

A slight smile came to her face. "Interesting name."

"He seems to be the head of the pack of kids that were using your house as a hangout. The last time I confronted him and kicked them out, he wet his pants. I don't know his real name, so Piss Boy it is."

"Were those the kids you took the phones from?"

"Yup. And he seems to think throwing a brick through your window is going to get me to give him back his phone."

"But you're not?"

"Not tonight."

She pushed me in the shoulder. "You forgot to fill the wine glasses, dummy."

CHAPTER 24

BRITTNEY

ZACK HAD BEEN A GOOD LISTENER, AND IT FELT GOOD TO FINALLY tell him what had happened, why I couldn't come back or get in touch these past few years.

I flicked on the TV as instructed and searched through the listings. I chose *Sweet Home Alabama*, a light rom-com. I had no idea if it was the kind of thing that suited Zack, but he'd told me to pick.

He returned with the wine glasses.

I examined mine. It was less than half full, but his was the same. "Kind of miserly with the wine tonight."

"I don't want you getting ahead of me, and I plan to keep my wits about me this evening."

"Do you think he'll throw another brick tonight?"

"Nah."

The movie started.

"Come on, not a chick flick," Zack complained as he reached for the remote.

I kept it out of reach. "I did what you said. You told me to pick, so shut up and watch. You might even like it."

"Fat chance."

"'Live with your choices,' you told me. Are you gonna tell me you don't like Reese Witherspoon?"

"She's kinda hot," he admitted.

I felt a pang of something I wasn't used to feeling when he called her hot. I couldn't be jealous of an actress on the flat screen—that didn't make any sense. I was just upset he didn't share my taste in movies, wasn't I?

"But it's still a chick flick," he whined.

I stopped talking and settled in next to him.

When the doorbell rang, I paused the movie.

Zack returned with our aromatic dinner, and I restarted the film while we ate.

He shoved away his plate after demolishing a huge part of the pizza. His arm came protectively around me, and his warmth gave me the first peace I'd felt in a long time.

Relying on someone else wasn't in my nature, but Zack was worth an exception. The more I thought about it, the more it made sense. Zack was the one I could depend on—he always had been. He was big and strong in more than just a physical way. He had strength of character, and he stood behind his words.

I snuck a peek up at him.

"What?" he asked.

I stretched up to kiss his cheek. "Thank you."

He merely gave a man-grunt in return, a reminder that I was cuddled up next to the other half of the species—the half that didn't verbalize emotions. The half that would complain about watching a love story, but instantly pick up his gun and charge into the fray to protect me.

I blinked back a tear and snuggled closer to my protector.

As the movie went on, we both got to laughing at the funny parts, as Melanie worked herself deeper and deeper into a hole with the two men in her life.

For a guy who didn't want to watch a movie like this, Zack seemed to be enjoying it—not that he would admit such a thing.

He had taken to stroking my shoulder and arm with lazy, slow movements that relaxed and excited me at the same time. Back in the day, we'd watched plenty of movies together, the three of us, but never like this. This was different, in a comfortable, cozy way.

The warmth of his body soaked through the fabric separating us and made its way to my chest, where my heart interpreted it as a need to beat faster.

My hand slipped from my leg to his thigh, not entirely unintentionally. My fingers began a slow circle, which he didn't resist. I had trouble concentrating on the plot of the movie as this afternoon's conversation with Serena kept replaying in my head. *"He's had a crush on you since the seventh grade."*

I couldn't get those words to stop repeating in my ears.

"Sunshine?" he said.

"Yeah?"

"This isn't half bad," he murmured.

"I promise not to tell anyone you said that."

He chuckled. "You better not."

"You want to know something?" I asked.

"Sure."

"I kinda like being here with you."

There, I'd gone out on a limb and admitted it.

"That's the wine talking," he said.

I sighed and pulled my hand back. He meant the rebuff in a humorous way, but it still hurt.

A minute later, he gave me a quick squeeze with his arm. "Me too," he added.

Two words had never been more welcome. What I hadn't admitted to Serena, of course, was that I'd had a crush on Zack since even before the seventh grade. These might not be the ideal circumstances, but I dared to hope his feelings hadn't changed in the years I'd been away. A lot had happened, though.

We'd just been kids back then. How would it work if the adult versions of us played out our younger fantasies?

The wine was taking its toll on my bladder, so I excused myself to pee. In the untangling process, my breast rubbed against his arm, and the sensation had me wondering how it would have felt without the clothing between us. My nipples tightened.

Checking myself in the mirror before returning, I made a choice. I ditched the bra and chose a scoop-neck T-shirt. I liked what I saw in the mirror after the change.

When I walked in, he was leaving a message on the phone. His eyes lingered long enough on my chest to tell me he'd caught the difference, and the look on his face was approval, and maybe a little more.

"Telling Wendy I won't be in tomorrow."

"Why not?"

He grinned. "Fixing your house is more important."

"Underwires suck." I answered the question inherent in his raised eyebrow as his eyes came to my chest again.

It was a useful enough lie. I retook my seat next to him and snuggled closer as his arm draped behind me again.

His eyes were on the screen every time I checked.

The movie was almost over. "Did you ever wonder what would have happened if—"

I didn't get a chance to finish the question.

"Stop it," he insisted.

I pulled away. I hadn't even decided how to ask about us before he'd interrupted me. "Stop what?"

"You're always worrying about the past. You can't change or fix that. It's a waste of time, and all it does is drain the energy you need to move forward. Take stock of the situation, and make today's choices to move toward the future you want. Deal with the present. It's the only thing you can affect. Focus your energy forward, not back. You have to learn that. Whatever happened, happened. It's not your fault. Benji was a bad choice. Get over it and make better choices in the future."

He didn't get me at all.

I stared him down. "I wasn't talking about Benji."

"It doesn't matter. Dwelling on past events that can't be changed doesn't help anybody."

I sighed and sat back. I couldn't possibly talk to him while he was in this frame of mind. "You're impossible."

"I'm pragmatic."

I moved closer. "Can we stop arguing and just enjoy the movie?"

"Come here, Sunshine." He opened his arms to me, and I moved to snuggle up next to my infuriating protector.

I purred contentedly, hoping nonverbal would work better than verbal with him.

He kissed the top of my head and pulled me closer. "I'm all about making you happy, Sunshine."

So long as he didn't have to talk to me, he should have said. *Guys.*

I felt like kissing him, but I also felt like punching him. How could I be attracted to somebody so exasperatingly bossy and know-it-all? Mom had once told me, "*the heart wants what the heart wants,*" and now I got it. No amount of self-deceiving logic was going to change how I felt. I knew he was annoyingly sure of himself, bossy, and argumentative—and at the same time irresistible.

Why does the moth fly into the flame and burn itself? Because it's a moth, silly.

I shifted closer. The tingles signaled clearly that the attraction hadn't dulled from my perspective. I was the moth, and he was my flame.

What I couldn't tell for sure was how he felt. He smiled at me, and he said nice things at least some of the time, but then the roadblocks would go up. The warning signs flashed, and he would distance himself.

The movie was nearing the wedding scene, where Melanie would be forced to walk down the aisle to marry the guy from New

York—and also tie herself to the mother-in-law from hell. Logically, she should marry the guy. She was a clothing designer back in New York, and he was a fit, in spite of his mother.

I moved my hand back to Zack's thigh, and his hand resumed its motions on my shoulder.

When the scene started to play out, however, I wasn't rooting for her to go through with it. The audience knew what Melanie hadn't realized yet, and in the end, she didn't marry him.

Zack fist-pumped the air. "Yeah."

The wicked mother-in-law had just gotten what she deserved, and Melanie set out in the rain to find the down-home Alabama guy.

I saw the parallel. Melanie finally chose the one she'd known from long ago, regardless of how infuriating he'd been recently. She got it. She understood the bond they had, and she had to choose him regardless of the consequences, regardless of his stubbornness, regardless of the distance.

I needed to do the same. I inched my hand toward Zack's crotch. I could let my actions replace words.

He looked over and pushed my hand away. "Careful there."

"Why?"

"You know why."

I shifted to lay my head in his lap and look up at him. "I'm old enough."

I could feel the surge of his cock under me.

He bit his lip. "You're Doug's sister." There it was. The bro code had reared its ugly head, just as Serena thought it might.

"So?" I needed to get him to talk about it.

He pushed my shoulder. "Sit up."

I fought it successfully and rolled my head toward the TV. "I want to finish the movie first."

He huffed, but stopped struggling.

"I want to." I didn't say what. I thought it was evident enough.

"No, you don't. You're a nice girl, and I don't do nice. And besides, you're Doug's sister."

177

I pulled the hem of my shirt up, so his hand at my side was now on bare skin. The feel of his touch was electric. I turned to my back to look up at him, and his hand slid to my stomach.

I snaked a hand behind his neck and pulled him down toward me. "You're talking too much."

His mouth moved closer, and he started to say something, but the words didn't come.

I knew what I wanted. "You told me to make my choices in the present for the future I want, and this is my choice." I pulled at his wrist and drew his hand to my breast as I pulled myself up to meet his lips.

I opened to his tongue, and the walls between us crashed down.

He took control of the kiss. His tongue searched out mine, stroking me, teasing me, claiming me, and igniting my blood as fireworks exploded behind my eyelids. He tasted of wine and pleasure and need. He fondled my breast and tweaked my nipple before moving to the other one.

I melded my mouth to his. Heat pooled between my thighs as his erection grew beneath me. He smelled of pine and maleness. I'd been kissed by boys before, but never like this. This was a new experience. A man. A man with a hint of animal.

Things are going so fast.

It didn't matter. This had been my choice. I had no regrets. I'd wanted this—and more—for longer than I could remember. I twined my fingers in his hair as I held on for dear life. My heart thundered against my ribcage as I relished the heat of his hand on my breasts, the rod of his desire underneath me, the scrape of his stubble on my cheek. The smell of his hair. The taste of passion on his tongue.

Time slowed, and the world melted away as I grew more drunk from his kiss than the wine. It didn't matter that Doug wouldn't approve… Nothing mattered, so long as Zack and I held each other.

When he broke the kiss, I whimpered a bit, or maybe I imagined it. Things were fuzzy as passion clouded my brain.

Why did I wait so long? Why had we waited?

He pulled at my shirt.

I lifted, and it came off.

His eyes feasted on my breasts, and his smile widened. "You have marvelous tits."

I pulled at his shirt. "How come I'm the only one getting naked here?"

He stood and removed his shirt, followed by the rest of my clothes. "My God, you're more beautiful naked than I ever imagined."

I felt oddly proud. The heat of a blush rose in my cheeks as I held my arms out to him and laid down on the couch.

He joined me, and we were finally skin to skin—at least partially. He'd kept his jeans on.

His mouth claimed mine again as a finger parted my folds and traveled the length of my soaked slit, teasing my entrance. He circled and stroked my clit as I rubbed his cock through his jeans.

I arched my hips to get more pressure, but he withdrew and continued to circle and tease, making me wetter by the minute.

He broke the kiss and turned his attention to my breasts. He continued to caress and lick and suck at my nipples as a finger entered me, moving slowly in and out and around, farther and farther. His thumb found my clit again. He alternated kissing and sucking my nipples with blowing softly. The cool air brought shivers to my wet skin. A second long finger joined the first as he stretched me and continued circling my clit with his thumb.

He let go of his lip-lock on my nipple. "You need to come for me, Sunshine."

I pressed into his hand, finally getting more pressure as he worked his thumb over and around my swollen bud, bringing me closer and closer to the edge. I clawed at his back and tried to pull him closer, but his mouth stayed focused on my breasts. He kissed my chest, moving occasionally to my collarbone and my neck, nibbling at my ear.

I tried to pull on his belt buckle. "I want you inside me."

He pulled my hand away. "I won't last if we do that. You need to come first, baby." He pulled my chest to his as he sucked and bit lightly on my earlobe, his breath loud in my ear. He increased his pressure and tempo on my sensitive nub as he pushed me up the pleasure slope.

The peak came quickly. I gasped for air, my pussy clenching on his fingers, my body spasming as he held me tight. Waves of pleasure crashed over me as lights flashed against my closed eyelids and blood rushed in my ears. I was helpless against the onslaught of my climax and the tremors in my core, an orgasm unlike any I'd experienced before.

In college, guys had wanted to get a finger inside me and squeeze my breasts on the way to getting into my pants, but they were certainly all clitoral-knowledge challenged. Zack had left them in the dust.

As I came down from my high and regained muscle control, I tugged at his belt again. "Please."

ZACK

SHE HAD MADE DELICIOUS LITTLE YELPING SOUNDS AS SHE CAME on my hand.

I wasn't going to be able to hold out much longer. Any manual foreplay from her and I'd end up coming in my pants like a teenager.

I stood and quickly dispensed with my jeans and boxer briefs.

She reached for me and grasped my length while I searched for the condom in my pocket. She wouldn't let go, and the feel of her hand was almost too much.

I located the packet and tore it open.

She held out her hand. "Let me."

I handed it over and stood in front of her.

The sweet torture of her rolling the latex down almost undid me before we'd started. The heat of her touch was something else.

I pulled her off the couch and positioned her kneeling toward it with her head on the cushion. As I got behind her, she spread her knees and reached back to guide me in.

I started with small strokes. "You're so fucking wonderfully tight."

She moaned and rocked back into me.

I pushed in farther and leaned forward to let my finger find its target. I began to circle and press her engorged clit, yielding more moans and groans. As I pushed in all the way, I stilled a bit before resuming little thrusts, just slow enough that I could hold off while I worked her toward the edge again.

Her breathing became more erratic as she came closer to the end of her rope. She met my increasing thrusts, rocking hard back into me as I upped the tempo.

Her yelps began again as she spasmed around me.

I rammed home over and over, deeper and stronger. The pressure behind my balls built to overload, and with a sudden tensing, I came inside her, pulling her hips hard into mine.

She moaned contentedly and shifted forward to lean on the couch.

I shifted with her and collapsed on her back.

"We shouldn't have waited so long," she mumbled into the cushion.

"Yeah" was the only answer I could manage.

I agreed. This was too long in coming.

Spent, I untangled myself from her and went to discard the condom in the trash.

She was still breathing heavily when I returned. She gave a little squeak as I picked her up and carried her upstairs. I set her down on the bed, her bed.

She got up to use the bathroom, and I followed when she was done.

When I returned to my room, she was there. I didn't complain. Instead, I turned off the light and settled in next to her.

She draped an arm over me, her warm tits pressed up against my side. "Thank you."

"For what?"

I couldn't tell if she meant the orgasms or letting her into my bed.

"For not pushing me away, and for being here for me."

I stroked her hair. "Get some sleep, Sunshine."

My thoughts were swimming, and I didn't have a better answer for her.

I had to follow my own advice now and not look back. I may have made a disastrous choice when I kissed Brittney, but there was no turning back and no undoing it—and absolutely no sense in second guessing. I didn't do second guessing.

I stroked her back, and the softness of her skin brought me back to the problem: She was soft, vulnerable, and fragile.

She needed protection. That was the imperative, and I was the one to provide it. There was so much I wanted to provide her that I didn't know where to start.

Doug was going to be pissed when he found out, and probably want to kill me. Hell, I'd told him to stay away from my sister Kelly.

"What are you thinking about?"

"What I'm going to tell Doug."

Her hand moved to stroke my hair. "He'll understand."

"The fuck he will."

She was quiet for a moment. "Let me tell him."

I touched her nose with mine. "No way. I fight my own battles."

"It's just—"

I cut her off. "I said no."

She snorted. "You're doing it again."

I pulled her close. I didn't want to argue right now. "Sorry. Please let me handle it."

"Okay. It's your funeral."

I laughed. "That's what I'm afraid of."

She didn't bring it up again, and before long her breathing slowed to the steady rhythm of sleep.

As I lay with Brittney next to me, I couldn't believe how lucky I'd gotten. The girl I'd always wished for had come back to me.

I'd broken Rule Number One, and now Rule Number Two came into play: If you break Rule Number One, leave the country for your own safety.

My own dictates said I couldn't second guess my past decisions. All I could do was make a plan for the future and execute it. I had to decide what kind of man I would be tomorrow.

Before today, the logical choice would have been to end it with her tomorrow and stay true to my best friend. That man would've called this a mistake, a lapse in judgment, a lapse of self control. That man would've been contrite about his mistake.

But that was the weakling's way, not the brave way. For all my father's faults, he raised me to be brave enough to stand up for what I believed, and I believed Brittney was worth the hard choice. I'd always wanted her, and now that she wanted me—nothing else mattered.

Sleep overtook me as I envisioned a day when I didn't have to deny how I felt about her. I was going to make tomorrow that day. Screw Rule Number Two. I wasn't backing down, and I wasn't running. Brittney was mine, and Doug or no Doug, I wasn't giving her up.

Tomorrow was going to be a great day.

She deserved a great day.

CHAPTER 25

BRITTNEY

LIGHT STREAMED IN AROUND THE CURTAINS AS I BLINKED MY EYES open. I smiled as I took in the sight in front of me. Inches from my face, Zack's deep blue eyes stared into mine.

"Morning, sleepyhead." He shifted forward to place a kiss on my nose.

I pulled my arm over him and moved us closer together, pressing my breasts to his warmth, wanting more than just a kiss on my nose.

He obliged with a kiss reminiscent of last night.

Our evening was coming back to me now as my skin melted into his—an evening that had started off so terribly and ended so wonderfully.

He broke the kiss.

My hand traced its way down his side to his abdomen and finally to my prize. I found his morning wood, warm and hard.

He pulled back. "We don't have time for that this morning."

I tugged harder on his cock, trying to get him to come back. "Why not?"

"We're burning daylight. We have a lot to do today." He wrested my hand loose and rose from the bed, his cock standing at attention.

Last night I'd known he was big, but in the morning light I could see he was packing the grande burrito.

"What are you staring at?"

I giggled. "My new toy. I'm going to have to give it a name."

"We're not doing any stupid naming."

"I'll think of something." I shifted the sheet down to uncover my breasts. "Are you sure you don't have a little time?"

He wasn't biting. He turned to leave. "I'll shower first."

I had a better idea. I followed him.

After he was in the shower, I pulled the curtain aside and joined him.

He didn't complain. Instead his smile grew and he grabbed the soap to help me with my breasts—a definite tit man.

If his cock was my new toy, my boobs were his.

I took the soap from him and lathered up my hands before grabbing for him.

"Your turn to come for me."

"We don't have time for this," he complained again.

"You'll just have to concentrate and be quick."

He gritted his teeth, barely holding back a complaint, but turned his back to the water and braced himself against the wall.

Several minutes of massaging, stroking, and playing with his cock and balls yielded the stiffening of his muscles that said he was getting close. I took some more soap and applied both hands to the job of making him lose the control he was so proud of.

I continued to work him, bringing one hand up and over the crown, squeezing as my hand slipped over the end followed by the other, and again and again, until...

He groaned, his legs shook, and a spurt hit the wall, followed by another, and another.

He panted, grunted, and pulled me to him for a kiss. "I'll get you later."

I knew he meant it too.

After that we got serious about washing and shampooing.

The sight of the water running down his muscled chest was too tempting. I traced the underside of his pecs and the groove that led to his belly button.

He retaliated by hefting my breasts in his hands. "Stop that, or you'll regret it."

"I doubt that."

He reached around and swatted my ass. "I'll spank you so hard you won't be able to sit."

"What if I like it?" I shot back.

He took my shoulders and turned me back toward the water. "Cut it out. We have a tight schedule."

"Yes, boss." I skipped the conditioner and quickly took a razor to my legs after he climbed out to shave at the sink.

I rinsed the razor and turned off the water. "What's the big hurry anyway?"

"We're going to San Diego."

I climbed out. "Not me. I've got more cleaning to do next door."

"I said *we're* going," he corrected.

I grabbed my towel. "And I said no thanks."

He turned and growled. "You are coming with me. Your cleaning can wait. Now stop arguing."

"What are you going to do? Grab me by the hair and drag me there?"

"If that's what it takes, yes. But you're a smart-enough girl to come willingly."

He said smart enough, but what he probably meant was pliable enough.

Still, I gave up. This wasn't worth the argument. "I have work on Thursday," I reminded him.

"I'll have you back in time."

Then I saw something I hadn't seen before, and a pang of jealousy overtook me. "Who's Deb?"

"Huh?"

I wrapped the towel around me and pointed at his ankle tattoo: **DEB**. "Your tattoo."

"Deborah Ellen Benson, my cousin who was kidnapped."

I shrank a few inches. "I thought it was… never mind."

He turned from the mirror to look at me. "I know what you thought, Sunshine." He grinned.

"I'm sorry. I'd forgotten about her." The tattoo looked fairly new, and the childhood abduction had been so long ago it hadn't registered.

He rinsed the razor under the water. "The tattoos were Dennis's idea. We all decided to get them a few years ago." He went back to shaving.

"Did they ever find her?" I didn't mean the question to be cruel, but I couldn't recall the details.

He shook his head. "No. The kidnapper died in a gunfight with the cops." He shivered.

I could tell this was hard for him, so I changed the topic. "Why San Diego?"

He ignored me. "The ransom note said she was buried with enough air for two days. With the kidnapper dead, the FBI stopped looking after two weeks. Dad and Uncle Seth paid to have investigators continue the search, but they ran out of leads. So, no, we never did find her. The tattoos are so we don't forget."

He took a deep breath and pulled the razor down his cheek.

I repeated, "Why San Diego?"

He made a stroke with the razor under his chin. "I decided I know what your problem is."

"I don't have a problem, except maybe you."

He ignored me. "Your happiness reservoir is empty. I need to help you fill it."

"You're nuts. I have things to do here."

He splashed to rinse off his face. "Those can wait."

"You're trying to tell me what to do again. I don't like it."

He patted his face dry and faced me. "Trust me on this, Sunshine."

I huffed, but gave up arguing, at least in the nude.

"Pack things for a few days, and don't forget a swimsuit, the skimpier the better."

I snapped my towel at his butt as he left the bathroom. I missed.

After the door closed behind him, I got busy drying my hair. I smiled. The idea that he was worried about my happiness was growing on me. No guy had ever suggested he and I take time to fill my happiness tank, and the idea was kinda cute.

Maybe he was right. I'd been running from one disaster to another, always in less than the best of moods, and that hadn't been good for my disposition. I wasn't working yet, despite my best efforts, so when was I going to have another chance like this?

I cracked open the door and yelled one more time, "Why San Diego?"

He yelled back from his room, "Why not?"

I didn't have an answer to that, so I wrapped the towel around myself and went to my room to dress and pack.

Pulling on a sweatshirt over my jeans, T-shirt, and Reeboks, I packed a few changes of clothes, and a string bikini I was sure would meet his definition of skimpy.

Zack knocked on the open door frame. "And bring something for a nice dinner out as well," he said with a devilish grin. "I'll meet you downstairs."

I didn't have a lot of choices, but I located a short red dress that would do and threw a pair of heels in the suitcase before zipping it up. I decided against bringing the heart-shaped pendant.

Lugging my suitcase downstairs, I found Zack pouring coffee into two travel mugs.

He checked his watch. "Time to go."

"Let's at least have breakfast first," I suggested.

He shook his head. "No time. You get the best of McDonald's on the way. Let's go."

"You take the suitcases, and I'll be right behind you."

He shrugged and lugged both suitcases out the door and down to the garage.

I heard the garage open as I went to gather the fruit. I knew what he was doing by rushing me, and I wouldn't give up that easily. I opened the backpack and added apples, peaches, and kiwis, along with bowls, napkins, forks, a knife, and a small cutting board for my lap. An extra plastic bag for garbage and I was ready to go. Slinging the backpack and my purse over my shoulder, I brought the coffee mugs outside, set them down, locked up, and joined Zack by the idling car.

We climbed in, and I set the backpack at my feet. The coffee mug had to go between my seat and the door. This car was built before cupholders were the rage.

As Zack pulled onto the street and turned toward the freeway, a kid on the far sidewalk flipped us off.

I turned to look back at him as we passed. "What's his problem?"

"That's Piss Boy, your local brick thrower."

I was tempted to tell Zack to back up so I could give the punk a piece of my mind, but I held my tongue. Today was for filling my happy tank, not the opposite.

After a few minutes Zack found a McDonald's with a drive-thru on this side of the 405 freeway, and we loaded up with three egg McMuffins, two hash browns, and two orange juices between us. The mouth-watering smells of grilled fast food filled the car.

I opened the wrapper for Zack so he could eat one-handed as he drove. My breakfast sandwich was warm, gooey, and tasty. The hash brown was crispy and perfect when dipped in ketchup.

Zack glanced over from behind his aviator sunglasses. "What's in the backpack?" He handed me the now-empty wrapper from his second McMuffin.

I retrieved his hash brown from the paper bag. "It's a little something for later," I answered over the rumble of the engine.

He'd been right that this car was all go and no frills, but I was enjoying it. The occasional thumbs up from other Mustang drivers we passed showed that car aficionados on the road knew our ride was something special. The traffic was heavy but moving—the advantage of a late start.

When we passed Long Beach, I opened the backpack to pull out my supplies: cutting board, knife, and a bowl for the cut fruit. I started to peel the first kiwi.

"Hey, stop that. No food mess in the car," Zack complained as soon as he saw the dreaded fruit.

I kept peeling. "You thought you'd avoid fruit by eating on the road. I'm wise to you, buster."

"Stop. You can't make a mess in my car."

"You promised to eat your fruit. It's your fault for trying to pull a fast one."

"I said no."

I finished peeling the first kiwi and started slicing. "Stop whining like a baby. This isn't going to hurt you. And last night you promised to eat two this morning."

"I just want to keep the car clean."

"Bull-pucky. Now suck it up and grow a pair." I picked up a slice and leaned over to get it to his mouth.

He frowned for a moment before giving up and taking it.

We continued down the road, him objecting, and me feeding him slice after slice until he finished two of the delicious green fruits he despised.

I'd won this round.

"I've also got peaches, if you'd like one of those," I offered.

He *tsk*ed. "Maybe tomorrow."

He downshifted and roared around the slower car in front of us to end the conversation.

After slicing and eating one of the peaches myself, I wiped off the board and knife before storing things away for the rest of the drive.

Past Irvine, the endless urban expanse of the Los Angeles area gave way to hills and countryside. Passing Dana Point, the freeway joined the coastline for the rest of the journey to San Diego.

"Going to tell me where we're going?" I asked twice.

Each time the response was the same. "You'll see when we get there."

I gave up and settled in my seat.

Zack rolled down his window, and I followed suit. The noise of the engine and the wind whipping my hair around was invigorating. I guessed this was halfway to the experience of riding a motorcycle.

I was looking out the window at the ocean when his hand found my thigh, and the tingles started again.

"Are we having fun yet?" he asked.

I intertwined my fingers with his. "Uh-huh."

When I looked over, warmth radiated from his smile.

The drive took more than two hours, but we made it to San Diego. Zack took the exit to the Coronado Bridge, and halfway over, I had a guess about where he was taking me.

In high school, Samantha, Doug, and I had once planned a weekend trip with our neighbors, the Waltrips, to the Hotel Del Coronado, but it had been called off when Mr. Waltrip's business trip was rescheduled. It had been a heartbreaker for us, and we never got another chance that summer.

We grew up, life intervened, and I'd forgotten about it until now.

I wasn't positive, so I didn't voice my guess, but when the iconic red cupola of the hotel came into view and Zack turned into the parking lot, I could barely hold myself back.

"You remembered."

"How could I forget? It was all you talked about for a month straight."

He had that part right. We had looked forward to it forever.

We parked and unloaded the suitcases.

Wanting to memorialize this visit with photos, I opened my

purse to get my phone. It wasn't there. "Fuck. I left my phone on the charger at the house."

My swearing got his attention. "You're not allowed to be upset, Sunshine. Besides, you won't need a phone down here."

"But I want a picture," I complained.

I sounded like a spoiled little kid.

He pulled his phone from his pocket. "Here, use mine."

"Thanks." I accepted the phone. We could transfer the pictures later. "What's the code to unlock it?"

He put his hands in his pockets. "0-4-0-4."

I started to type the numbers in. "My birthday?"

"I changed it this morning," he said with a grin.

The gesture sent a tingle down my spine and tugged a smile out of me even though I resisted. I unlocked it and took a shot of the hotel, then moved to get one with him *and* the hotel.

As soon as I finished, he started rolling his bag toward the building.

I floated after him with my suitcase trailing behind as we made our way to check-in.

We were expected, and when Zack pulled out his black Amex card, the desk clerk's smile went up two notches.

A bellhop arrived, and we followed as he pushed the luggage trolley to the north end of the property. When he stopped and Zack opened the door, I couldn't believe it. This wasn't a common hotel room. This was a beach villa suite, complete with multiple rooms and a kitchenette. The living room and patio bordered the beach and faced the ocean waves across the sand. Staying with Zack at his rundown old Victorian, and riding in his fifty-year-old car, I'd forgotten how different our backgrounds were. I stayed at Motel 6 or a Holiday Inn. He booked ocean-view villas when he traveled. The rich were different, after all.

Zack tipped the bellhop and closed the door.

"Like it?" He walked up behind me and kneaded my shoulders.

I fell back into him. "What's not to like? But you didn't need to splurge like this. A regular room would have been fine."

His arms came down to wrap me up. "Nonsense. I want to spoil you, Sunshine."

"Well, you succeeded."

He released me. "I'm not done yet. You'll need sunscreen and a hat. Let's go."

I collapsed onto the couch. "Can't we just relax here for a while?"

"Humor me." He extended his hand.

I took it, and he pulled me up.

"I need to use the bathroom first," I told him.

He pulled out his phone and dialed. "Hey, Phil. I need a little help... Hold on just a sec." He took the phone from his face and waved me toward the bathroom. "I'll wait," he told me. "Yeah. Do you have some time this weekend?" he said into the phone as he walked out to the patio.

I closed the bathroom door behind me and stopped. It took me a moment to figure out it wasn't a second toilet, but a bidet in front of me. I skipped the opportunity for a tush wash and used the one I knew how to work. How did you dry off afterward anyway?

CHAPTER 26

ZACK

IT TOOK A LITTLE COAXING TO GET BRITTNEY OUT OF THE VILLA and on the road again.

But the drive to SeaWorld was a short one, and once we got inside, the smile on her face as she watched the porpoise and sea lion shows was priceless. Getting splashed by the orcas because we sat in the first row had been part of my plan, and she screeched like a little kid—a sure sign she was having fun.

Happiness was today's goal, and places like this always delivered.

We stopped for a lunch of hot dogs and fries.

Brittney sipped her soda while we waited for the food. "You forgot to leave the phone for the kid you hate so much."

I pulled out my phone. "I'll have Phil leave him something."

"You're not giving back the phone?"

"Absolutely not. I told him he had to write me a letter of apology to get it back, and those are still the rules. But I am going to give him something that's gonna make his day."

She looked at me apprehensively. "Just give it back and be done with it."

"You can't appease bullies that way. He needs to be taught a lesson in a language he'll understand."

I dialed Phil Patterson, hoping he had what I needed.

"Hey, I'm just getting things together for that project," Phil said as he answered. "And we missed you at the Ironhorse yesterday."

I winced. In my anger with Brittney, I'd skipped the normal restaurant stop on the way back from the Habitat site, and I'd let the guys down.

"Sorry about that. We had to rush home," I explained.

"Right," he said dismissively.

"Anyway, the reason I'm calling is I was wondering if you have one of those pirate packages left?"

He laughed. "I've got two. You prefer skunk or fart?" he asked.

"Skunk, if you can spare it."

"I thought you might like that one," Phil said. "No problemo."

"Could you do me a favor and drop it by the house? I need it put under the planter on the porch of the house to the right of mine."

"Got it. Porch planter. Who the fuck's this for?"

"A guy who threw a brick through my friend Brittney's window."

"Friend, huh? She's hot. I bet I know what kind of friend."

I didn't acknowledge his inherent question.

"Well?"

I stayed silent.

"I get it. She's fucking there with you."

"Uh-huh."

"Does she have a sister?" A typical Phil question.

"Yes, but I'm not your dating service. The package?"

"Sure. I'll get it placed this afternoon."

"Thanks, bud."

"If you want to thank me, introduce me to her sister."

We hung up, and I shook my head. Phil still didn't get that he needed to clean up his act, because under the rough exterior and bad language, he was a nice guy.

Brittney's eyes narrowed. "What was that about?"

I sat down across from her. "Phil had a problem a while back with porch pirates making off with his Amazon deliveries."

She nodded. "That sucks."

"So he made up a couple dummy packages. I'm getting the one with skunk oil. When Piss Boy opens it up, he and the room he's in are going to get sprayed, and it'll take forever to get the smell out."

Brittney giggled. Even she thought that was funny.

"After that, he's guaranteed not to mess with us again." I joined her laughing at the mental image.

She shook her head. "Don't you think that's a little extreme?"

"You don't think a brick through a window is extreme?"

She tilted her head. "I guess."

"It was your window, by the way," I pointed out.

She put her soda down. "Damn straight. I'm liking the idea more and more. But wouldn't it still be easier just to give back the phone, or talk to his parents or something?"

"You don't give in to bullies. That just encourages them. I'm going to fix this for you so it stays fixed."

I should have said I'd fix it for both of us. Piss Boy was becoming a pain in the ass, and I didn't relish a brick through my window either.

Our food was ready, so I retrieved it from the counter.

Brittney quietly people-watched as we started in on the food.

My phone dinged with a text message.

WENDY: Your father is looking for you

Dad could wait.

Brittney cocked her head.

I put the phone down and ignored her unasked question.

She nodded toward the phone. "You sure you don't need to take care of that?"

"Today is about happy, right?"

She picked up a fry and dipped it in the ketchup. "Sure is."

"That means it can wait."

My phone rang, proving me wrong. Dad's name lit up the screen.

Brittney leaned forward to look. "You need to take that."

Part of me wanted to throw it in the bushes for interrupting my day with my girl. Just thinking the phrase *my girl* was odd. Brittney had always been Doug's sister, and that definition couldn't allow her to be anything else. What a difference a few days could make.

"Go ahead," Brittney said, breaking my trance.

I picked up my electronic tether to the real world and accepted the call. "Hi, Dad."

Brittney smiled and blew me a kiss, approving of my decision. She was the adult here.

"Zachary, Wendy tells me you're not coming in for a few days. What's the problem?"

"No problem, Dad. I'm out for a few days taking care of something for a friend."

"I see… Well, how long will you be? The Bartolo deal is going sideways, and Mario thinks it needs your attention. Can you make it in tomorrow?"

The problems changed day to day, and week to week, but the theme was always the same. Mario always threatened that if I didn't help him out, the deal might drift away to the competition. The job was like a treadmill: a lot of activity, but the next day we were in the same place. When I finished my rotations through the divisions and got to join Dad at the top of the pyramid, that's when it would get easier.

"No. I'll be out longer than that. I'll call in and get it taken care of." My brother Josh would be my first call. Mario wouldn't dare tell Dad Josh wasn't a good enough replacement.

"That sounds good. And my regards to Brittney."

He was no dummy.

"Thanks, Dad. I'll be back in as soon as I can."

Brittney was frowning when I looked up. "Is there a problem at work?"

"Dad says hi."

She glared, demanding an answer to her question.

"There's always a problem. It's nothing new."

"And your father wants you back?"

"That's also nothing new."

She stood. "We should go. I don't want to get you in trouble."

I pointed to her chair. "Sit down."

She put her hands on her hips, threatening to talk back. Obstinate Brittney had replaced my happy Sunshine.

"Sit," I repeated, pointing again to the chair.

She took her seat again, albeit reluctantly.

I leaned forward. "Sunshine, this is where I want to be. I'm prioritizing my time. You come first. They can do without me for a few days. The only thing I'm doing today is filling up your happy reservoir, get it?"

Her mouth formed a thin, flat line. "Got it."

I gave her a thumbs up. "Good. Because being with you today is what makes me happy too."

BRITTNEY

I WAS SURE I'D HEARD HIM CORRECTLY. FIRST HE'D TOLD HIS father he was helping a friend. Then he told me he was prioritizing his time, and I came first. *I came first*—the thought went through me with a warmth I wasn't accustomed to.

Zack was telling his father to shove it, although politely, and I was more important than his work, his family's company, his duty to his father, his duty to his family—the same duty he'd told me was paramount.

I watched as a family walking by stopped in front of us. Two middle-school-aged kids squabbled with their father about which ride to go on next. Dad was threatening to cut the day short. Mom wasn't amused, and Dad wasn't wearing his happy face when she sided with the kids. The children went running ahead, and the parents followed, no longer holding hands.

Suddenly I didn't relish being the cause of family friction between Zack and his father. "I want to go back home."

Zack looked up, surprised. "What?"

"I've had enough today. I'm tired."

His eyes narrowed. "Work will be fine. Trust me."

"I'm done. Let's go home."

"Dad understands my choice, and in his day, he made the same one."

"But I don't want to get between you and your father."

A grin replaced his stare. He'd guessed right. He reached across to take my hand. There was almost a literal spark as he touched me.

"Sunshine, it's cute that you're concerned, but don't be. Dad is always pushing, and I'm always pushing back. He's trying to teach me to watch all the details, and I'm trying to teach him it's the long-term plan that matters, not the day to day."

"And you think arguing is good?"

"He respects me for not rolling over. He's making progress teaching me what he wants me to learn, and surprisingly, I'm making progress getting him to see my perspective. He's already changed."

"I don't want it to be my fault that you argue."

He squeezed my hand. "Stop with the fault already. Nothing we do is your fault. Nothing anybody does is your fault."

It was the same thing he'd been saying, but it didn't make it true.

"I only want to be here with you," he added.

I could see the sincerity in his eyes, and I needed to be happy about that and block out my negative thoughts.

I sighed. "Me too. What do you want to do this afternoon?"

He let go of my hand, and an evil grin appeared. "There's not enough privacy here for what I want to do."

I giggled as heat rose within me, and I wished we were in a more private place right now. But that could wait.

"I meant here." I nodded toward the center of the park.

Zach insisted I pick, so we saw the sea lions again and went on some more rides before spending an hour just walking hand in hand along the paths. Everything he did made me feel special: the way he hugged me, kidded with me, held my hand. The way he'd asked about my time in Arkansas and truly listened, which was more than I could say for any of the guys I'd met since coming back to California.

By the end of the afternoon, I'd had enough fun and more than enough sun for the day.

We made our way back to the car, and I got another loud, wind-in-the-hair ride back to the hotel.

I decided his car wasn't old—it was special, and riding in it with Zack was a special gift.

CHAPTER 27

Zack

I OPENED THE DOOR TO THE SUITE AND USHERED MY GIRL INSIDE.

After the door closed, she wrapped her arms around my neck. "It's private here…"

Her suggestion hung seductively in the air.

I unwrapped her arms from me. As much as I wanted to, we didn't have time. "We have a dinner reservation, and you have to get ready."

She grabbed my waist and brought herself close again. Her breasts rubbed against me as she fingered my collar. "We could order room service."

The offer was tempting.

I took her shoulders and pushed her away. "I'm taking you to a proper dinner, and I intend to show you off."

She walked toward the bedroom. "Then you're right. I'll need some time to get presentable."

I shucked my shirt off on the way to the bathroom and started the water in the shower.

She joined me after stuffing her hair inside a shower cap.

I took the time to soap her down thoroughly, paying appropriate attention to all the areas I intended to worship later this evening. I pulled a towel off the rack to dry off.

Being naked with her in the shower had led to the predictable situation that prevented me from getting my dick in my pants. It took several minutes in the other room, away from Brittney's nakedness, to deflate me enough to pull my slacks on properly. A clean button down shirt and a blazer was all I needed to be ready. Women took more time. Checking my watch, I hoped she wouldn't spend too much time—I hated being late.

While I waited, I pulled out my phone and dialed my brother Josh.

"Hey, Zack. I hear you're out with your new girl."

News certainly traveled fast.

"That's sort of why I'm calling. I need a few days off to help her with some things, and Dad called today."

"Let me guess, he thinks you need to be at work?"

"Naturally," I replied. "He said the Bartolo deal is going sideways. You think you could spare the time to get involved and help me out?"

"I would if I could, but I'm in Atlanta today and Rome tomorrow."

That certainly put a hole in my plan.

"I'll be back next week, if that helps," he added.

"I'll let you know. Thanks anyway. Have a great trip."

"Good luck with Dad."

Without Josh around, I'd have to figure out some other strategy for Bartolo...

I scrolled through my phone contacts, trying to come up with a better idea than me going back to work and leaving Brittney alone.

After what seemed like an eternity—but was probably only fifteen minutes—I poked my head around the corner to check on Brittney's progress.

She was a sight to behold, a beauty packaged in a tight red

dress with a skirt short enough to get everybody's attention. She was leaning over the counter working on her makeup.

I approached quietly.

She jerked. "Hey. Don't sneak up on a girl doing her eyes."

I raised my hands in surrender. "Sorry. I didn't think it was such a big deal."

"You try stabbing your eye with a mascara brush and see how you like it."

Appropriately admonished, I retreated back to the living room. "I'll wait out here till you're ready."

"Good plan," she called through the doorway.

~

BRITTNEY

AFTER I JUMPED AND MADE A MESS OF MY MASCARA, IT TOOK A few extra minutes before I finally finished. Turning sideways to check myself in the mirror, I decided I looked pretty damn good if I sucked in my tummy a little. I'd hoped to be able to skip the bra, but the fabric was too thin and my nipples were a little too pokey for a fashionable dinner, so I'd grabbed my Victoria's Secret special push-up bra.

It had been a long time since I'd gotten dressed up to go out to dinner, and it felt good to be rocking a tight, short skirt. Plus, the bra was doing its thing. All I had to do was avoid tripping in these heels. I only wobbled a little as I strode into the living room.

Zack's eyes said it all as he looked me up and down. It was the look of hunger every girl hoped to get in a dress like this.

"You look fantastic, Sunshine."

"Thank you. I hope the restaurant's not far, 'cuz these shoes aren't made for walking."

That was no understatement.

"It's in the main building."

"I think I can handle that."

"Good, because I'm not letting you take those off tonight."

He chuckled, and I felt a rush of heat to my core.

"Promises, promises," I replied as I went back to retrieve the matching purse I'd brought.

I quickly dumped out the contents of my larger purse and fumbled through for what I wanted. I stopped at the pink envelope that was meant to remind me to be a better person. As penance for what I'd done, I always carried it with me, and this wouldn't be an exception. I folded it, put it in tonight's purse, and added lipstick, tissues, and my wallet.

"Now I'm ready," I announced on my return.

Zack held the door open for me.

The main building wasn't that far, but I almost wished we'd called a golf cart or something. These shoes looked great, but they were sheer torture after a hundred yards.

The restaurant was busy, with a large group waiting to be seated.

Zack introduced himself at the desk and discreetly passed a bill to the hostess. We were shown to a perfect table at the edge of the patio, facing the beach so we would have a wonderful view of the sunset later.

Zack held out my chair, and I sat, eager to get the weight off my poor feet.

Our waitress arrived, attired in a white shirt, a gray vest, and bow tie—another reminder that we weren't at Denny's. "May I start you off with something to drink this evening?"

After the briefest perusal of the wine list, Zack made a selection. "Chardonnay okay with you?" he asked.

I nodded. "Sure." If it came in glass with a real cork, it was better than I was used to.

"A bottle of the Trefethen chardonnay, please."

She smiled and left us to enjoy the bread and water.

Zack held the bread basket for me to pick.

I made a selection and broke off a piece. "You said you need to switch departments at the company. How does that work?"

He opted for the heel end. "Nothing much to tell. I get told to move, and I do."

"And that's it?"

"That's it."

"Did you ever consider working any place other than for your father?"

He chewed his bread for a moment. "Not really. It's my responsibility, and I want to do it."

"And all of you join up, just like that?"

"Not all of us. Vincent left to go work in Boston for Bill Covington. Dennis was at the company for a while, but he spun off a section, and that's where he is now."

He wasn't volunteering much.

"So you could too?"

Our waitress returned with the wine, which she had Zack taste.

I took the time to pick my dinner from the menu. The lamb shank looked good. It came with toasted saffron pasta pearls, olives, rainbow chard, and gremolata salad, whatever that was.

The waitress left after pouring us each a glass of wine.

I prodded my date. "You were saying?"

He twirled his glass and took a sip. "That was his choice. I owe it to Dad and the rest of the family to stick around. It's important to me. No... make that imperative. I'm the oldest son in the company now, and running it will fall to me some day. The family legacy will be my responsibility. It's who I am, I guess."

"And you don't get a choice?"

He looked over his wine glass at me. "Like I said, it's my responsibility, and I want to do the right thing." He sipped his wine without a hint of discontent on his face.

"And the department switching?"

"Dad wants us to get involved in the business. And that means that we rotate through different responsibilities in the company. He thinks it's essential to know how everybody does their jobs if you're going to be their boss. Before marketing, I worked procurement, and I'm scheduled to move to finance next."

Our waitress stopped by to take our orders.

I asked for the lamb shank I'd been liking. I was too embarrassed to ask what gremolata was—I'd settle for being surprised.

Zack predictably chose the filet mignon.

I handed my menu to the waitress as she left. "How do the other people at the company feel about you moving around like that?"

"What do you mean?"

"Do they feel okay working for a guy who just flits in and out of departments?"

"I don't flit."

"You know what I mean."

He thought for a moment. "I don't know. I never thought about it. It's a family company. That's just the way it works."

I wasn't surprised the question hadn't occurred to him.

He ate a piece of bread in silence.

"I think you're really lucky to be so sure of your destiny," I said after a moment.

He didn't say anything in response.

I took a sip of my wine during the pregnant pause.

He peered into his glass, then looked up. "I guess you're right, but I'm not going to apologize for being born a Benson."

After more reflective silence, the waitress brought our dinners.

I took a bite of my lamb—delicious.

He cut a piece of steak. "How do you like being a hygienist?"

"I like it, and it pays the bills—that is, when I can get enough hours."

"I know you're waiting for an opening at the office here, but is that a problem?" he asked.

"It was with my dentist in San Jose."

"Why?"

"Money. She didn't give any of us enough hours. I think she

didn't want to pay benefits. Actually, I'm sure it's because she didn't want to pay us benefits."

"That sucks."

"No kidding."

"What was the hardest part of that job?"

"Knowing that nobody who was coming in wanted to be there with me. Patients are always happier when they leave than when they arrive. And it's not because they've enjoyed my company. It's because it's over, and they don't have to endure me any longer."

"It can't be that bad."

"The good part is knowing I'm helping people be healthier. Did you know poor oral health and heart disease are correlated?"

"I've heard that."

"So, in addition to helping people to keep their teeth, I might be helping them stay heart healthy. At least that's what the literature says."

"You should be proud."

"I am."

He lifted his wine glass, took a sip, and put it down with a grin and an odd look in his eyes as he stared at me.

"What did I say?"

"Nothing. It's the way you look."

I checked quickly that I hadn't spilled on myself. "What?"

"I don't think you could look any more beautiful."

Heat erupted in my cheeks. I took a quick sip to cool myself down as the unexpected compliment washed over me.

"How's your steak?" I asked as I looked down to fork another piece of lamb.

"Pretty good." He stared at me over his glass again. "But it's the view here that's really the best." His eyes didn't leave me for the beach.

Now we were getting into three-alarm territory with his compliments.

His phone rang. He flipped it to silent and sent the caller to voicemail before setting it down on the table. "Now, where were we?"

"You were telling me how much you liked your dinner."

"I thought I was referring to dessert." His grin grew as his gaze held me. The eyes of the hunter appeared, and I was his prey.

His phone vibrated on the table again.

"You better get that."

He sighed and flipped the phone over before showing me who was calling.

My brother.

ZACK

"HEY, DOUG. HOW ARE YA?" I SAID IN GREETING.

I checked my watch. Okinawa was sixteen hours ahead, so it was midmorning tomorrow there.

"Fine. Just fine, but I'm worried about Brit. I've been calling, and she's not picking up her phone. She always answers."

He was speaking so fast I couldn't get a word in edgewise.

"I need you to check on her to make sure she's okay."

"She's around."

Brittney's eyes went wide, and she shook her head, warning me off in a way I didn't understand.

"Can I talk to her?" he asked.

"Sure. Let me find her," I answered. I waited a few seconds before handing her the phone. "Doug's calling."

"Hi," Brittney answered. "I'm fine... The battery died... Yeah, I'll get it fixed... No... Why would you say that?" She looked exasperated. "No. There's nobody, and if there was, it wouldn't be any of your business anyway... He wants to talk to you." She handed me back the phone.

"You gotta watch after her for me," Doug said.

"I'll keep her safe."

"More than that," he insisted. "The last time she acted like this, she'd just hooked up with that Benji creep."

"I don't understand," I said.

"I'm not there to protect her, and I need you to fill in for me."

"I'll keep her out of danger."

"That's not what I mean. She's got terrible taste in men, or it's just bad luck following her around. She moves to a new town, and she hooks up with the first creep she meets."

He didn't realize he was talking to the creep right now.

"You gotta find out who this guy is, 'cuz I'm gonna kill him when I get some leave."

"Well, maybe you're wrong."

"I'm not wrong. I've got a sense about this. You gotta find this guy."

"Sure. I'll keep my eyes open."

"She's my sister, and I swear I'm gonna kill the guy. Promise me no guy will get his hands on her."

"I got ya covered, Doug. She'll be safe."

"I knew I could trust you, Zack. See ya soon."

"Yeah, soon." I hung up the phone.

What the fuck was I going to do now? I'd just lied to my best friend, and slept with his sister.

My future held one hell of a fight, or maybe a coffin.

CHAPTER 28

BRITTNEY

WHEN ZACK HUNG UP, HE HAD TURNED PALE.

"What's the problem?" I asked.

"He thinks you're in a vulnerable time."

"It's none of his business. I'm not a little kid."

He took the last of his broccoli on his fork. "He's just looking out for you."

"What does he know?"

My brother could damn well keep his nose out of my business.

Our waitress came by and asked to take our empty plates.

I sent a wink his way. "It's early. Maybe we could go dancing."

He shook his head, obviously less than enthused. "Nah. Maybe another time."

His countenance carried another message—maybe never.

"How about drinks at the bar then?"

That suggestion didn't get any better reception. My brother's call had certainly put a damper on things.

The waitress returned. "Can I interest you in dessert, or perhaps coffee or an after-dinner drink?"

Zack waved her off. "I think we're done." He refused the menu.

I held my hand out. "I'll take a look at that."

She gave me the maroon tablet.

I sucked briefly on the tip of my thumb. "I think I'd like something to suck. Would you happen to have any popsicles?" I licked my lips while looking straight at Zack.

"No, I'm sorry. But we do have a nice sherbet."

I perused the choices. "I think the pistachio crème brûlée looks good." I glared at Zack. "And I think my date would like something sour. What would you recommend?"

She looked at me, perplexed.

Zack broke the silence. "I'll take one of those as well, please."

The waitress retrieved the menu and hustled off.

"Something sour? What has gotten into you?"

"I just thought it would match your mood."

"Now, hold on. Who says I'm in a bad mood? I have a lot to think about."

"Yeah, so much that you don't know what you want to do or not do anymore."

He shrugged.

I stood. "Well, I know what I want."

"Calm down and sit," he commanded.

"I need to use the ladies room." I snatched my purse and marched off.

I was washing up when two other ladies came in, chatting up a storm.

I unzipped my dress, removed my bra, and re-zipped.

Their chatting stopped.

I smiled at them. "I'm hot." I pulled my panties down and stepped out of them. My bra and panties went into my purse. I checked the mirror before I left the speechless pair. Their look was just what I was after. I was going to get his mind off of the call with Doug and back on us. Fuck the bro code.

As I walked back with an exaggerated bounce, it was obvious Zack noticed the double-barrel salute from my nipples.

A wicked grin returned to his face. Mission accomplished—at least partly.

I rounded the table and leaned over to whisper in his ear. "Hold these for me, will you?"

I dropped my panties in his lap before returning to my chair. After taking my seat, I leaned forward. "You may not know for sure what you want, but I do."

Our desserts arrived and were as delicious as they looked.

I stared into his eyes and deliberately licked my lips before every bite I sucked off my spoon.

His eyes got wider by the minute, and I could only imagine what his pants would look like when he stood.

He dropped a few large bills on the table, and we were instantly on our way back to the villa.

With his arm around me, he urged me faster than the damned heels wanted to take me.

I'd touched a match to the fuse, and I was about to reap the whirlwind.

He threw open the door and pulled me inside, where the pace instantly slowed.

He kicked the door closed and backed me into the bedroom. "Stand still and don't say a word."

I froze in place. My eyes slowly acclimated to the partial darkness. Moonlight through the window provided the only illumination.

He walked around me.

I shivered with anticipation as he traced a finger over my collarbone, my shoulder, my back, and returned to just under my neck.

I lifted my hands to bring his face to mine, but he pushed them down.

"Still."

He walked behind me and inched my zipper down.

Returning to my front, he slid the dress off my shoulders.

"Zack," I whispered as it slipped to the floor.

A finger to my lips reminded me of his previous command. He didn't want me to talk. This wasn't a time for words. It was a time for touching, a time for hands and lips and tongues.

He knelt and lifted one of my feet and then the other, recovering the dress and tossing it aside.

"My God, Sunshine. You're fucking beautiful," he said in a raspy voice coated in lust.

I couldn't control the blush that overtook me—not that it was visible in the moonlight. He'd said it before, but tonight the conviction in his voice conveyed more than the words. The passion in his eyes sent the true message.

He moved closer, and my nipples scraped against him.

He had commanded my silence, and I didn't have the words for him anyway. All I could do was show him. I circled one hand around the nape of his neck and speared his hair with the other, pulling myself up. I kissed him like it was our last night together.

As I covered his mouth, my tongue began the dance with his. We exchanged breath and a hunger for each other. He tasted of pistachio dessert, lust, and need.

He gave me back all that I offered and more as his hands found my back and my ass, pulling me against him. I didn't care that I could barely breathe. I was in his arms and he in mine.

I broke the kiss and pushed away enough to reach his belt. I fumbled as I tried to undo the thing while he removed his shirt. Finally it loosened, and I was able to pull the zipper down. I wasted no time hooking my fingers into his underwear and pulling them and his pants down to his ankles, freeing his cock.

He pulled me back onto the bed on top of him, heels and all.

I straddled him as I rubbed my soaked slit along the length of his cock. I leaned over, my eyes conveying my wordless wishes to him as my breasts rubbed against his chest.

When I sat up, he kneaded my breasts and tweaked my nipples, sending shocks through me.

I moved down and took him in my mouth to get him to come for me. To get him to give in to me. To get him to give up control. To taste him.

"Not tonight, Sunshine." He pulled me up and rolled us over.

Pinned below him, I clawed at his back. I was his to have as he wished, but I wanted him inside me. He hovered there on arms extended at my sides, his eyes taking me in, pulling me in.

"You are so fucking beautiful," he repeated.

I felt tears building as his emotions shone in his eyes.

I worked my hands over his torso, his arms, his neck, feeling the bunched muscles as his eyes continued to dance over me.

He left me for a moment and came back with a condom, which he handed me.

I tore open the packet and rolled the latex slowly down his length. His eyes widened and his breath hitched with every stroke. I spread my legs to welcome him. Slowly, he positioned himself at my entrance and pushed in.

I pulled my knees up and grabbed my ankles. "I kept them on like you asked."

The sensation as he entered me was pure bliss. He began to thrust, and the sensation grew exponentially. If this was high-heel sex, sign me up.

We fit so perfectly and he filled me so fully, it was as if his cock had been made for me and me for him.

When he was inside me, whether gliding in and out, thrusting in and out, or pounding in and out—it didn't matter. The way he made me feel was nothing I had ever expected to experience.

With every thrust, I clenched more tightly around him. He brought me closer and closer to the cliff, building pressure within me as sensations crashed over me. The tension within me built to a crescendo. But I didn't want to come, because I didn't want it to end.

I held off my orgasm as long as I could. All I wanted was to stay like this, joined with Zack. I wrapped my legs behind him and pulled him in with my heels.

I rocked into him, giving him all I could, all I had. I was his completely. I needed to be his, to stay his forever.

With several more hard thrusts, Zack reached his limit and exploded inside me. He thrust harder and deeper, pushing me over the cliff into a soul-shattering orgasm as we screamed out each other's names.

I unclamped my legs, and he collapsed on top of me, panting, sweating, and kissing my neck.

"You're beautiful," he said over and over.

My pulse banged in my ears, and the pounding of our hearts against each other's chests overtook my thoughts.

I had given him all I had, offered it for him to take, and I would do it again and again.

As our jagged breathing slowed and the pulsating of his cock inside me dissipated, he rolled off me to the side.

I nestled up against him, my arm over his chest, my head on his shoulder, sensing the beat of his heart—the heart I wanted so much to win.

He got up to dispose of the condom.

I shed my heels and spooned with Zack, his hand cupping my breast, claiming me. Sleep came quickly.

CHAPTER 29

BRITTNEY

ON WEDNESDAY AFTERNOON I LAID BACK ON THE BED AND CLOSED my eyes while Zack was off settling the bill.

Our time in San Diego replayed in my mind. He'd taken me to SeaWorld with the magnificent and funny seal and sea lion shows. I'd gotten to feed and pet a dolphin—and had the fish-smelling hand from the bait for an hour to prove it. We'd gone on roller coasters, wandered, and just hung out. He'd taken me to the zoo, where a morning of watching the animals had been relaxing, except when we got to the African penguin pool and leopard sharks were in the water. The signs assured us that the sharks and penguins got along well together. Who knew?

They had a bird that ate bees by catching them mid-flight and removing the stinger before swallowing. The baboons were too loud for my taste, but the panda bears were the opposite—three-hundred-pound versions of a kid's fluffy stuffed animal. The Komodo dragons were scary. Just knowing they occasionally attacked people put them on my *avoid* list.

Zack had also taken me jet skiing in the bay for an afternoon.

He'd offered to get me surfing lessons as well, but that could wait until next time. I'd voted for relaxing by the pool instead.

It didn't matter if it was the ritzy hotel restaurant or the local burger stand, wherever Zack took me to eat, I was across from the most handsome and attentive man in town.

He had gone all-out to provide a mixture of fun and relaxing escapes from the day-to-day grind of LA. The one time I'd brought up my house and the work to be done, he'd set me straight that San Diego was not the place to discuss anything having to do with LA and my situation. We were on a vacation from reality he'd told me, and it had been far, far from reality.

In the real world, responsibilities, money issues, even doing the laundry needed to be dealt with. Ignoring them wouldn't make them go away. But those had been the ground rules for our days in San Diego, and the problems had receded temporarily from my consciousness, replaced with smiles, giggles, and the best company a girl could wish for.

Zack had brought me from the darkness of despair at my situation to the sunny side of future possibilities. He'd insisted I just needed to figure out a plan for the future instead of looking back at the failures in my past.

He opened the door and pulled me back to the present. "Ready to go?"

"Yeah." I got up from the bed slowly.

"We can stay, if you want."

"No, it's fine. I've got work tomorrow."

I followed Zack to the car and let him open the door for me as he liked to do—ever the gentleman.

"Back to the real world," he said.

I took one last look at this magical place. The bright red cupola might be merely an audacious hotel roof, but to me it now anchored memories of two wonderfully happy days. Me, Zack, and San Diego. Sunshine, smiles, and laughs. But he was right. Our few days in fantasyland were over, and now I was taking a ride back to my world of no money, no house, no job, and no future. A two-hour trip from carefree to reality, courtesy of Zack's ferocious Snake.

Zack laid his phone on the carpeted transmission tunnel behind the shift lever.

"When do I get to drive the Snake?"

"The tenth of never."

"You said that last time," I noted.

He started up the big engine without answering me.

I found a hair-band in my pocket and pulled my hair back into a ponytail. I didn't need the tangles.

"I like it better down," he informed me.

"You're not the one who has to comb out the knots."

"I will when we get back." He stared at me, not putting the car in gear.

"What?"

His eyes shifted to my lap.

"Oops." I grappled with the seat belt halves and shoulder belts. This was one thing that was difficult about the Snake.

He was still staring at me when I finished.

I rolled down my window. "I'm ready."

"Down, please," he said.

"Fine. But I'm holding you to that promise about the combing." I pulled the band free and shook out my hair.

He peered over his shoulder and put the car in reverse. "Thank you."

I smiled to myself, remembering the *Animal Planet* show on gorillas. They groomed one another as a sign of affection, and now my bossy, gruff Neanderthal was offering me the same treatment. In some ways, we weren't that removed from the primates.

It was a beautiful sunny day as we motored north, even if I didn't get a turn driving.

"How's your tank?" he asked as we passed La Jolla.

It took me a second to get his drift. "Almost full."

He had done a masterful job refilling my "happiness reservoir," as he'd put it.

"How come almost?"

"Because you won't let me drive the Snake," I quipped.

"Then you'll have to settle for almost."

He was in full Neanderthal mode. *Me drive, you ride* was only one step removed from *me hunt, you cook*. I was riding, and I'd been assigned the cooking duties too.

I looked over at my driver, my protector, my happiness coordinator, and yes, my lover. I laid a hand on his shoulder. "Thank you."

"For what?" His hand came from the steering wheel, his fingers lacing with mine.

"For giving me these days."

"I promised to fill your happiness reservoir, and I keep my promises."

"And for being you," I added.

He glanced over. "You sure about that?"

"I'm sure, because I know you're going to let me drive."

He disentangled his hand from mine with a laugh. "Fat chance."

"I'm sure."

I wasn't going to give up trying. Sooner or later I'd catch him in a moment of weakness. And until then, I was still happy he was the way he was.

Before long we left the shoreline and climbed into the hills, then quickly descended again into the urban sprawl of the LA Basin.

We made good time in spite of the late-day traffic and passed the LAX exit without hitting any serious slowdowns.

I decided to try his technique of visualizing a better future for myself. I closed my eyes, ignored the wind whipping my hair in my face, and thought about what I wanted most. I wanted a phone call from Dr. Fosback saying I could start tomorrow. And I would get four days a week, and I was getting a raise.

That would put me in a happy place, a place where I could envision paying for Samantha's school. A place where I could start to pay down the awful debt Benji had saddled me with. A calm warmth filled me as I visualized that call.

My phone rang, yanking me from the dream.

I opened my eyes and blinked several times as I tried to swipe the hair from my eyes and locate the ringing phone.

I found it and answered. "Hello?"

"Hi," a surprised voice said. "This is Phil Patterson. Is Zack around?"

I took the phone away from my ear momentarily. I'd answered Zack's phone. He'd gotten the call, not me.

"Hi, this is Brittney. We met Sunday at the Habitat house. Zack's driving right now. Can I give him a message?"

"Brittney—I remember. Tell him the first stage is done."

"Got it. Anything else?"

"No, that's it. Thanks."

"I'll tell him."

Zack looked over. "Tell me what?"

"That was Phil Patterson. He said the first stage is done. I hope that means something to you."

He smirked. "It sure does."

"What's so funny?"

"Nothing," he answered. "I'm just happy about the news."

"Which is?"

"Later."

He clearly didn't intend to be more forthcoming. In Zack-speak, *later* could be shorthand for *never*. Like his statement that maybe later he'd eat his fruit? Translation: don't get your hopes up, girl.

I settled into my seat, closed my eyes, and went back to visualizing the call I wanted from Dr. Fosback to put my life in order. It had worked once to get the phone to ring—wrong call, but a call nonetheless. I concentrated, but I only heard wind noise and the thundering engine. No phone. I checked my purse for my phone to make sure it wasn't on silent.

Fuck.

I'd totally forgotten I'd left it at the house, which is why Doug had been unable to reach me before he called Zack the other night.

Zack's pleasant holiday had completely erased my brain. I'd been using his phone for pictures the whole time.

Zack slowed for the exit, and we left the freeway for the surface streets.

"Can we work on the water pipes after we get back?" I asked.

I liked being with Zack, but I desperately wanted to make the house that was supposed to be mine and Samantha's livable. I wanted to stake a claim to some space I could call my own.

"No," he said brusquely.

I recoiled at the word. "But we have daylight, and I want to."

"No," he repeated.

"But this is supposed to be one of my happy days," I complained.

"Exactly."

He made the final turn onto Snakewood. This time the street was empty—no one giving us a middle-finger salute.

I folded my arms.

He turned into his driveway and slowly drove to the back. "I have a surprise for you."

"Sure. But I'd rather make progress on the house."

"If you're going to have a poor attitude, I won't tell you."

"I'm listening."

"I had Phil work on the house while we were away. He got the water fixed and turned on today."

"Really?" I undid the seatbelt and lunged for my boyfriend, wrapping him in a hug.

He put a finger to my nose. "Yes. Really."

I opened my door. "The first thing I'm doing is flushing those horrid toilets." I jumped out of the car.

"Hey," he called.

I'd forgotten to wait for him to open my door. "Sorry, I was in a hurry."

He exited his side. "I'll get the bags inside. You go check it out."

I bounded through the gate and up the steps, before I realized I'd been in such a hurry, I'd left my purse with my keys on the floor of the car.

I retraced my steps, with the keys this time, unlocked the back door, and entered the kitchen. I turned on the sink, and water sputtered out. I left it on and turned to go to the downstairs bath.

My heart stopped, and I shrieked.

A dead rat with a knife through it lay impaled on the cutting board.

The note was in dark red letters.

**NOT FUNNY BITCH
GIVE ME THE KEY**

I turned and lunged for the door.
It couldn't be him.

Zack

I HAULED THE SUITCASES INSIDE AND GRABBED A COKE BEFORE leaving to go see my happy girl in her house with running water.

I'd started up the back stairs when I heard her scream. I rushed the final few steps.

She came barreling through the door and straight into me. My Coke went flying, and she almost bowled me over.

I grabbed her and held her tight. "What's wrong?"

Instead of pulling away and running, she gripped me tightly and planted her face in my shoulder.

"I've got you," I reassured her, stroking her back.

She shivered before she managed a few words. "We have to go back to the other house."

Her words didn't make any sense.

"What the hell's wrong?"

She sobbed. "It's him."

I pried her loose from me. "Stay right behind me," I commanded. If there was someone in the house, I was dealing with this now. With one hand holding hers, I slowly opened the kitchen door and looked inside before entering, dragging her with me.

Inside, the scene was horrific. A rat had been stabbed dead in the middle of the kitchen table. When I got closer, I saw the note.

NOT FUNNY BITCH
GIVE ME THE KEY

My first thought went to Piss Boy and his crew, but the note didn't make any sense. He wanted his phone, not a key.

She was crying again.

The blood pooled by the rodent was still wet. The message writer could still be in the house.

I turned off the water running in the sink and backed her out the door. I closed it behind us. "I like your idea of going to the other house."

With an arm around her, I led her back to the gate and inside my house through the back kitchen door.

I deposited her in one of the kitchen chairs. "Stay here and lock the door after me. I'm gonna go check it out, but I want you to stay inside."

She nodded.

I hurried to the drawer with my gun safe, opened it, and pulled out my Sig Sauer. If the pistol was good enough for the Secret Service, it was good enough for me. And if he had a knife, I wanted a gun—a real one this time.

As I passed back through the kitchen, Brittney's eyes widened at the sight of my weapon.

"Just in case," I assured her.

As I descended the stairs again, I heard her latch the deadbolt as I'd told her.

Good girl.

I took off the safety before I reached her house and mentally prepared myself for Piss Boy, or whoever else I might find.

Going through each of the rooms one by one, I confirmed the house was empty. With the flashlight on my phone I did the same for the cellar. I didn't put the safety back on until that was complete.

If this was that ex-whatever she'd run from in San Jose, he was dangerous. Why hadn't she told me?

When I returned, I found her with a suitcase.

"I can't stay now that he found me." She sniffed.

Fuck that shit. I planted myself in front of her. "You are not leaving."

"You don't understand. It's not safe for me here. I've gotta go."

I pointed to the kitchen table. "Sit."

"Stop telling me what to do," she yelled.

I grabbed her arm and yanked her to the table. "I said sit."

She fussed, but complied after a moment.

"Out there is where you're not safe. Here with me, you are. Running from this problem, whatever it is, won't solve it. I'll help you, but confronting the problem is the only way to fix it."

"But…"

"But nothing," I yelled. "I'm not fucking letting anything happen to you, and if that means tying you to the fucking bed so you can't leave, then so be it. I said you're staying. End of discussion."

She stared at the table, no longer arguing, but not accepting the inevitable either.

I took the other chair. "Now you need to tell me what's going on."

She looked up with teary eyes.

I locked eyes with her. "You have to trust me."

She nodded.

"You're safe here with me. I won't let anything happen to you."

She blinked back the tears, and the slightest hint of a smile appeared.

"Are you going to tell me what's going on?"

She gave me a shrug and a nod.

I took her hand and pulled her up. "Go sit down, and I'll get the wine." I pointed her toward the couch. "White or red?" I asked.

"How about stronger? I'll take that Jack now."

"Wine, until we talk."

She shook her head. "Easy for you to say."

I walked after her and took her into a hug.

She was shaking.

I rubbed her back and kissed the top of her head. "You need to explain what that note means. Now, go sit down."

She did as I asked and took a seat on the couch.

I poured us each a large glass of wine, and returned to her.

"When do I get the whiskey?"

Pulling the gun out of my waistband, I placed it on the coffee table, sat beside her, and offered her the glass. "Start with this."

She accepted the wine and quickly drained half the glass.

"Did Benji whoever leave you that present?"

"No… At least I don't think so."

I waited for her to continue.

She drained the rest of her glass and handed it to me.

I put it on the coffee table.

"I'll take a second," she said.

"Not yet. Not till we finish here. You know who wrote the note, don't you?"

"Maybe."

"You said you had to leave now that he found you. Who is he?"

"One of Delgado's people."

"What does a key have to do with anything?"

"Delgado is after me, and if I stay, I'll just put you in danger."

I nodded toward the gun. "But I can fight back."

Her explanation hadn't completed the picture, though.

"What about the note?"

"Todd told me he and Rick had hidden the money Rick stole somewhere, and only they knew where the key was. I never saw a key, and he never told me where one was, but I always figured they got the key or location or whatever from him before they killed him in Mexico. I mean, it would be sort of stupid not to, right?"

"These guys are not always the brightest bulbs in the pack."

"It has to be one of Delgado's guys, because he's still in prison."

"Are you sure?" I asked.

"He got twenty-five to life."

"How would they know you moved back?"

She shook her head again. "I don't know. Maybe somebody saw me?"

"But you haven't been in town a week yet. Could it be this Benji asshole? Did he ever know about the key?"

She thought for a moment. "I got talkative one night. More than a little. I was pretty drunk. I must have said more than I should have, because the next day he said it sounded scary. I don't remember what I said, but he never asked me about a key."

I reached for my glass again and took another swallow.

"I'm sorry I kept it from you," she said. "Can I have my whiskey now?"

I rose from the couch and took both our glasses. "Just relax for a minute, okay? We're doing pizza and a movie again tonight."

"And Jack?" she suggested.

"No. Better than Jack."

After ordering the pizza, I poured us each a glass of the hard stuff. "I think you'll like it."

She took a sip and nodded. "This is smooth. Glenfiddich?"

"Macallan. Now I have a call to make to get us some help."

"Help?"

"Protection for you. The professional kind."

She opened her mouth to object, but seemed to think better of it and instead took another swig of her scotch.

I went to the kitchen and called Bob Hanson of Hanson Security.

"Hey, Zack. What can I do for you? It's sort of late."

I started slowly. "You provided some security for the Covingtons a while back, is that right?"

"Yeah. Quite a clusterfuck for a few days. This crazy lady and her brother were after the lot of them—burned down a house, torched a car, and tried to abduct Emma. We got in late, handling protection and surveillance. The two perps are cooling their heels in prison on arson and attempted kidnapping raps right now. They won't be a threat for a while. And then they had another brother out east. Screwball family, if you ask me. What's your interest?"

"I have a friend who needs protection for a while till we can figure out her situation."

"Tell me a little about it," he said.

"When we got back today, we found a disturbing message in her kitchen."

"What kind of message?"

"A rat knifed to the table and a note."

Hanson's voice filled with concern. "Zack, that's serious."

"I get that. That's why I'm calling. Can you spare somebody?"

"Sure. I'll pull Winston off his surveillance first thing and send him over. I take it the protectee is a woman?"

Having Winston was good news, as ex-FBI, he was a solid guy. I'd met him at the Habitat weekends, and the Covingtons liked him.

"Yeah. My girlfriend." It felt odd to refer to Brittney that way without asking her, but it was how I felt this morning.

"Then Constance will head the team. She's ex-Secret Service, and with women it helps if one of the team is also female, if you know what I mean."

"I hear ya."

"Give me your location, and I'll have them there in the morning, unless you think we need to start tonight?"

"No, the morning works."

"One more thing—are you packin'?"

"Yeah, a Sig."

"Have you been to the range lately?"

"Why?"

"If Constance and Winston aren't comfortable with your abilities, we take your gun for the duration. Those are the rules. Can you live with that?"

"Do I have a choice?"

"No," he said flatly.

I gave him my address and returned to Brittney.

She needed additional alcohol and a movie tonight to calm down.

CHAPTER 30

Zack

Brittney was snoring lightly, facing me, when I woke the next morning.

For a few minutes I lay there quietly watching my woman, my perfect woman. The woman who had finally come back to me, back where she belonged. Just the words *my woman* felt so right. She always had been the one for me.

It had taken a long time and a fair amount of alcohol for her to finally fall asleep after finding the sick present in the kitchen next door.

She deserved to sleep late, so instead of kissing her awake the way I yearned to do, I slipped slowly out of bed. I palmed my Sig from the nightstand before softly closing the door behind me.

My sweet Sunshine deserved happiness and safety, not the torment the note writer had brought to her. Last night hadn't been the end I'd envisioned to our San Diego outing. It made clear why she'd left with no notice years ago. Whoever these guys were, *scary* and *unhinged* only began to describe them.

Downstairs I made a quick tour of the house, checking

windows and doors before I stuck the gun at the small of my back and started breakfast. In no time, I had two plates of scrambled eggs, English muffins, and even bowls of apricots in a nod to her need for fruit at every meal. At least with apricots, I didn't have to worry about the seeds getting caught in my teeth.

I was checking my phone for messages when she padded in, wrapped in my bathrobe. "Hey. Breakfast is my job."

I pulled the plates of eggs from the oven. "You looked like you needed the sleep."

She rubbed at her eyes. "I guess I did."

Adding the English muffins to the plates, I brought them over. "Are apricots okay for morning fruit?"

She sat. "Who are you and what did you do with my boyfriend?"

The boyfriend comment surprised me, but I tried not to let it show. It was a definite step up from brother's friend, and not one I was going to refuse. "Can't I make my girlfriend breakfast for once?"

The smile she wore went up several notches. She liked her new status as much as I liked mine.

I poured cranberry juice for both of us. "Coffee?"

She nodded. "And Advil."

I located the Advil bottle in the cupboard and poured two mugs of coffee. "You should have slowed down on the scotch."

"That was seriously good stuff. What did you say it was?"

I handed her the painkillers. "Macallan." I didn't add that it was aged eighteen years and cost over two-fifty a bottle.

After swallowing the pills, she ate slowly, mostly pushing the food around on her plate and sipping her coffee.

"It'll be okay, Sunshine. I promise."

She sighed. "I'm scared, Zack, and I don't want to drag you into this mess."

"We went through this last night. I'm not letting you leave. We are dealing with this together.'

Her eyes lifted from her plate, and a smile emerged. "Thank you."

It had taken a long time last night to get her to see I wouldn't back down on this.

"But they're dangerous," she said.

I pulled my gun from behind my back and laid it on the table. "So am I."

She gave up the argument and went back to her plate. Eventually she finished her apricots, but barely touched the eggs. She pushed the plate away. "I'm not very hungry."

I didn't tell her to finish the way she would have told me. "I'll keep it warm if you want it after your shower."

She stood. "A shower sounds like a good idea." She came around the table to me.

I stood and took my girlfriend into my arms.

"Thank you for breakfast," she said.

I kissed her and sent her upstairs. "Anything for you, Sunshine. Anything."

~

BRITTNEY

BEFORE GOING BACK DOWNSTAIRS, I HAD A CALL TO MAKE.

"Why haven't you been answering my calls?" Benji complained when he answered.

"I blocked you because you've been an ass."

"I need to see you."

"I want my papers back. I know you took them."

"Tell me where you are, and I'll bring them over."

That's one thing I *wasn't* doing. "Give them to Lillian at the Pig."

"No. I said I'd bring them over. We still have to talk."

231

I had to hold back to keep from yelling. "Give them to Lillian, or I'm calling the cops."

"I want to talk to you." He was just a broken record at this point.

Benji wouldn't have been able to lie like that if he knew where I'd moved. I felt confident now that he hadn't been the one to write the note.

I hung up and went downstairs. Zack was scrubbing dishes at the sink.

"Could you go next door with me?" I asked.

He put the pan off to the side. "Sure. We can go after you meet your protection detail."

"I'm not sitting around locked up with a bunch of goons with guns. I told you I have to go to work. I can't afford to lose this job."

"Give it a chance. This is for your safety."

The determination in his eyes meant he'd gone into full stubborn mode.

"It's not fair that I don't get a say," I shot back.

"Fine," he said, surprising me. "Meet them before you make up your mind though." He turned back to the dishes.

A half hour later, the doorbell rang while I was upstairs. Peering out the window, I located two black SUVs parked on the street: the goon squad. I went downstairs. Like Zack said, it wasn't fair to tell them to leave before meeting them.

At the base of the stairs, I was surprised by what I found. One of them was the hulking, buzz cut guy from the Habitat project the other day—Winston, if I remembered correctly. The surprise was his partner, a short woman with a bob haircut in a leather flight jacket. He looked like the dumb gun jockey I'd expected. She did not.

The big guy extended his hand. "Winston Evers, Brittney. I didn't expect we'd meet again so soon. By the way, thanks for the apple on Sunday."

My hand disappeared in his massive one as we shook. "At least somebody around here likes fruit." I shot a sideways glance to Zack.

The woman extended her hand. "Constance Collier."

I took her hand and received a surprisingly firm handshake. "Brittney Clark."

"Constance is ex-Secret Service," Winston noted.

Constance smiled.

A few moments of awkward silence ensued before I asked, "So, Winston, how do we get started with this?"

He turned to Constance. "What do you say, boss lady?"

A blush rose in my cheeks for making such a stupid assumption.

"Let's start with assessing the threat," she said. "Mr. Benson, you said there was a note?"

"Zack," he corrected her. "Yes, it's next door."

"Winston, why don't you and Zack go check it out," Constance suggested.

I waited until the door closed and the boys were outside before I spoke. "I'm sorry. I didn't mean to—"

Constance waved her hand dismissively. "Not an issue. I'm used to it."

"Coffee?" I offered.

"Water will be fine."

I led her into the kitchen and poured water from the fridge for her and an orange juice for me.

She accepted the glass and took a sip.

I twisted my glass. "Secret Service? Were you ever assigned to him?"

"No, not the president. I was on the First Lady's detail. Boring as hell."

"Really?" I wouldn't have guessed that.

"Protection detail is barely supposed to be seen, and certainly never heard." She stifled a laugh. "I was on that detail so long, I was afraid I'd forget how to talk."

"And this is better?"

"Tons," she said before taking another sip. "Better pay, better hours, and better partners—like Winston, top notch."

I could see we were going to get along fine.

The men came back in from next door.

Winston showed Constance some photos on his phone. "Pretty standard gang threat."

I cringed, recalling the sight from last night. "Normal?" I obviously led a sheltered life.

"I didn't mean this is normal so much as it's something we see a lot," Constance explained. "It's meant as intimidation."

"Mark me down as properly intimidated," I answered.

Winston pocketed the phone. "What key is the note referring to?"

I look to Zack for confirmation, and he nodded. "That's the problem. I don't know. It has to be related to a key they thought Todd told me about. But I never knew where to find any key."

"You think you know who left this?" Constance asked.

"You better start at the beginning," Zack told me.

I swallowed. "I testified in a murder trial that put a guy away—Luis Delgado. He's in prison, so I can only guess this is someone associated with him."

Winston put his hand up to interrupt me. "Can you spell that?"

I did so slowly.

"Go ahead," Constance urged me.

I told them about my ex-boyfriend Todd's brother getting murdered, then Todd disappearing in Mexico, and the messages about a key.

"And there's no way this could be anybody else, any other key they're referring to?" Constance asked.

"It's the only key that makes sense," I answered.

Constance turned. "Did anyone else know about this key? Did you tell anyone?"

I thought back. "Just the detective on the case, Detective Swenson."

"Who is he with?" Constance asked.

"LAPD," I told her. Then I remembered one other person. "I also told Benji one night."

Winston looked up from his computer. "Who is he?"

"Ex-boyfriend in San Jose."

"Recent?" he asked.

I nodded.

Winston hovered over his keyboard. "Last name?"

I looked to Zack for a moment.

He mock covered his ears.

"Sykes, S-Y-K-E-S," I told Winston.

He typed into his laptop.

Constance looked up from her notepad. "If you were to guess, who would you think did this?"

"I'm guessing one of Delgado's friends or relatives," I responded. "He got sent away for twenty-five to life, so it can't be him, and Benji doesn't make sense. I didn't even tell him I moved here."

Winston stood. "That's not quite true."

"What's not true?" Zack asked as he moved to see what Winston had on his screen.

"Luis Delgado was released from prison ten days ago. The conviction was overturned on bad jury instructions."

I shivered. I'd stopped checking the detective's emails long ago, and I didn't pay much attention to the news.

"He's one ugly son of a bitch," Zack said as Winston turned the screen so we would all see it.

The mug shot made Delgado look even more menacing than I remembered.

"At least he'll be easy to spot," Constance said.

The picture showed tattooed red teardrops under each eye, as well as the red star tattoo on his forehead. Those are what had made my testimony so damning at his trial. With those markings, there wasn't any guesswork involved in my identification, and that had been clear to the jury.

"So if we go on the assumption that this is Delgado, what do we know?" she asked Winston.

"We know he is risk averse," Winston offered. "Luring your boyfriend down to Mexico instead of confronting him here was a smart move. The closure rate on homicides in Mexico is extremely low. Also, leaving you a message when you weren't home means he's afraid to confront you directly."

"Afraid of me?" I asked.

"More like afraid of circumstances he can't control," Winston said.

"I agree with Winston," Constance added. "He's taking the low-risk approach in each case. That's good for us. Because it means he's not likely to make a crazy-ass move straight at you the way some gangbangers might."

"I don't see how that helps," I admitted.

"It means he's not going to try to come through us to get to you. He'll be looking for an opportunity where you're not protected."

"Wait—for how long?"

"That's not something we can answer right now," Constance said.

"I've got a question," Zack said. "How did he know she was here? She only arrived a week and a half ago."

Constance shook her head. "Brittney, who knew you were planning this move?"

"Nobody knew ahead of time. I left on the spur of the moment."

"And who have you told since you arrived?"

"Only my brother and my sister," I said.

"And since you've been here?" Constance asked.

"I've only been to Dr. Fosback's office, the Rusty Bucket, and the grocery store—and Home Depot to get some supplies. That's it," I answered.

"Winston, that's your assignment for this morning," Constance told him.

"What assignment?" Zack asked.

"Check out the employees," Winston answered.

"You can do that?" Zack asked.

"If anybody can, he can," Constance assured us.

I checked my watch. "I need to get ready for work."

"No, you don't," Zack said.

"I'll go with her," Constance said. "It'll be fine."

Zack backed down.

I went upstairs to change and get ready.

"Want me to tag along? I don't order much, but I'm a good tipper," Zack asked as I picked up my purse.

I kissed him on my way to the door. "Thanks for the offer, but no."

I left the house with Constance just a step behind me. I would finally be getting back to work and earning my own way. As I approached my car, Constance unlocked the closer black SUV with her key fob.

"I'll drive," she said.

I wasn't in the mood to argue this minor point. But she wasn't going to be following me around at work. "Do you know where it is?"

"Sure do. I've been there once or twice. I like the place." She didn't strike me as our normal clientele, but maybe off the clock she was more laid back.

"How does this work?" I asked. "You can't just shadow me."

She looked over, smiling for the first time. "It's nothing like that. I'll hang out where I can watch the entrance. There's only one entrance, right?"

"Yeah. Just one entrance off the street. The fire exit in the back is alarmed. A drunk crashes through it about once every two weeks, but that's only near closing. The lunch crowd is better behaved."

"What about the kitchen? I assume there's a back door for deliveries."

"There is, but Max is super strict about keeping it locked. It doesn't even have a handle on the outside, and deliveries are early in the morning, except for the beer distributor. He comes in the afternoon."

"Sounds simple enough," she said, turning down the main drag. "Delgado should be easy to spot."

"No kidding. With those tattoos, you can see the guy a block away."

"Is there anyone else I need to watch for?"

"Not that I know of," I told her.

She pulled into the Bucket's parking lot and stopped the SUV. She extracted a pendant on a gold chain and handed it to me. "Wear this around your neck. If anything happens and you need me, press the center stone and I'll be right there. Try it now."

I examined the pendant—cheap costume jewelry—located the central stone, and pressed it.

Her phone chirped.

I put the alarm jewelry around my neck. "Cool."

"Only if there's trouble," she warned me.

"Understood."

I climbed down from the truck and walked toward the door.

"I'll be in as soon as I check the back. Remember, I'm invisible."

As soon as I opened the door, Max called out to me. "There's my girl." He strode over and handed me a menu. "The menu's changed a little. You should check it out."

I took it. "I thought I'd be behind the bar."

His brow crunched up. "You said you wanted the first thing that came up, and this is it. Celeste has the bar today, and you've got section three."

"Sure, section three. That's great." Section three was nearest the pool tables, and always the slowest—a beer here and there, and nachos or poppers once in a while. The real lunch eaters usually took tables closer to the door.

After a few minutes memorizing the menu changes, I noticed Constance take a table near the side wall with a good view of the front door. Not once in the several times I looked over did I see her glance in my direction. They probably had classes in watching without being noticed at the Secret Service. Occasionally I saw her looking at what looked like a Kindle in front of her.

I was being fucking guarded by the Secret Service, was that ever a trip.

On my first trip to the bar, Celeste ignored me for a minute, and when she arrived, her scowl was icy. She'd probably heard the exchange with Max and thought I was trying to ace her out of tending bar.

"Welcome back," she finally said.

"Thanks. It's good to be back."

Lunch wasn't as slow as I remembered from before, and a few of my tables ordered more than just appetizers.

Maria stopped me by the kitchen entrance. "Why have you been checking out my tables all shift?"

I stepped back with the plates I was balancing. "What do you mean?" I instantly knew she was talking about my frequent glances in Constance's direction.

"Stick to your own section," she warned me. A moment later, she said something to Max.

As I returned from delivering food, Max's voice stopped me in my tracks.

"This ain't Starbucks. If you wanna read all day, go get a coffee or whatever." It was Max, telling Constance to take a hike.

I turned, and my mouth must have dropped as Constance rose and left without a word.

Max marched back to the kitchen and motioned for me to follow.

The kitchen door swung closed behind me.

Max had his hands on his hips. "Who is that lady you been watchin' all shift?"

"What?"

"The book reader who thinks this is a fucking Starbucks or something."

Maria and our cook, Paul, stopped what they were doing to catch the fireworks.

"My protection," I said in a low voice.

"Protection from what?"

"My ex," I whispered.

Max's expression softened, and he put a hand on my shoulder.

"Brittney, I'm all the protection you need. If'n he comes in here, you tell me, and I'll take care of it, permanent like."

I nodded. "Thanks, Max."

Maria pushed past me to the door.

Max looked me in the eye. "I take care of my own. Now get back out there, and don't worry about nothin'."

Max left first, and I followed.

As I left, I could see Maria huddling with Celeste. Celeste wasn't wearing a happy face.

Fucking great.

Now everybody was going to know my business.

CHAPTER 31

BRITTNEY
(Three Weeks Later)

FOR A LITTLE OVER THREE WEEKS ALREADY, I'D BEEN "UNDER protection," as Zack called it. Three weeks that felt like three years, and I was plenty tired of it. So far every time I asked if they'd tracked down Delgado, the answer had been no, maybe tomorrow.

We'd spent much of the day working on Zack's floors. It was hard work, but since it was Sunday, I had him here with me. Tomorrow he'd be off to work, and I'd be cooped up with my protection detail until my shift at the Bucket.

For now, I was cuddled up next to Zack on the couch. He had picked tonight's movie, so we weren't watching what he would call a chick flick. It was a thriller called *Paycheck* with Ben Affleck and Uma Thurman. I hadn't seen it before, and it got a little intense, at least for me. But when the end came, the good guy beat the bad guy, and the girl got her man.

Zack's arm around me pulled me tighter. "That wasn't so bad, was it?"

"A little scary for my taste. I thought for sure the bullet would hit him."

He kissed the top of my head. "But it didn't because he learned the lesson."

"What lesson would that be, oh wise one?"

"His future wasn't preordained the way it looked. He focused on a split-second change to the present when he was on the bridge to affect his future. That saved him, and the world."

The movie had indeed been about that, and I'd totally missed it. It was a variation of what he'd told me half a dozen times. I obviously wasn't a good enough student.

I looked up at him. "I got a different lesson from it."

"Yeah?"

"We should invent a shot like the one he had to erase memories, and use it on the bad ones."

He stopped being my pillow, stood, and pulled my hand. "Up."

"Why?"

"I said up." He pulled again.

It wasn't worth the argument, so I stood.

A second later, he'd picked me up and was carrying me to the stairs. "Your problem is you need more good memories to outweigh the bad ones."

I hung on his neck. "Really?"

He started up the stairs with me. "I aim to fix that."

I giggled as wetness pooled between my thighs.

He kicked the door closed behind him, and I had only the light from the full moon to see the grin that had eaten his face. He deposited me on the edge of the bed one second, and was yanking at my top the next. In short order he had me naked, with unmistakable lust in his eyes as he stood over me. The eyes of the predator were back.

I worked his belt while he pulled off his shirt, and with only a short struggle to free his erection, he soon stepped out of the clothes, his nakedness matching mine.

He pulled me to him, and the kiss he laid on me was worthy of his earlier promise to make tonight a wonderful memory. His strong arms clamped me against him as we traded breath and our tongues dueled for position. The pine scent of his hair tickled my nostrils, and the raspberry on his tongue was a reminder of his efforts to please my fruit obsession. The thickness of his arousal between us was a promise of what was to come.

He settled us down on the bed, our mouths still devouring each other with a hunger that wouldn't stop. He pushed my legs apart, and his fingers traced my folds as his kisses moved to the sensitive skin of my neck.

"You're going to come for me, Sunshine."

With one hand I grabbed his hair, with the other, I grasped his cock. "No. If tonight is my memory, I get what I want."

His finger slid forward to my clit, and his attack began. "I know this is what you want."

He got better every night at teasing me with just the right pressure, just the right circling, just the right rubbing, or sucking to drive me instantly crazy. He wasn't wrong that his ministrations were something I wanted, but only *one* thing. I wanted more.

I worked my hand on his cock, pulling, squeezing, and twisting. "That's not all I want."

His fingers continued to send electric shocks through me with every touch. "You'll get that too," he whispered as a finger entered me and exited.

I let go of his cock, pushed his shoulder over, and moved to straddle him.

"You want to be on top?"

I rubbed my wet folds over his length. "That's part of it." I leaned forward, placing a hand on either side of his head. I placed a gentle kiss on his lips. "But that's not all."

As I straightened up and slid forward and back over his cock, his hands came to my breasts, and his other talent came into play as he held them, fondled them, and circled the nipples playfully, teasingly.

I lowered a bit, and he brought his head up to take first one nipple and then the other into his mouth.

His breathing hitched just a bit every time I slid myself forward and over the tip of his cock.

He stretched to reach for the nightstand.

I tugged on his arm. "If it's my night, I should get to write the script."

He relented and his hand came back to my breast.

I leaned forward, my face an inch from his. "You said I could have a wish."

"Uh-huh."

I kissed him again lightly before whispering, "I'm on the pill. Can you guess my wish?"

His smile grew. "I'm clean. It's your script."

I lifted up and positioned his cock with my hand. "Me too." I pushed down just a little and lifted up, teasing his tip several times before his hands went to my hips and urged me lower.

He gasped as I slid down, taking much, but not all of him. "You're torturing me, baby."

I pushed down, taking him to the root. "My script."

He thrust up into me. I leaned forward to give his mouth access to my breasts. The sensations grew with each successive thrust as we glided against each other.

He pushed up into me. "Oh baby, you're so fucking good."

I rocked down on him again and again, my nerves firing harder each time he filled me to the end. I wanted to keep it up, to keep feeling him inside me, filling me as he was meant to, but the tension was building, and I wouldn't be able to keep my orgasm at bay for long.

The tension in his muscles and the gasps that came with each thrust said the same was true for him.

I clenched more tightly around him and pinched his nipples as he pulled me down hard with each push. I couldn't catch a breath as he picked up the tempo, and without warning, the waves of my climax rolled over me. I was over the edge into a sea of bliss as the spasms took over.

He tensed and pushed one last time with a groan and came undone himself, emptying inside me.

As I melted into exhausted limpness, I fell forward onto my man, panting to catch my breath and feeling the rapid beat of his heart beneath mine—the heart I hoped I'd won. I could still feel the pulsing of his cock within me.

He ran his fingers through my hair and kissed my ear. "I told you, you just need to add good memories to push the bad ones to the back."

"You won't leave me, will you?" My question escaped my lips before I could stop it.

He gave me a squeeze. "Of course not. I'll protect you always."

I kissed him. I wanted to stay like this, connected man to woman for as long as I could, and he let me.

He stroked my back and my hair as I listened to his heartbeat.

Eventually, I slid off to his side, and he got up.

I instantly missed his presence.

He returned with a warm washcloth for me to clean up and climbed back into bed.

I nestled against the man who had claimed me as his and promised to always protect me. Nothing could have warmed me more. I fell asleep as contented as I had ever been.

CHAPTER 32

ZACK

MONDAY MORNING, I WOKE WITH MY WOMAN SNORING SOFTLY IN bed beside me, where she belonged.

I slipped out of bed and out of the room as quietly as I could, taking my clothes to dress in the bathroom. Brittney deserved to sleep in after all the pressure she'd been under these last few weeks.

Once downstairs, I found Winston already up, in front of his laptop with a steaming cup of coffee in hand, as always.

He raised his mug. "Hey, boss."

"Anything new?"

"Maybe. I heard from a contact in Sacramento that he might have something for me later today."

I knew better than to get my hopes up. This was probably the fortieth lead, all of which had yielded zilch so far on Delgado.

"You should know this protection is getting on her nerves," I said.

"It can be tough. She just has to be patient."

I sprayed oil on the frypan. "She joked about giving you guys the slip to get some private time."

He put his cup down. "You better talk to her. That's not something to joke about."

I opened the fridge to get eggs. "I did, but you guys should be aware."

"Thanks. I'll let Constance know."

I added the eggs and dry ingredients to my bowl and had the batter whipped up quickly.

I got the other ingredients sliced and the pan heated by the time Brittney made it downstairs in her robe.

"Hey, that's my job," she said when she realized what I was doing at the stove.

"Sit down."

"No, that's my job."

I turned and pointed my spatula at the table, where Winston was closing his laptop and preparing to leave. "Sit. I'm doing breakfast this morning."

Winston stood.

"And you stay," I told the big guy.

He sat back down with a slight eye-roll.

Brittney fussed for a second, but decided against further argument and took her seat. "What are we having?"

I flipped the last crepe in the pan. "You'll see in a moment." I pulsed the blender a few times for the topping.

A minute later I had two folded crepes on each plate and brought them over.

"Looks good," Brittney said, raising her fork.

I rushed back for the blender. "Hold on, I'm not done yet." I poured the raspberry sauce over each crepe. "Now it's ready."

Brittney took a bite with a smile. "Delicious," she proclaimed. "And with fruit. I've converted you."

"I wouldn't go that far," I replied. I dug into mine and was proud of the result, even if I'd have to floss after to get the seeds out of my teeth.

Winston sipped his coffee. "This is good. I vote we let him cook."

Brittney shot him a questioning glance.

"Once a week," he added.

The warmth of Brittney's smile as I looked over to her made even cooking something fruity for breakfast worth it.

She blew me a kiss when Winston wasn't looking.

I pursed my lips in a kiss in return.

"I got an email this morning from Benji," Brittney announced.

That got both my and Winston's attention.

"And?" I asked. Nothing good ever came from her interacting with that jerk.

"I called him because I still need my papers back."

"You shouldn't have done that," I told her.

Her fork hit the plate with a clank, and her glare could have frozen a steaming cup of coffee. "Hold on a minute. You're the one who told me to take actions in the present to create the future I want. Well, I need those papers, so instead of waiting around, I did something, and I'm not second guessing it."

Winston leaned back from the table to avoid being between me and Hurricane Brittney.

I put my hands up. "Okay. No second guessing. So what happened?"

She calmed down and lifted her fork again. "I told him to bring them all here this weekend, but then the asshole said the drive was too far and I should buy him tickets on Southwest. Do you believe that?"

"You didn't agree to that?" I asked.

"Of course not."

"Did you give him the address?" Winston asked.

"No. I'm not stupid. I told him we'd meet at the Bucket."

That was a relief, the last thing we needed was him knowing where she lived.

"I don't think that's wise," I said. "How about if I take you to San Jose this weekend and we do the exchange there?"

"No way. I'm not having you get arrested for assault. You have no idea how underhanded he can be. He'll fall down and claim you hit him. He'd stab himself and claim it was you. He's a looney toon."

I was about to argue the point, but Winston beat me to it. "I'll go with you instead. How about that?"

Her head tilted as she considered the offer. "That'll work." She smiled as she took another bite of her crepe.

"I'm coming too," I announced.

Winston shot me a disapproving eyeroll. "Constance and I are probably better suited to handle this than you are, boss man. And it would be safer that way for Brittney, which is our top priority, right?"

I nodded, unable to argue with his logic. "I'm coming, but I'll stay in the car. How's that?"

Winston stated the obvious. "It's Constance's call. She's the lead."

I didn't have a fallback position for that. Hanson had made it clear from day one that Constance called the shots.

When Brittney left to take a shower, I gathered up the dishes.

"Thanks for nothing," I said.

"Take your argument to Constance. I'm just calling it as I see it, and frankly you can be a loose cannon. We don't need to add unpredictability to the situation. Brittney's safety is our primary concern, isn't it?"

"Of course it is." I returned to doing the dishes, appropriately admonished.

Winston went back to his laptop in the other room.

The morning sun shone brightly through the window of my kitchen—her kitchen now, the kitchen she'd re-arranged, as she had my whole life.

Her return had brought a clarity I'd been missing. She was the tornado that blew everything around, and when the pieces finally settled, things made more sense than they had before. Order had replaced disorder, and it was an improvement.

I reached into my pocket and rubbed the Lombardi coin on my keychain. It was time to have a difficult conversation with Dad.

CHAPTER 33

Zack

That afternoon, I was back at the house, sanding the spindles on the staircase railing.

Dad hadn't been in the office, so I hadn't stayed long.

Constance had decreed that I shouldn't go along on the San Jose trip. "Too many variables," she'd said—shorthand for agreeing with Winston that I was likely to do something stupid.

Brittney had the dinner shift at the Bucket today, and she and Constance hadn't been gone an hour when I got up to deal with the fruit Brittney had made me promise to eat this afternoon: plums. I pulled three from the fruit basket to slice up between Winston and me.

I always saved the pits to show her, but there was no room to cheat anyway. Winston had finked on me the first time I'd tried to fudge how many apricots I'd eaten, and that had cost me with Brittney.

Fucking Winston was as honest as the day was long, and nothing I could offer him would sway that, so Brittney always double checked with him.

He thought it was funny, and had fully committed to helping Brittney reform me on the fruit angle.

After peeling and slicing, I brought the bowls to the table. "Fruit's up."

Winston closed his ever-present laptop and came over. "Looks good."

I didn't echo the sentiment, although this was getting easier.

Winston had gotten through half his bowl when his phone chimed. He checked the screen. "This might be something," he told me before dialing a number. "Detective Wilmont, what's up? … That's great… Where does this come from?" He thanked the guy on the other end before hanging up and dialing another number.

He rose and grabbed his coat and gun, his phone clutched to his ear. "Constance, we got a lead on Delgado. I'm leaving to go check it out before it goes cold. You okay to hold down the fort for a day or two?… I'll be in touch."

"Where's the lead?" I asked after he hung up with Constance.

"Sacramento."

"That doesn't make sense. Didn't he always live here?"

He checked his weapon's clip, as he always did. "Not unusual. A lot of guys held at Folsom don't land far from the prison, at least at first. His conviction was thrown out, so since he's not on parole, he can live wherever he wants."

"How solid is our lead?" I used *our*, although my only part in this was to pay the bills.

"One of Wilmont's CIs said he knows where we can find Delgado, so I'll go check it out. Informants aren't always reliable, but you never know till you check." He loaded his laptop and charger into a backpack.

In a few minutes I was alone in the house, with a bowl and a half of sliced plums in front of me.

~

Brittney

It had been super hectic for a Monday evening at the Bucket, and it wasn't over yet. Eddie hadn't shown up to tend bar, and Max was filling in. I could do a better job than he was, but waiting tables didn't suit him.

Celeste emerged from the back, holding her stomach and carrying her purse. She headed for the door. She'd been scheduled to stay till closing.

Right on cue, Max waved me over to the bar from the table I'd just served. "You need to stay late. Celeste had to leave."

"Sure, no problem," I responded.

I needed all the work and tips I could get since Dr. Fosback still hadn't scheduled a start date for me.

"Good girl."

I pulled out my phone and typed a message to Constance first.

ME: Working late

Her response was immediate as always.

CONSTANCE: OK

Table twelve was motioning for their check, so I took care of that before texting Zack as well.

ME: working late be back when I can

His text didn't take any longer than Constance's had.

ZACK: Miss you

ME: Miss you more

ZACK: Miss you most

It was our standard back and forth. I'd tried to skip the more line and claim the most title a few times. That hadn't gone well. It was against some set of rules I wasn't allowed to challenge—no way, no how. I found it kind of cute the way I could force my man into his bossy mode. If I pushed the right buttons, he couldn't help himself.

His bossiness always came from a caring place though, and made me feel wanted and protected when it reared its head.

I just had to accept it as his way of showing he cared.

On my way to greet another table, my phone announced another text.

ZACK: Text when you leave

He hadn't added please, but I knew that's what he meant. Then he surprised me.

ZACK: Pls

I smiled as I put the phone away and took the table's drink orders.

I texted him back on my way to the bar.

ME: Wilco

Doug had taught me that bit of military lingo meaning *will comply*, and I knew Zack would appreciate it, because *comply* wasn't always in my dictionary.

"Two chardonnays, a Bud Light, and a whiskey sour," I told Max when he slid down in my direction.

"I hope we aren't interfering with your social life," he said sarcastically.

I straightened up. "You asked me to stay late, and I had to let people know." I wasn't in the mood to let Max push me around.

He poured the two glasses of wine. "Good enough." That was as close as he got to saying I was off the hook.

As Max poured the whiskey sour, I noticed Constance come in and make her way to the restrooms.

Max handed me the drink and started pouring the beer. He nodded toward Constance. "She could at least buy something."

I pulled a five out of my apron and slapped it on the counter. "Here. You're the one who told her she wasn't welcome."

He grumbled something unintelligible and pushed the money back at me. He'd just finished the beer when a commotion caught his attention by the pool tables. "Those fuckers again. I swear, I'm gonna break their faces."

I looked over, it was that idiot Chuck and his stupider wingman Todd. They'd managed an argument at least once a month or so when I worked here before, and apparently that hadn't changed.

Chuck yelled at an equally big guy in a cowboy hat and boots. Chuck knocked the guy's hat off, and the fight started.

Max hurried around the far end of the bar to break it up.

I grabbed some towels to wipe up the inevitable mess and walked in that direction.

Before I got there, Todd was on his ass, and Chuck was howling like a stuck pig.

Mr. Cowboy picked up his hat.

Constance had Chuck in an arm lock. "Now, you apologize to the man before I break your arm."

Todd stood and backed away.

Before Max could get there, Constance had made Chuck apologize, and Chuck and Todd were on their way to the door with her right behind.

I still had some beer to clean up, so I got busy.

Max made apologies to the two closest tables and offered them a round of drinks, which lightened everyone's mood.

When I made my way back to the bar a little later, Max pulled me aside. "What's her name?"

"Constance."

"Well, she's all right. Tell Constance tomorrow that she's welcome back in here anytime, even if she only buys an iced tea."

I smirked. "I'll tell her."

"And tell her thank you from me. The last time those two got into it with the cowboy, it cost me two chairs."

"I'd tell her that too, but I'm not allowed to text on duty."

"Don't be smart with me."

I slid into the kitchen and typed out my message. It was time to leave well enough alone.

ME: Max says thanks

Another immediate response followed.

CONSTANCE: no problem

She was the best.

I pocketed my phone and went back to my tables.

A half hour later, Maria came looking for me. "Max wants two more cases of beer from the back." Every night, Maria seemed to think I was the only one capable of carrying a box of beer bottles. It seemed to be her version of new-hire hazing, even though I had worked here for years before leaving.

"As soon as I fill this drink order."

She nodded and left for the kitchen while I visited the bar for margaritas and a beer.

Done with my tables for the moment, I went through the kitchen to the dark hallway with Max's office and the storeroom.

Maria unlocked the storeroom door for me. "He wants two boxes."

I went inside and flipped the switch. The light didn't come on.

Max had told Joey to change it, and in typical Joey fashion, it wasn't done yet.

Behind me, the back loading door squeaked open.

After a few seconds of acclimating my eyes to the dim light, I located the beer boxes along the wall. A faint skunk scent wafted in the air.

Another skunk had gotten run over in the back alleyway or some dog had gotten sprayed.

I leaned over to pick up the top box.

A hand grabbed my hair, yanking me back, and another brought a cloth to my mouth. The cloth was wet and sickly sweet.

I tried to scream, but the cloth and a hand muffled my attempt.

I struggled against the hand holding the cloth over my mouth. It was large and rough, definitely a man.

Moments later my knees buckled.

The world went dark.

CHAPTER 34

ZACK

CONSTANCE'S NAME APPEARED ON MY PHONE AS ITS ANNOYING ring started.

"Hey, Constance—"

She cut me off. "Do you know where Brittney is?"

I sat up. "With you at work, I thought." I checked my watch. It wasn't closing time yet. My mind started going in all the wrong directions.

"She skipped out. Did she tell you anything?"

My heart stopped. "Not a thing. Yesterday she was complaining about how confining this all was, but she seemed resigned to it when she left with you."

"Fuck. We need Winston. Her car is still here in the parking lot. The owner, Max, came out to tell me she went out the back door and didn't come back."

"How long ago?"

"From what I got from Max, less than an hour. He was pissed she skipped out on the tables."

"That doesn't sound like Brittney. No matter what, she would have seen to it somebody took care of the customers."

The pit in my stomach grew. Brittney took her job responsibilities seriously. She would never up and leave unless it was an emergency.

"She didn't call or text?"

I paced back and forth. "Not in a while. She said she'd text when she left work." That was another thing—Brittney had committed to text me, and she wouldn't blow me off like that. "What about the pendant?"

"That's what doesn't make sense. If she was forced to leave, the range on that is a mile or so. She would have had plenty of time to press the button."

I slammed my hand on the table. "What do we do now?"

"Her phone's off, so I can't get a location on her. I'll call Winston to see if he can get a bead on her with any surveillance cameras in the area."

"What can I do?"

"Just sit tight. If she just bugged out for some privacy, she'll probably call you, or show up, and you need to be there when she does."

"I will. Keep me up to date."

"Of course." She hung up.

I was sweaty, and my legs felt jittery. This wasn't fight or flight, this was fight *and* fight some more. Only I had no target to vent my anger on. Delgado was in Sacramento, maybe.

Scrolling through my phone, I located the app and tried to ping Brittney's phone's location. No luck, just as Constance had said. There was no current location data, only her last location at the Rusty Bucket.

Kicking the leg of the table earned me a sore toe, but no change in the app's ability to find her.

What the fuck?

Could she really have run off to get some peace and quiet like she'd threatened? The sour state of my stomach told the answer. I didn't believe that for one stinking minute. She was obstinate and impetuous, but leaving her car didn't make sense—that was a stupid move, and she wasn't stupid.

∿

BRITTNEY

As I BLINKED MY EYES OPEN, A WAVE OF NAUSEA ROLLED OVER ME. I closed them again.

The putrid smell of skunk was unmistakable.

The lurch of the floor bumped my head against the cold surface and hurt my hip.

My moan of pain and frustration didn't escape the tape over my mouth. All I managed was a loud hum.

I went to rub my eyes, but couldn't. My hands were tied together and connected somehow to my feet. My heart started to race.

The floor bounced again, and I blinked my eyes open a second time.

The sound, the movement, the dim light, the metal wall in front of me—I was being driven, in a van.

Slowly, I started to process my surroundings.

Maria lay on the floor facing me, bound in duct tape with her mouth taped as well. Her eyes bugged out, and she shook her head slightly, telling me not to—not to what?

I had no idea.

She lay between me and the driver.

The vehicle slowed to a stop and started again. A stoplight passed through the portion of the windshield I could see beyond Maria. It was still night, or nighttime again.

As we passed under a streetlight, I made out the driver, a man. The passenger seat was empty.

I craned my head to look behind me. The nausea that returned in force told me that was not a good idea. I was near the back of the work van. It was just the two of us in here.

My pendant. I tried, but couldn't pull my hands up high enough to reach it. I pulled up, but they pulled against my ankles, and I couldn't pull my feet up enough to reach.

I was such an idiot. Instead of struggling against the hand holding the cloth to my face, I should have reached for my pendant to signal Constance.

It was my fault we were in this situation. I should have gone for the pendant. Why hadn't I?

Constance would have flattened this asshole, or better yet, shot him in the head. Scratch that—in the nuts, then the head. That's what he deserved, whoever he was.

The driver started to whistle softly.

I knew that from somewhere, but where? I closed my eyes and concentrated. I knew that whistle.

My eyes jerked open with the realization.

Delgado.

The two days I'd spent at the trial, he'd whistled like that each time he was taken out of the courtroom.

Luis Delgado was the driver. This couldn't get any worse. First Todd, and now me and Maria.

A skunk hadn't gotten run over behind the restaurant—it had been him coming in through the back door. He'd gotten the skunk package Zack had meant for our local juvenile delinquent. Delgado had been behind the brick through my window. Somehow he'd known I'd come back to town only days after I'd arrived.

He turned his head back toward us.

I shut my eyes and played possum.

The van stopped and started again before I chanced another glance. There was no way I could stand and get to the door, much less open it or run if I got it open.

Controlling my breathing was becoming difficult, but with my mouth taped up, there was only so much air I could get in through my half-plugged nostrils.

Yelling for help was a non-starter with this stupid tape.

How long would it be before Constance noticed I wasn't in the Bucket anymore? How long had it already been? Neither of those questions had an answer. Where was he taking us?

If only I'd accepted Zack's offer to come tonight. What could I do?

My God, I needed Zack. There was so much I hadn't told him. So much I wanted to tell him.

If Zack was here, he'd have an idea. What would Zack do?

First thing, Zack would have been smart enough to hit the emergency pendant. Or maybe not—maybe Zack would have over-powered Delgado.

I closed my eyes, and for a moment I envisioned how the fight would've played out. Delgado would be a whimpering mess on the floor in a few seconds flat. I wanted to smile, but the tape prevented it.

Zack would have saved me. Zack would have kept me safe.

Why are you wasting time, girl? Get it together. You have to rely on yourself right now. Zack's not here.

I'd just wasted valuable time wishing for what I couldn't have instead of figuring out what to do. Zack would tell me to make a plan for the future. Visualize it, and make it happen.

I tried using my tongue to wet the tape near my lips to loosen it. But my saliva was no match for the industrial-grade tape. It wasn't loose enough for me to try to bite through either.

What did they do in the movies? They found something sharp to rub against to cut the rope or the tape.

He turned to look at us again, and I played comatose one more time, counting to ten in my head before venturing to crack an eyelid open.

As often as he was checking on me, there was no way I could move toward the back wall and feel for a sharp edge. Unconscious women stayed put, and that's what I was pretending to be. It was the safest course of action—or inaction—at the moment.

The chain on the emergency pendant settled down my shirt, out of reach. I used my chin against my neck to pull on the chain. It moved just a bit. Another scrunch move, and it slipped to where I couldn't reach it with my chin.

"I see you're awake," his evil voice came from the front.

Fuck.

I hadn't checked to be sure he was eyes-forward when I tried to the pull the chain.

"You bitches and I are going to have a nice, long talk. I want that key."

I shivered.

I didn't have the key. How could I give him what I didn't have?

I was fucked. We were fucked. Poor Maria. It was all my fault for not pressing the pendant.

CHAPTER 35

BRITTNEY

THE VAN STOPPED.

I could see a roll-up door moving through the windshield.

Delgado drove us in after it finished opening. He turned the engine off and got out.

The sound of the mechanical door closing came through the van's walls, and the lights came on outside the van.

I closed my eyes, dreading what would come next. I'd tried to use my chin to pull the pendant within reach—without success.

The sound of the van's back door opening behind me got me to open my eyes.

With a forceful yank, he rolled me over to face the back.

He had a knife in one hand. "You and I are going to have a little talk." The darkness in his eyes was pure evil, and the grin as he spoke was a bad sign. He ripped the tape off my mouth.

I trembled.

People who said it was easy if you ripped it off all at once were definitely wrong. It felt like my skin had been ripped off.

"I don't know anything," I mumbled.

He laughed. "Then this is going to be a very long night. I want the key."

"But I don't have it."

He waved the knife slowly. "In prison, we had a debate about how many cuts the body could endure. *Mi amigos,* they thought one hundred. I told them two hundred at least. Maybe tonight I find out." He laughed again.

I tried to squirm away from him, but ended up against Maria behind me.

He brought the knife to my shoulder. "Hold still, or this will be worse." He cut me with a quick slice.

I screamed at the pain.

"Only one hundred and ninety-nine more to go." The evil laugh reappeared.

I was going to die in here, and nobody could help me. Zack, Constance, Winston—none of them knew where I was.

He grabbed for my purse, which I hadn't realized was by my feet, and turned it upside down on the metal floor. "Is it in here?"

I shook my head, but didn't speak.

He rummaged through the contents that had spilled out. After a minute, he was convinced the key wasn't in my purse.

I started to hyperventilate.

"Is it at your house?"

That was my one chance.

I shook my head vigorously.

"No? I don't believe you. The house it is." He'd taken the bait.

I could only hope Zack and Winston could help if he took me to the house.

Delgado tore off a fresh section of tape, and I was once again gagged.

My shoulder stung.

The van door slammed shut.

~

ZACK

IT HAD BEEN A HALF HOUR SINCE CONSTANCE'S LAST CALL WHEN the phone lit up with her name again.

"I've canvassed the nearby streets, the coffee shops, and the diner. There's no sign of her in the vicinity," Constance told me over the phone. "Is there anybody she could have gone to see?"

I wracked my brain. "None that come to mind. Her sister is still out east. I'll join you, and we can cover twice as much ground."

"Not a good idea. I've called my boss, and he has two other agents on the way to help me. You need to cover the house. She could return there to pick up clothes or something. You should wait and watch."

Her advice sounded rational. It assumed that Brittney had left on her own and was dodging her security, and probably me too.

"Okay," I answered reluctantly. I hated being inactive.

Ten minutes later, I left my spot in the front room and went back to the kitchen for something to drink.

I chose grapefruit juice. A small gesture toward what Brittney would have wanted seemed like the right thing to do.

After rinsing the glass in the sink, I flicked the kitchen light off to return to the front. That's when I noticed the dim kitchen light on next door at Brittney's house.

It hadn't been on before. She was back.

My heart leaped in my chest.

Movement—I caught movement I couldn't make out. Running to the switch, I doused the lights in the TV room so I could see next door more clearly, and she wouldn't be able to see me.

Two people. No, three.

Brittney, another woman, and a man.

The man turned my way.

The red star tattoo on his forehead was unmistakable—Delgado, and he was waving a gun and a knife in Brittney's face, then the other woman's.

My stomach soured.

If fucking Winston hadn't confiscated my gun, I'd be able to take him, but now I had to do it unarmed.

I rushed to my phone and redialed Constance. "He's here, and he has Brittney and another woman."

"Slow down, Zack." I heard the screech of tires over the phone. "I'm headed your way. Tell me what you see."

Breathlessly I recounted it. "Delgado is here. He's got Brittney in the kitchen with another woman. He has a gun, and he's waving a knife in their faces too."

Constance was cool under pressure. "I'll get LAPD SWAT there as soon as I can. Don't make a move. The most dangerous thing you could do is try to take him on by yourself. Leave this to the professionals. I have to hang up now to call the police. You keep an eye on what's happening from your house. Call me with any change." She clicked off.

No fucking way was I sitting still while that whack-job had my woman.

I ran my fingers through my hair.

Need a plan.

I ran back to my darkened kitchen.

They were all still in Brittney's kitchen at the back of the house. The front was dark. I grabbed a big carving knife from the knife block, then decided I needed something easier to wield and chose a six-inch chef's knife, one I'd sharpened this week.

My plan was idiotic—bringing a knife to a gun fight—but if I snuck in through the front of the house and got behind him before he saw me, I stood a chance. It was my only chance. The only chance we had, and doing nothing was not a plan, not an option.

I walked calmly toward my front door. "Control your breathing, dickhead. You have to sneak up on him," I said to the empty room.

I found my key to her house on my key ring. I was prepared. I opened my front door and found what I was *not* prepared for.

Piss Boy.

He backed away from the door and eyed the knife I was carrying. "Calm down, man. I brought the letter." He held up an envelope. "I just want my phone."

Change of plan. He was just what I needed. I slid the knife in my back pocket. "Cool. Your phone is next door."

"You said here," he complained.

"I left it next door," I told him. I pointed to Brittney's house. "I've only got a key to the back door. You go to the front door, and I'll go in through the back."

"Why don't I come with you?"

"Because I said so, that's why."

He huffed, but didn't argue again.

"You go to the front door and ring the doorbell in two minutes. Ring it twice then get off the porch. Got it?"

"Yeah, man."

"Doorbell, two minutes, then off the porch" I repeated as I passed him to descend the stairs.

"Whatever." He followed me down the steps.

We'd taken to locking the back gate between the properties, so I scurried down her drive and around the gray van that had to be Delgado's. Sliding silently to the back steps, I climbed them, skipping the creaky one. It was a short crawl across the porch to the back kitchen door. Two panes of its glass were broken. That had to be how he'd gotten in.

"I don't know where it is." I heard Brittney crying clearly through the broken door.

"I'm going to cut you again. Every time you give me a wrong answer," Delgado yelled.

Brittney screamed.

It was all I could do to hold back and not break in, but a gun against a knife wouldn't end well, and that wouldn't save Brittney.

I heard the doorbell ring.

"Who's that?" Delgado asked frantically.

"I don't know."

"Maybe it's your boyfriend, and he can join us. We'll have a little party, the four of us. Maybe you tell me when I start cutting *him*."

The doorbell rang again.

I heard footsteps and chanced a peek through the window.

Delgado was going to the front door as I'd hoped he would.

I silently turned the key in the deadbolt, just in case. Leaving the key in the door, I twisted the handle and pulled the door partly open.

Neither of the girls had noticed me yet. They both had their wrists duct-taped to the arms of the chairs, and their feet to the legs.

I clamped my hand over Brittney's mouth from behind. "Shhh." I turned her head to me and took my hand away. She had two short bloody cuts on her shoulder.

The other woman coughed.

I turned to her and put a finger to my lips to silence her.

I quickly cut Brittney's hands loose.

"You came," she mumbled with tears in her eyes.

My heart was pounding so hard I could barely hear her. "Shhh," I reminded her.

I could hear Delgado arguing with Piss Boy. "Get the fuck outta here."

I cut Brittney's legs loose. "Leave," I said quietly nodding toward the open door.

"Not without Maria." She had to choose the worst possible time to be obstinate.

"Not till I get the phone," Piss Boy yelled. "The guy said he'd give me back my phone."

I cut at the tape securing the woman's wrists.

She yelped in pain.

I'd been careful not to nick her, but I slowed my cutting just the same.

The front door slammed.

I pushed Brittney toward the door and shifted to Maria's legs.

Brittney didn't budge.

I'd gotten the second of Maria's legs loose when the shot rang out.

It splintered the floor in front of me.

Looking up, I found Delgado in the doorway, his gun pointed right at me. I had a knee down to reach Maria's ankle, and Delgado was too far away for me to lunge from this position and have a chance.

"The next one goes through your boyfriend," he yelled from the doorway.

CHAPTER 36

BRITTNEY

DELGADO WAVED THE GUN TOWARD THE CORNER WITH THE PANTRY. "Close the door, and over to the corner, all of you."

Moving on jittery legs, I closed the door and followed the other two.

This was going from terrible to horrific in a hurry.

Zack had wanted me to save myself, but I couldn't leave him and Maria here with this monster.

Delgado moved back. "Slide the table over in front of the door."

Zack moved slowly, eyeing Delgado every second. He pushed the table to block our escape through the back door.

Delgado slid a chair toward the sink. "Now tape the fat one to the chair, and we can continue our little conversation."

Maria sneered at him, but moved to the chair and sat.

Zack lifted the roll of duct tape from the counter, keeping his eyes glued to Delgado.

"You are going to tell me where the key is," Delgado said, his dark eyes glaring. "I guarantee it." He trained the gun on me, then Zack, then back to me again.

"I think you should," Zack said, drawing Delgado's attention.

What the hell was he thinking? Zack knew I didn't have a clue; we'd talked about it.

Delgado smiled. Zack's comment pleased him as much as it tormented me. "Tape her to the chair." He waved his gun at Maria and Zack.

Zack started rolling the tape around Maria's wrist and the arm of the chair. "Tell him about the safe," he told me, nodding toward the pantry.

Delgado pivoted to me. "Yes, tell me about the safe, bitch. Where is it?" The amusement in his face went up a notch.

I looked to Zack. How could he be doing this?

He winked.

Confusion tinged my terror. I didn't get what Zack was up to, but he had something in mind.

"So where's the fucking safe?" Delgado asked again.

Zack nodded toward the pantry. "In there."

Delgado waved his gun, motioning me away. "Move."

I slid down the counter, looking toward Zack for a clue.

Delgado opened the pantry door, keeping his gun pointed in our direction.

Zack mouthed something I couldn't make out as Delgado turned away.

I shrugged. Not risking a word, I mouthed *what*? I still couldn't lip-read his indecipherable message.

Delgado opened the door wider and turned back to us. "Open it," he commanded.

My legs were shaking as I went to the pantry and knelt in front of the safe. Damned if I could remember the combination Grams had told us once.

"I don't remember the combination." I looked back to Zack for a clue as to what he meant to accomplish with this.

Delgado's evil grin returned. "You better." He pointed the black gun toward Zack's knees. "Or he won't ever walk again."

Zack's face showed a confidence I couldn't echo. He nodded toward the floor twice when Delgado looked back at me.

I turned back to the safe and started twirling the knob. Doing something was better than nothing.

Grams had told us the combination as little girls, and it had been a birthday, but I couldn't remember whose.

"Don't you remember? You waved it in my face the night you came back," Zack said from behind me.

I looked back. "What?"

Zack's eyes shifted to the floor. "You waved it around."

Big help he was. He was hallucinating.

Then I caught on.

He wanted me to stall.

I turned back to the black steel box.

"I'm not waiting forever," Delgado said.

I raised my arms. "Quiet," I yelled. "I need to think."

"Faster," Delgado spat.

A birthday, and it had a seven in it.

I ran through our birthdays, including Grams's and Gramps's. No sevens popped up.

Fuck, I was sure she'd said a birthday.

What other birthday could it be?

I moved a container of colored sprinkles out of the way. Red, white, and blue. The answer was simple. Our country's birthday—seven, four, seventy-six.

I spun the wheel four times to the right, stopping at seven, then back around to the four, and back toward seventy-six. As I did, I saw what Zack had been hinting about on the floor beside the safe.

I shifted right to conceal the can before twisting the knob the final bit to seventy-six. Praying silently that I'd gotten it right, I tried the handle, and it turned with a satisfying clunk, unlocking the door.

"I got it." I didn't open the steel door.

"Let me see," Delgado demanded.

I turned and palmed the can, hiding it behind me as I rose.

"Out of the way," he said, approaching, eager to see the interior of the safe.

I slid sideways and waited. When he got close, I stepped to the side, raised the can, and gave him a full dose of pepper spray, right in the eyes.

He squealed as his hands went to his face.

Zack charged from behind, slamming him against the pantry door, and the gun skittered across the floor.

The two men threw fists.

I lunged for the gun.

Zack fell back from a wicked punch.

Delgado, his eyes closed from the stinging spray, lunged in our direction, a knife in hand, flailing at the empty space between us.

I raised the gun and pulled the trigger.

The explosive recoil ripped the gun from my hand.

Delgado fell back.

Maria screamed and leaped up, dragging the chair by the arm taped to her wrist.

Zack pulled me to the far wall and cradled me in his arms. "You're okay." He kicked the gun away.

Maria pulled the knife from the floor and cut at the tape holding her to the chair.

"I thought you'd never figure it out," Zack said in my ear.

Maria finished cutting herself loose from the chair. With the knife still in her hand she screamed, "You killed my brother."

Her eyes were wild, and anger filled her face. She stooped to pick up the gun.

Zack shoved me out of the room toward the front. "Run."

I ran for the front room, and a shot rang out. Bits of plaster from the wall stung my face.

Zack was right behind me when Constance appeared in the doorway. She raised her gun at me, shifted right, and fired.

As I reached her, she pushed me and Zack to the side. "Get outside." She advanced toward Maria on the floor.

I looked back, and she kicked the gun Maria had been holding to the side before holstering her gun. "Call an ambulance."

She rolled Maria over and applied pressure to her shoulder.

"Delgado's in the kitchen," Zack told her.

"Get outside," she repeated.

I was so hyped up on adrenaline I couldn't tell how long it took for us to be swarmed by LAPD officers and paramedics. It seemed immediate, but it probably wasn't.

CHAPTER 37

ZACK

THE FIRST TWO PARAMEDICS RUSHED INSIDE, AND I GRABBED THE next one I saw for Brittney. "Here. Over here. She's bleeding."

The cops were everywhere. A guy in a suit jacket, probably a detective, gave directions to the uniforms.

Paramedics wheeled Delgado out on a gurney.

"I'm going to get you," he said through the oxygen mask. The look he gave us was pure evil.

If that day ever came, I wanted my Sig back from Winston. Delgado had been let out of prison once, so there was honestly no telling what might happen in the future, but I would be ready. We would be ready.

Brittney shivered in my arms—not from any cold, but from fear and the massive amount of adrenaline this horrific night had induced. After a few minutes the paramedic began cleaning and bandaging her shoulder.

"The cuts are clean," he told her. "If you get theER at the hospital to stitch you up tonight, I don't think the scars will be noticeable after a while."

"Thanks," she replied.

The guy in the suit came over after talking with Constance for a minute. He asked our names and introduced himself as Detective Ryan, handing me a business card.

"Miss Clark, I'm glad you're all right."

"Thanks," she answered.

"Sir. You were in the house when this happened?"

"Yeah."

"I'm going to need a statement. Could you please come with me for a moment?"

I didn't budge. "I'm not leaving her." "Sir, two people have been shot. You need to step over here, please."

Brittney patted my leg. "It's okay. Go."

Reluctantly, I rose and followed the detective.

I ran through the sequence of events while he took notes.

"Miss Collier told us she advised you to wait for us to arrive. Why didn't you?"

"It looked too risky. I thought I could get them out of there with a distraction."

"That didn't work out so well, did it?"

"Only because Maria alerted him while I was cutting her loose."

"How?" He checked his notes. "You didn't mention that earlier."

"Sorry. I probably went too fast. When I was cutting her loose, she yelled like I'd cut her. That brought Delgado back to the kitchen early."

"But you hadn't cut her?"

"No, but I didn't know it at the time. We didn't know she was his sister."

"You said that. And you put the local boy you sent to the front door in danger as well."

I nodded. I hadn't considered that in my rush to help Brittney.

"Tonight could have ended very badly for all involved because you didn't wait."

"I made my choice, and it's done. I did what I thought was best at the time. I'm not going to spend a lot of time second-guessing myself."

"That's your prerogative, Mr. Benson."

He asked a few more questions about details of my statement, and I answered them.

"One thing I still don't understand…" He closed his notebook. "Why do you think she didn't give him the key?"

"Because there is no key—at least not one Brittney knows anything about."

"That's obviously not what Mr. Delgado thinks. Guys like him are dangerous, but they kidnap people for a reason. He thinks there's a key, and he thinks she knows where it is."

I shrugged. "I can't help that."

~

BRITTNEY

ZACK RETURNED TO ME AFTER ANSWERING DETECTIVE RYAN'S questions.

Shortly after that, Constance finished with another detective and came to sit with me, too.

"You should have hit the pendant," she said.

That was an ode to obviousness.

"I didn't have time," I lied. "He drugged me with something." Also, I hadn't been thinking clearly enough. I'd probably had time, but I didn't have the right instinct. I'd fucked up, pure and simple.

"Why was the other waitress chasing you with a gun?"

"Maria, that's her name, said Delgado was her brother."

Constance nodded. "That explains a lot."

"Will she be all right?"

"Looks that way to me. I only winged her. You two were in the way, and it was the best I could do under the circumstances. Delgado's injury doesn't look life threatening either. You guys did good."

The anger welled up in me, thinking about poor Todd and what Delgado had been about to do to us. "I wish I'd killed him."

"No. Trust me, you don't. It seems right in the moment, but it would haunt you for a long time."

Her words made sense. I shouldn't want to sink to his level. I still needed to cool off from the horror of tonight.

"Did you ever?" I asked.

She didn't respond. Her eyes told the story, though. She'd advised me about regret from personal experience.

I switched subjects. "I forgot to thank you."

"It's the job," she said, tilting her head. "But I appreciate it. Three years on the First Lady's detail, and that never happened."

"A situation like that?"

"No." She laid a hand on my arm and smiled. "A thank you."

I reflected for a moment on how that must have felt to her, giving up a normal life to keep somebody else safe, and not getting any gratitude in return. No wonder she left that job.

"I saw an open safe in the kitchen. Is that where the key was?" Constance asked, fishing for an explanation.

"There is no key. The safe was empty except for some old papers. It was just a diversion to get to the pepper spray."

"Not to worry." She smiled. "It's all over now except the nightmares. Delgado and his sister won't be seeing daylight for quite a while."

The nightmares comment didn't help. It had taken long enough to get past them after Todd's disappearance.

"Will they be out on bail?"

"Not a chance. Kidnapping and assault? No way."

Her confidence was reassuring. I didn't relish hiding again.

Detective Ryan came back, this time accompanied by Detective Swenson, who I'd dealt with years ago during Delgado's murder case.

"Miss, Detective Swenson will be taking your statement."

Zack didn't looked pleased to let me go.

I walked with Swenson, and we settled on the front room couch.

"I thought you left the country," he started.

"Well, I'm here now." I hadn't trusted anyone but my family with the truth, and I didn't care to go into that with him.

"Miss Spear, let's start by having you walk me through the events as you remember them."

"It's Clark now," I corrected him.

He took a note, obviously surprised.

"I changed it after the trial," I explained.

"I didn't know."

"Nobody did."

"Well, Delgado obviously did," he retorted.

I'd been thinking about this, and now it made sense. "He didn't either. I only came back to town a couple weeks ago, but I went back to work at my old restaurant."

"And?" he asked.

"Maria, his sister, took my application paperwork. She knew me from before, and the application had my new name and this address. I never knew she was his sister."

"When did you find that out?"

I huffed. "Tonight when she screamed that I'd shot her brother, and then came after us with a gun."

We went over the events of the night three times before he let me get back to Zack and Constance.

Z_{ACK}

THE EVENING DRAGGED ON. NOW THAT BRITTNEY AND I HAD BOTH been questioned, I hoped we'd soon be free to go.

I wrapped her in a tight embrace. "You're still shaking."

"A little. But it's getting better. I've never been so scared."

"I've got you now, Sunshine."

She looked up at me, and her smile told the story before her words did. She nestled her head against my shoulder. "I know."

"You two can go now," Detective Ryan said as he approached.

Brittney disengaged herself from me. "Can I have my purse back?"

"Purse?" he asked.

"It was in the back of the van."

Ryan backed up. "I'll check to see if it's been processed yet." He moved down the driveway.

"I'll bet you could use a glass of wine," I told her.

"Make mine a bottle."

Detective Ryan returned with her purse and told us again that we could leave.

"Not so fast," Constance told us.

With what we owed her tonight, I wasn't arguing.

She jogged to her Denali and returned carrying a gun.

It took an okay from the detective for her to get past the cop at the sidewalk.

"They took my piece...evidence," she told us. "Now we can go."

"You don't need to babysit me anymore," Brittney complained.

Constance addressed me. "I've learned that often the most dangerous time is directly after an attack." I knew she was telling me because I was the one contracting them.

"Do you think Sacramento was a deliberate red herring?" I asked.

"That would be my guess," she replied.

Brittney wrung her hands.

None of this made me more comfortable, especially the thought that there could be someone else out there.

"I'll drive," Constance offered. "We still need to get you to the ER for those stitches."

⁓

THE ER VISIT HADN'T TAKEN LONG AT THIS TIME OF NIGHT, AND Constance had been with us the whole time. Brittney and I had each already downed a glass of wine and were on our second when Winston finally arrived back at the house.

He had aborted his trip to Sacramento after hearing about Brittney's disappearance.

His return gave Constance the right to pour herself a glass of wine, down it, and pour a second. "I gotta catch up to you guys," she explained.

Brittney scrolled through the movie choices after her second glass of wine.

"Stop," Constance called. "Go back two. Yeah, that one."

Brittney shot me a grin.

"Constance has earned the right to pick tonight," I told her.

Brittney nodded and punched the button. *Sweet Home Alabama* started up.

Constance settled into the couch. "Ever since *Legally Blonde*, I love her movies."

A minute later someone knocked on the door, and Winston rose to answer it—with his gun, of course.

"Winston, put that thing away." My sister Serena's voice sounded from the front of the house.

With loud footsteps, she hurried our way. "I heard what happened. Are you okay?" she asked Brittney.

Brittney leaned against me. "Thanks to these two. Just a few stitches is all."

Constance hoisted her glass. "The good guys won this one." She took a gulp.

Serena looked at me and laughed. "I heard it was the good gals. Brittney shot one, and Constance shot the other one." She pointed at me. "Saving your ass."

I shrugged. "What can I say? I surround myself with strong women."

Constance rose and took the chair. "Have a seat," she said to Serena.

Serena shoved my shoulder to get me to make room, and Brittney and I moved down.

I ended up with women on both sides of me.

Serena insisted on talking over the movie. "I wish you'd killed him. He deserves it after what he did to poor Jonas," she said.

This was the first time my cousin's name had come up in years.

Brittney looked as perplexed as I was.

"What do you mean?" I asked.

"Delgado was Jonas's dealer, sold him the stuff that killed him." Serena leaned forward to talk around me. "Jonas is, was, a cousin of ours. Died of an overdose. Not something the family talks about much."

"You sure Delgado was his dealer?" I asked.

"Absolutely. Didn't you know that?"

"Didn't pay attention, I guess," I said.

Jonas had steered himself down his own road of self destruction, and she was right, it wasn't a topic we dwelled on.

"It's a good thing she only clipped him," Constance interjected. "The guilt of actually shooting a man is not something you want to wish on her."

"I still say he deserves a bullet." Serena sat back. "I love this movie."

Ten minutes later, my sister elbowed me. "I came over to see that you were all right too."

I squeezed her shoulder. "Thanks."

She did care, and it meant a lot to me.

We had to pause the movie several times as the family grapevine activated and my phone rang. One by one my parents, brothers, and my other sister called to see how we were doing.

CHAPTER 38

BRITTNEY

I WOKE TUESDAY MORNING WITH A MILD HEADACHE. I SHOULDN'T have let Zack switch us to red wine. Or maybe it had been Constance who'd requested red—anyway, it had been a bad idea.

Last night had been a late one.

It had taken several glasses of wine and two movies to relax from the terror of the evening.

By three in the morning, I'd finally been calm enough to sleep.

Zack's side of the bed was empty. I dragged myself out to join him.

"Morning, sleepyhead," he said as I wandered into the kitchen. He pulled a plate with a stack of waffles from the oven. "Been keeping these warm for you."

"Thank you."

Winston was parked in what I called the TV room on the couch, hunched over his laptop.

Zack brought over bowls of sliced papaya without me having to bug him.

I took a seat. "Hey, Winston. Want to join us for breakfast?"

He waved me off. "Thanks, but I already ate.

"Where's Constance?"

Winston looked up from his computer. "She went to the police station—something about an extended interview about last night."

I put some of the papaya slices on my waffle and cut a bite, which I stuffed into my mouth. This morning was not about being a lady. The taste was heavenly.

Zack pointed his fork at me. "How's the shoulder?"

I stretched it. "Not bad. It's the keep-it-out-of-the-shower-for-a-few-days part that will bother me."

"You'll just have to let me give you a sponge bath."

I looked up to see the devilish grin I loved on him. "You won't have to twist my arm."

Serena appeared, wrapped in Zack's bathrobe. "I shouldn't have switched to red last night. It gives me a headache."

"Red is healthier for you than white," Zack countered.

I got up to pour her a glass of OJ. "I didn't realize you stayed over."

"I wasn't in any shape to drive."

"She's a lightweight," Zack added.

I handed her the glass of juice. "We have waffles and papaya, unless you want something else."

She slumped into a chair. "Sounds great, but I think I'll start with Advil."

My purse was still in here from last night. "Sure. Generic ibuprofen good enough?"

She nodded and drank some more juice.

I poured four tablets into my hand for her, and two more for me. I tried to swallow mine dry. That was a mistake. I raced for my juice glass before delivering the tablets to Serena.

Zack wolfed down his waffles. "I need to go into the office," he said between mouthfuls.

I had hoped for more alone time with him after last night, but office time was clearly becoming an issue with his father. A family-member boss was more understanding in some ways, but the leeway only extended so far.

Five minutes later, after a quick kiss, he was gone.

Serena leaned forward after the door closed. "Dad wants to talk to him about London. I think you'll like it there."

I jerked back. "What?"

She cocked her head. "Zack's next rotation."

Zack had mentioned that he was due to start his finance rotation at some point, but London had only come up as a trip he'd canceled weeks ago.

Serena forked a slice of papaya. "Dad told me he wants to move up the timing."

I waited for her to explain further.

She finished chewing. "I found it an amazing city when I was there. I think you will too."

The lump in my throat prevented me from swallowing the bite of waffle I'd taken. I finally got it down with a swig of juice.

Zack had kept this from me. Moving to another city was a big deal—another *country* constituted a gargantuan big deal, not the kind of thing you forgot.

After an awkward silence, Serena finished the last of her breakfast and took her plate to the sink. "I can stay longer if you want to talk."

"No, I'm fine."

"Okay. You've got my number. Maybe we could have lunch later this week."

"Sure," I answered.

I stood and brought my plate to the sink.

She gave me a hug and was off.

I went to wipe down the table. With Delgado and Maria in jail, I should have been feeling better than I was, but the London news hadn't thrilled me. I knew Zack had to do this rotation bit for his father, but my hygienist certification didn't extend to foreign countries. Being the hanger-on girlfriend waiting all day for my boyfriend to come home didn't appeal to me. And, that was even assuming he wanted me to come along. He hadn't told me about it. What did that say? Nothing good.

I was sick and tired of being told what to do, and the next command was going to be to uproot my life and go to England with him? Hell, I didn't even have a passport.

I washed a plate and moved it to the drying rack.

This discussion should include me, not just Zack and his father, shouldn't it?

As I went to place the glass in the drying rack, it slipped from my grasp, and as I lunged to catch it, I knocked my purse off the counter. I caught the glass, but the purse landed on the floor, its contents spilling across the hardwood. Like an idiot, I hadn't zipped it shut.

Kneeling, I gathered things and put them back into the bag one by one...until I got to the pink envelope—my penance envelope.

Whenever I wanted to torture myself, the contents of this envelope never failed. I unfolded the faded piece of paper within and read the names of the people I'd killed.

Twenty-seven in all. Twenty-seven people whose lives I'd cut short. Twenty-seven who would never see another sunrise, much less London. Twenty-seven sentences of damnation for me.

As imperfect as my life was, at least I was still alive.

This time as I read, I noticed something new. When I reached the thirteenth name, I burst into tears. I'd never known who it was until last night. His name had never been mentioned. I'd never considered that they could be related.

But the thirteenth name was Jonas Benson, Zack's cousin.

Karma could be incredibly cruel.

∼

*Z*ACK

. . .

287

THE LOOK ON WENDY'S FACE AS I APPROACHED SAID THIS WOULD not be just another Tuesday morning at the office.

"I heard what happened." Her eyes searched my face. "Are you all right?"

"Now that it's over, yes."

"I already told Stanton you wouldn't be calling this morning."

"Thanks." That was one aggravation I didn't need today.

She stood and took our coffee mugs in the direction of the caffeine dispenser. "I'll get the coffee today. The usual?"

"Please."

I had only just settled into my seat and opened my email when Dad arrived and shut the door behind him.

"Sounds like a harrowing night."

"It was, but Brittney's safe now, and that's what matters."

He took a seat. "You can expect a call from your mother. She's as worried as sin about you."

I could tell Dad wasn't. As Bensons, we got up, dusted ourselves off, and moved on to the next challenge. That's what this had been in his mind—just another challenge.

"I'm glad you're safe. I was worried too," he added, forcing me to reevaluate his feelings for a second.

"Thanks, Dad. I've never been that scared."

"It's when our loved ones are in danger, that it's the worst."

"That's for certain."

He shifted in his chair. This visit hadn't been merely to see how I was doing. Typical Lloyd Benson. He would have rushed in instantly to help me last night, straight into gunfire if necessary. But today, that episode was over, and it was on to the next item of business. That was one thing he'd taught me well. Don't dwell on the past—look to the future and deal with it.

"You wanted to talk?" I asked.

He fidgeted, very unlike his usual self. "It's about London. Harold's controller there has just given his notice, and that's going to move up the timing of your move." He hadn't phrased it as a choice, because it clearly wasn't intended as one. The timing had just been decided for me.

"How soon?"

"A week, give or take. You can talk with Harold about the specifics."

One week wasn't tomorrow, but it was a lot less time than I'd counted on to break the news to Brittney.

He rose to leave, but stopped at the door. "Have you decided what you'll tell her?"

Somehow he knew I hadn't broached the subject with Brittney. "Yes. I have."

He nodded and moved off down the hallway.

Wendy used Dad's departure as an opportunity to bring in my coffee.

I took a sip of the hot brew. "I need you to make me an appointment with Harry Winston."

Puzzlement crossed her face. "The name doesn't ring a bell."

"The jeweler."

She smiled as recognition lit her eyes. "Right away."

CHAPTER 39

Zack

After turning onto Snakewood, I could see Winston up ahead carrying things. Getting closer, I realized he was carrying clothes and paintings from my house to Brittney's.

I pulled into my driveway and parked in front of the garage.

"Brit?" I called, letting myself in through the back.

I made my way to the front of my house.

Winston opened the door and came back in.

"What's going on?" I asked.

"She asked me to help move her things next door."

"Why?"

He shrugged. "That's above my pay grade. All I can tell you is she was crying, but it's not my place to pry. She's next door. Oh, and she fired us."

"Huh? She can't do that."

"She doesn't want protection anymore. And maybe you can talk to her about it, but we can't force her. Constance already left for a new assignment in Long Beach."

I bounded out the door and over to her house.

At the front door, I stopped. Instead of bursting in as I wanted to, I rang the bell.

A minute later footsteps approached the door, and she let me in. Her demeanor was cool, with downcast eyes.

"We have to talk," I said as I closed the door behind me.

I moved to get close enough to kiss her, but she backed off. A bad sign.

She put a hand on her hip. "Really? Do you have something you want to tell me?"

The tone and the attitude said I was walking into a buzz saw.

I pointed to her couch in the front room. "Sit down."

I regretted the wording, but not quickly enough.

"Stop telling me what to do. I'm sick of it."

"Sorry. I meant, can we please sit down?"

She crossed her arms over her chest. "I can talk standing up. And I'm sure it won't take long."

Everything about this exchange screamed danger. The buzz saw was ramping up.

I took a breath. "I got called into a meeting with my dad this morning."

She shifted her weight and huffed. "I bet he had something really important to tell you."

"Sort of. You remember I told you I was doing department rotations at the company, and the next one was in finance?"

She shifted to the other foot. "Sure, I remember. But somehow I don't remember you telling me it would be in London."

My mouth must have dropped.

"Don't look so surprised. Serena told me. She let the cat out of the bag because she thought you'd already told me, but it must have slipped your mind somehow. I'm sure it didn't seem that important to tell me you'd be leaving the country."

I moved toward her, but she backed away.

"It wasn't like that," I protested. This was going south in a hurry.

"Right. It never is when guys plan on leaving the girl."

"Stop that," I said loudly. "And listen."

"You can't come into my house and yell at me." She pointed to the door. "Get out."

"No."

"No? You've got some nerve."

I pulled the box out of my pocket.

"This is not going the way I wanted, but I'm not leaving until you answer my question."

Her eyes teared up at the sight of the jewelry box I held.

I opened the box. "I want you to marry me and come to London with me this Saturday."

She sniffed.

"Not necessarily in that order," I added.

Somehow I was screwing this up, and big time.

She didn't say anything.

I'd forgotten something important. I went down on one knee. "Brittney Clark, will you marry me?"

She sniffed again. "No."

No?

~

BRITTNEY

IT WAS THE MOST GORGEOUS PRINCESS-CUT DIAMOND I'D EVER laid eyes on, and certainly ever would see.

But now everything was completely confused. He seemed sincere about wanting me to come with him to London this weekend, but he certainly hadn't given me much time or input on the decision. And then there was what I'd realized about my penance list.

I didn't even have a passport, but that wasn't the big problem.

How could I marry him after what I'd done?

It was the hardest thing for me to say, but I didn't have a choice other than telling him no.

He held out a hand. "I love you, Sunshine."

Sure, he said that now.

A typical guy move. They said it in high school when they tried to get inside your bra. They said it in college when they wanted to get in your pants.

He'd had opportunities before, and I'd longed for it. I would have welcomed it and cherished the words. But after realizing who the thirteenth name on that list belonged to, *I love you* was a phrase I couldn't bear to hear.

Zack wouldn't love me for long. Once he found out the truth, he couldn't. The feeling would still start with an L, but it would go from *love* to *loathing* and never change back. It couldn't after what I'd cost him.

The guillotine would come down on those feelings, and what we'd had, what we'd shared, would sink in the quicksand of hatred and regret. He could never forgive me. It would be better if he never knew. So as hard as it was, I repeated myself.

"I said NO. Now please leave."

His brow creased in confusion for a moment before it fell into disappointment, and he stood. He walked toward the door, but before he opened it, he looked back. "This discussion isn't over."

Yes, it is. I said the words mentally, unable to find the strength to utter them aloud. It was over—the discussion, the relationship, the future, all of it.

The door closed behind him, and with it all my hopes for a better future. Life sucked, and it was my fault. If only I hadn't run, if only I'd had the courage earlier. But this guilt would haunt me for the rest of my life.

I locked the door and walked into the kitchen. After opening a bottle of chablis, I grabbed a water glass. I needed a big sturdy cup for what I had planned. My tears flowed freely as I trudged up to my room. I chugged the first glass before falling onto my bed, a whimpering mess of a woman.

My phone rang.

I ignored it.

It went to voicemail. A rational conversation with anybody was out of the question right now. It was probably Zack anyway.

My entire life had come crashing down around me in less than a day.

My phone chimed with distinctive notes that meant my sister had sent me a text.

SAMANTHA: Please call

I realized my sister had been the call a minute ago, not Zack. But I still couldn't manage a conversation.

As hard as I tried, I couldn't outrun my past. Nothing could erase my sins, and all I could do now was deaden my senses enough to escape into sleep.

I turned off the phone and refilled my glass.

Another followed it a minute later.

CHAPTER 40

BRITTNEY

I WOKE UP WEDNESDAY MORNING TO KNOCKING AT THE DOOR, AND
the bell ringing over and over.

I stumbled to the stairs, but didn't descend them.

"Brittney, Sunshine, we need to talk." Zack's slurred voice
came from outside the front door.

Talking to him would only make it worse, especially with him
drunk. I couldn't even handle a sober Zack.

Silence was my only weapon at this point.

After a few more drunken tries, he gave up and left. At least I
thought he left, but I didn't dare peek for fear he'd see me.

Avoidance was my strategy, but it wasn't working well enough.

How could I explain it to him? It would only cause him more
pain, destroy any good memories of me he still held. Every time I
tried to understand it myself, a buzzer sounded in my brain. A big
red X flashed. Game over. Does not compute.

Living like this, next to him—with him constantly reminding
me of my sins and me constantly reminding him of what could

never be—would be a hell I couldn't endure. And it was one I shouldn't put him through.

Once again, despite what I might want, leaving was the only alternative. I had no choice. At least this time I had a way to finance it, thanks to Grams.

I left a quick message for Max that I wouldn't be in for a while, and that I'd call later. He deserved better, but right now I couldn't give him two weeks' notice.

I returned to my room to pack. I wouldn't need a lot. The rest of my things could wait here, including the boxes Lillian had sent from San Jose. I hadn't even unpacked those yet.

Two suitcases, a backpack, and a duffle later I had enough to do me for a month or so. Quickly checking the bathroom and my drawers, I came to my makeshift plastic jewelry bag and added that to the duffle.

Downstairs, I checked the windows before venturing out the back to load up my car. When I finished, I went back inside for the treasure that would finance my getaway. Pulling the painting down from the wall I'd just asked Winston to hang it on, I swaddled it in towels and tape to keep it safe.

The first gallery I stopped at thought I was joking, and I left when they decided my painting had to be stolen if I was in such a hurry to sell it.

The second wasn't much better. My grand plan was washing out. Showing up at galleries in my little shitmobile, looking like the out-of-work waitress I was, didn't get me anywhere.

At the third gallery, I tried a different tack.

The salesman's first response was the same as the others. "Madam, I think you might want to try an establishment closer to the beach."

Translation, some place that sold hundred-dollar prints to the masses, not a real art gallery. A place where the clientele wore shorts and sandals, not skirts and heels.

I looked down. I was in jeans and my black work shoes, definitely not the skirt and heels look.

The salesman looked bored.

I had one more card to play. "Mrs. Covington suggested this gallery, but if you don't have the wherewithal to evaluate my painting, perhaps I should try uptown."

"Mrs. Covington?"

I pulled Lauren Covington's card from my purse and handed it to him. "Yes. William Covington's wife. He's on the board of the museum, and I expected her suggestion would be a good one, but if she was mistaken—"

"Not at all." He interrupted before I finished the rest of my threat and handed back the card. "You should have mentioned you were referred by the Covingtons. Right this way, and we'll have a proper look at your piece."

He and an older man looked over the painting before bringing over a third.

A fair number of *ooh*s and *aah*s passed between them as the towels were removed, and an under-the-breath mention of Bill Covington. After that, the older man went off to the corner to make a phone call.

After a few minutes they made an initial offer I knew was low, based on the research Zack had helped me with.

"Why don't we check the auction history for a moment first," I countered.

The older gent returned from his phone call and huddled with the other two for a moment.

"Perhaps eighty-five thousand would be a nice compromise," the old man suggested.

I waited for a few seconds, doing my best imitation of pensive before nodding. "That seems fair to me." It was actually on the high side of what Zack had estimated I might get for it.

A half hour later, the teller at my bank was calling the manager over to authorize an eighty-five-thousand-dollar deposit to my account, which probably showed an average balance a hundredth that size.

"This will require a five-day hold," the manager said.

"It's an in-state check," I pointed out. I handed him the gallery manager's card. "Please call Mr. Gundry to verify, if you wish."

One phone call and two minutes later, we settled on five hundred today and the remainder in three days. Bankers were the worst. I knew he wouldn't have treated Zack like this.

My gray envelope problem was finally behind me—goal accomplished. Samantha's schooling was safely secured, and my promise to Mom fulfilled.

The next step was up to Samantha. She'd do well. I was sure of it.

With money for gas and food, I had one stop remaining before I left town—the reason I had Lauren Covington's card in my purse.

I'd called this morning, and she'd graciously invited me to visit.

When I pulled into the circular drive off Wilshire, the massive black glass building seemed like it reached to the sky. I found a place to park and made my way to the door where—wouldn't you know it?—they had a doorman. In LA, nobody had doormen. That was a New York thing. In California we pumped our own gas and opened our own doors, but apparently not everybody.

The doorman's nametag read *Oliver*. "May I help you, miss?"

"I'm here to see Lauren Covington."

"And your name, miss?"

"Brittney. Brittney Clark."

He checked his clipboard. "Yes, Mrs. Covington is expecting you." He opened the large glass door for me. "Elevators are at the rear. Unit 2-2-1 on the twenty-second floor. It will be to your right as you exit the lift."

"Thank you, Oliver."

"My pleasure, Miss Brittney."

The large marble and stainless lobby would have put a good-sized bank to shame.

Inside the elevator, I pressed the button for twenty-two. The numbers didn't go any higher—no big surprise. My ears even popped on the way up.

Upstairs, Lauren had her door open, waiting for me.

Oliver had probably called ahead.

Little Wendell was on her hip. "Come on in. It's so good to see you again."

I passed through into the massive open space of their penthouse unit. "Thanks. You too."

"I heard about that horrific incident. That must have been terrible." Her eyes showed genuine concern.

"I'm trying to get past it," I told her.

I'd had my fill of talking about it. Reliving any of the time with Delgado was not something I cared to do.

She walked toward the kitchen. "Would you like anything to drink?"

I followed her. "Diet, if you have it." The kitchen was the size of my apartment.

"Diet Pepsi okay?"

"Perfect."

She pulled two cans from the massive refrigerator. And then a glass from the cupboard, followed by another. She dispensed ice from the door of the fridge. Everything was slowed by her having one arm around her baby.

Since I had two hands free, I popped the top and poured mine as well as hers.

She thanked me and added, "I hope Mr. Gundry treated you right." The call in the corner of the gallery must have been to her.

"Thank you. Yes, they were very helpful."

"A Wyeth is quite a nice painting to let go of."

I took a sip of my soda. "I need the money to pay for my sister's schooling."

"She's going to Wharton, I understand? That's an accomplishment to be proud of."

She was better informed than I'd expected, because I hadn't mentioned it at the Habitat weekend, that I could remember.

"We are."

She seemed to realize I was surprised. "Zack was bragging," she added. "That's how I knew."

"He has a big mouth."

"Mostly he was bragging about you. You have quite an admirer."

I felt the heat rise in my cheeks, even though I needed to stop caring what Zack said or did.

"You've got a keeper there. Zack's one of the good guys, through and through. A bit rough around the edges—sort of like my Bill—but sweet on the inside."

"He can be a little bossy."

She touched my arm and laughed. "Don't I know it. My Bill is the same sometimes. But trust me, it comes from the heart, and that's what matters."

Her laugh brought a big smile to her baby's face.

I was impressed by how every little while she'd tousle Wendell's hair, or bounce him on her hip.

"Would you like to hold him?"

I took in a breath. "I'm not sure. I've never…"

I'd never held anyone's baby before, although I'd admired them from a distance when one of the girls brought a child to work for a few minutes.

"Don't worry, he won't break." She hoisted him up. "Here."

I took him and situated him on my hip the way she had. "Are you sure?"

He didn't cry. Instead, he looked up at me and smiled.

"I could use the break, and he likes you."

The little guy grabbed at my shirt for a moment.

Lauren picked up her glass. "Want to go out on the patio?"

"Sure." I took a drink and followed her.

She snatched up a floppy sun hat on the way and plopped it on Wendell's head.

There was so much about being a mother I didn't know. I wouldn't have thought about the hat.

We sat outside, sipping our sodas as she asked and I answered her questions about Doug and Samantha, all while bouncing Wendell.

He was a happy baby, and I found myself wondering if my own would be as well behaved.

Talking with Lauren was easy, relaxing, comfortable.

Wendell was happy on my lap, looking around, but mostly at his mother.

"You said you were interested in using the lake cabin," she said after a while.

I hadn't wanted to bring it up right away and seem ungrateful: *give me the key—thank you—no, I can't stay—I have to go hide—bye.*

"Yes," I answered. "I need a little time away after everything that's happened."

"I think you'll find it's the perfect place to find peace. Did I tell you that's where Bill proposed to me?"

"No, you didn't."

"I'll tell you the story another day. I'm sure you and Zack will enjoy it."

I didn't tell her Zack wasn't coming. This didn't feel like the time. "Your description sounds lovely."

"It's the anti-LA, secluded and relaxing. I went there to escape and think." She laughed. "And I left having found love. The place is built for romance." Her eyes misted over. "I'll get you the key." She hurried off.

Wendell watched his mother leave, then fixed his gaze up at me and smiled and gurgled a happy sound.

I bounced him a bit while she was gone.

Lauren returned with the key and a slip of paper. "The address for Casa Nelson. The drive takes a little while. If you guys want to go today, you should leave soon."

I accepted the items. "Nelson?"

"We have such good memories from there, we didn't want to change a thing when we bought it, so we kept the old name," she explained.

I stood and balanced the baby on my hip. "Thank you so much."

Wendell grabbed for my breast this time.

"It's time for his next feeding. This part of a mother's job is never done." She giggled. She put her hands out, and I gave him up.

I thanked her again, and she told me we could stay up there as long as we wanted. I wondered if that would change when she found out Zack wasn't coming along.

I left the building with a baby-spittle mark on my shirt. I was now a certified baby handler, and happy to be one.

When I made it to the freeway, Siri told me to turn north, and I was on my way to the cabin and away from Zack.

Secluded and relaxing, she'd said. Just what I needed.

I WOKE THE NEXT MORNING TO THE SOUNDS OF BIRDS OUTSIDE. IT had taken forever to get to sleep. Actually, it had taken me forever to get up and locate some wine so I could sleep.

I sipped my water and looked out through the cabin's full-length windows that faced the lake. I'd have to make a grocery run to get juice and fresh fruit. This morning water and oatmeal would have to do.

Lauren had said this place was relaxing, and I could see what she meant. The view of the lake, with gentle windswept waves lapping the shore and the mountains beyond, was very *un-LA,* as she had put it—simple country splendor of the kind we didn't see in the concrete jungle of the city. Birds flew by, and the occasional fish breached the surface to feed on unsuspecting insects. Nature on display.

I opened the sliding glass door to breathe in the fresh air. Closing my eyes for a moment, the warmth of the sun on my skin and the faint pine scent of the air had me remembering a kiss with

Zack, except his body had provided the warmth and his hair the scent. Kissing him had always been wonderful.

I jerked my eyes open to banish the vision. I was here to forget Zack and get back to the old me, the pre-Zack me. The rational me that didn't believe in fairy tales. The me that understood how hard I had to work to get anywhere in life. The me that knew I deserved better than Benji, but the me that realized I would have to settle for a lot less than Zack.

Maybe somewhere in the middle of the alphabet, with someone like a Mark, or a Mason, or maybe a Matt, I could find better than Benji. Yes, an M-name wouldn't be as wimpy as Benji, or as bossy as Zack. Samantha would have an opinion on a good name to look for. It couldn't be any worse than the way I'd met men so far.

Someone knocked on the front door.

When I answered it, I stepped back a bit.

The old man had a shotgun under one arm and appraised me warily. "Good morning. The name's Sam Patterson. I'm two cabins up the lake. You friends of the Nelsons?" he asked.

He pointed down at the doormat that read Casa Nelson, same as the wooden sign above the door.

"No, Lauren Covington gave me a key." I fished out the house key to show him.

His demeanor immediately improved. "Good, 'cuz the Nelsons ain't lived here for years. I'm sort of the neighborhood watch on this part of the lake."

Apparently I'd passed his test. I nodded.

"Like to see that nobody's squattin' where they shouldn't be."

"Would you like to come in, Mr. Patterson?"

"That's very kind of ya, but maybe later. I got my rounds to make. You fish?"

I shook my head. "No."

"Mighty good fishin' on this lake. I go out every day, if the weather allows."

He expounded on the joys of fishing for a few minutes, and

explained that on occasion he also liked to walk the circumference of the lake. He excused himself after a while.

I closed the door.

Neighborhood watch with a shotgun. I was definitely not in LA anymore.

After my grocery run, I made myself a sandwich. I set out for a walk with a water, an apple, and two apricots in my backpack. Circling the lake sounded good.

CHAPTER 41

*Z*ACK

(Three days later)

"W HAT THE HELL DID YOU DO?" S ERENA SCREAMED AT ME, angering the fire ants that had invaded my brain.

Just opening my eyes hurt. "Don't yell." I squinted, trying to sharpen the image in front of me. It was daytime, but that was all I could tell.

She held a mostly empty bottle of Jack. "You're a fucking imbecile."

I reached for the bottle, but missed and ended up on the floor. "Give me that."

"Winston, put him back on the couch."

Winston?

Suddenly, powerful hands lifted me and dumped me on the couch. It was Winston all right.

I held my head. The creatures in my skull didn't like being jostled. "Winston, what are you doing here?"

Serena answered for him. "I asked him to let me in. You

haven't been to work and wouldn't answer the door or the phone. Dad said '*by whatever means necessary*'. Those were his words."

Winston chuckled and went to the kitchen.

Serena took the chair and scooted it to face me before sitting. "Tell me what the hell you did to her."

I shook my head. That was a bad idea. The fire ants hated being shaken. I put my hands to my temples to try to squeeze them out. "Did to who?"

Winston held out pills and a glass. "Here, swallow these."

I took them. But just my luck, it was orange juice.

"Brittney, of course. She went crying to Lauren and asked to use her cabin for a while to get away. I'm sure she meant away from you."

It was coming back to me…the terrible word she'd said.

NO.

I closed my eyes and lay down slowly. "How many days has it been?"

"Three. It's Friday. Now sit back up and answer the question."

"Stop telling me what to do."

Now I sounded like Brittney. I slowly righted myself to avoid being manhandled by Winston again.

"No fair ganging up on me."

Serena waved the bottle. "Judging by this bottle and the way you look, you need all the help you can get."

I started to stand. "Screw you. And Winston, I want my gun back."

He shoved me back down. "Not a chance. Not when you're like this."

I didn't know what he meant by *like this*, but I didn't care. The fire ants eating my brain prevented any real thought.

"Then get me a drink."

"No way," he shot back.

"What good are you?"

He smirked.

Right now it was a smirk I wanted to wipe off his face with a fist. Although I might have had a chance on a good day, I stood zero chance in this condition. One good hit from him would give a normal man a concussion.

Maybe that wasn't such a bad idea. A concussion might make the fire ants go away. Unconsciousness sounded better than the way I felt right now.

Serena got my attention by kicking my foot. "Tell us what happened. How did you fuck up so royally that she wants to leave?"

Putting the pieces together took a moment. "I asked her to come to London with me."

"And she didn't want to?" Serena asked.

"No. I don't think so."

"What do you mean you don't think so? How was she feeling about it before?"

I shrugged. "I dunno. I hadn't told her."

Serena kicked me again. "Why not, you dumbshit? You've known forever."

"I didn't know how to approach it, I guess."

"So you wait until just before you have to get on a plane to tell her? Smooth move, Romeo."

"I didn't know how."

"When you reiterated how much you love her, that must have helped, right?"

I slumped down and closed my eyes.

"Don't tell me you didn't tell her."

I shook my head.

"Not even once?" she asked.

I didn't want to admit how stupid I'd been.

Winston chimed in. "What did you expect? She's just a piece of ass to him."

"She is not," I shot back.

He continued. "Now that he's leaving, I think I'll have a taste of that honey."

I lunged for him and swung my fist.

He jerked sideways, and I missed. He grabbed my arm, swung me around, and pushed me back to land on the couch again.

I put my aching head in my hands and wiped my mouth. "I asked her to marry me."

Serena's mouth dropped. "And she said no?"

"Duh."

"That's a pretty big bomb to drop on a girl when you haven't even told her how you feel."

"Maybe I won't ask her out after all," Winston remarked.

I shot him a *shut up, asshole* look.

"And you're just taking no for an answer?"

"Hell, no." The memory was fuzzy. "I went back over, and she wouldn't even answer the door."

Stumble over is what I'd actually done. I lifted my elbow to check, and sure enough, the scrape from falling down on the way to her house was right where it should have been.

"Was her car there?"

I couldn't recall checking. "Dunno."

I also couldn't recall how many times I'd gone over. It seemed like more than once, but I couldn't be sure. There wasn't much I was sure of.

"That's because she hightailed it out of town, you idiot."

"What's her problem?" Winston asked Serena.

"What he said," I repeated.

Serena pointed at me. "How should I know? He obviously did something bad." She stood. "Better forget her and move on."

I sat up. "I don't want to."

The sudden movement angered the bugs eating at my brain. I hated that idea. Moving on was the worst idea ever. The time since Brittney's return had been the best of my life, even with the threat of Delgado hanging over us.

Serena laughed. "Then you better sober up and go after her before you lose her for good. Argue your case. Banish her doubts, or problems, or insecurities. And for God's sake, tell her how you feel."

"How is he going to do that if he doesn't know what her problem is?" Winston asked.

"Haven't you guys ever heard of talking about your feelings? People have been doing it forever. Well, obviously not guys like you two."

Winston stiffened at the slight, but I knew Serena meant the comment for me.

I stood, instantly regretted it, and sat back down. "Where'd she go?"

"First things first," Serena said. "You stink. Winston, put him in the shower while I make us something to eat."

Winston shoved the juice glass at me. "Finish this first."

I did. This time I actually enjoyed the orange juice.

"Can you make it upstairs on your own?" he asked.

I stood. "I'm not a baby." In spite of my throbbing head and unsteady legs, I was not going to be carried upstairs.

"Good. Because I'm not wiping your ass for you." He laughed.

AFTER BREAKFAST AND A SHOWER, I HAD FINALLY KICKED THE intervention duo out of my house.

Now I was attacking the flooring demo project I'd abandoned when Brittney came into my life. I was back to what was comfortable: prying up laminate and contemplating how marvelous the old oak would look after it had been sanded and re-finished. I could think while I worked.

My phone rang, and I checked it. But it was Wendy.

"Sorry to call you at home, but you need to know that your father is worried because you're not in."

"I got that message already." Dad had called directly after Serena had failed to bring me back, and I'd told him not to expect me for another day or two. "I talked to him at lunchtime."

"Is there anything I can do to help?"

"No, thanks."

The only help I needed was figuring out what I could have done differently with Brittney.

Serena had said I needed to be more open about my feelings. A typical girl point of view, but probably right, in retrospect. Still, the timing hadn't felt right, hadn't been right.

Winston said I should have been clearer up front about my family responsibility to go to London—another good observation after the fact, but not the way it had seemed at the time.

After doing physical battle with another section of recalcitrant laminate, I threw down my pry bar, and it skidded across the floor.

"Fuck," I yelled at the empty room.

I was doing the thing I'd vowed never to do. I was dissecting the past instead of acting in the present to affect the future.

What was wrong with me?

Five minutes later, I cleaned up. The paper towel I'd used to dry my hands wouldn't fit in the overflowing bin under the sink.

I grabbed the trash bag and went out back.

I felt a quick pain in my side and a huge arm came around my neck.

I couldn't breathe.

I dropped the garbage and yanked at the arm.

I kicked behind me, but failed to connect.

"I'm gonna kill you," he said.

CHAPTER 42

BRITTNEY

THE WALKS AROUND THE LAKE WERE LONG, BUT THEY HADN'T KEPT me from thinking about Zack. I hoped he was doing better than I was.

For a moment, I wished he were here to enjoy the walk with me, the way we had in San Diego. It had only been a few weeks since then, but it seemed both recent and so long ago. Reminding myself that this was for the best didn't make it easier.

My memories of San Diego were vivid—the zoo, SeaWorld, jet skiing, and walking on the beach. It all put a smile on my lips and a spring in my step. Zack had put his busy life on hold at a moment's notice to refill my "happiness reservoir." And refill it he had. I hadn't felt so carefree and content in forever.

He could have spent money on me, bought me beautiful things and wonderfully expensive meals. He had done that last one a little, but even the hot dogs at SeaWorld had been a special meal with him across from me, smiling the whole time. Instead of things, he'd given me his time and attention and shown me how happy we could be doing simple stuff, so long as we did it together. He'd shown me how to block out the world and focus on us—just him and me and the activity at hand. No worries about my past or my future, only a concentration on the present.

He'd shown me that it was possible for a guy—no, make that a man, because Zack was certainly more man than anyone I'd ever been with—to show his love in ways that weren't verbal.

I was just realizing that now.

I'd been wrong the day I pushed him away to think that had been the first time he'd said he'd loved me. It had been the first time he'd verbalized it, but not the first time he'd shown it. His love was something I could see everywhere when I looked back on our time together. He'd said actions spoke louder than words, and in his case, the actions spelled love loud and clear. I'd just been too stupid to see it clearly until now. He'd made me feel appreciated, and cherished.

But these memories of him, of us, were also distant, because I now had to categorize them as my prior life—a place I couldn't go back to any more than I could re-enroll in high school. Zack couldn't be a part of my future without me ruining it for him, for us, when the truth came out. And the truth always came out in the end. My sins would destroy him, and I couldn't bear that thought.

I'd made the right choice to leave. Leaving was always the right choice.

I would have to content myself with the short time we'd had together, and the memories he'd given me.

After stopping on the opposite shore for my lunch, I continued the walk, mentally berating myself for the mistakes that had gotten me to this point.

Twenty-seven names, and number thirteen was the worst.

Nearing Casa Nelson, I kicked the sand at my feet. A man waved from a small fishing dinghy. It was Mr. Patterson again.

I waved back.

His fishing pole hung off the back of the little boat as he puttered out to do battle with a wily fish somewhere on the lake. His life was so simple compared to mine. Man against nature. Get up, go fish, check the neighborhood, fish again, wash, rinse, repeat. No drama, no regrets.

I finally reached Casa Nelson and decided tomorrow I would pack more fruit and do two laps of the lake. It was a long way around. But long was good. I needed the exercise to tire me so I could sleep.

Last night I'd resorted to several glasses of wine, as I had every evening since arriving. It worked for a few hours, but I woke each morning way before I should have, and I hadn't been able to get back to sleep.

Wine before bed was one thing, but downing a few glasses at three in the morning to get back to sleep was not something I could do long term.

Unlocking the back deck door, I went inside and looked around.

Lauren had called this place romantic, and I could see how it would be if you had someone to share it with. A middle-of-the-alphabet guy, less Benji and more Zack, that's who this space needed. That's what I needed.

Fuck. I'd left without having Winston and Constance help me get my papers back from fucking Benji. Another mistake I could add to my list.

A check of the pantry showed another trip to the market was in order, and not just for food. I was also down to my last bottle of wine.

My little car started with a whimper, dependable as always. I goosed the gas before putting it in reverse. The whine wasn't at all like the roar and rumble of the Snake. Maybe I needed to spend a little of the money from Grams's painting on a new car. Less Corolla and more Mustang, that was the ticket. But it wouldn't be cheap to get a car that was half the ride the Snake was, if that was even possible.

As I walked the aisles of the market, I checked out the guys as much as the produce. What I already knew to be true quickly became obvious. It would be easy to find a guy more masculine than Benji, but it wouldn't be easy finding one that tipped the manliness scale at half of Zack's reading.

I added a bag of mandarins to my cart.

This was going to be harder than just finding someone with a name that started with M—a lot harder.

I might have to settle for one third of a Zack, or maybe a quarter-Zack.

~

ZACK

"HOW COULD YOU SLEEP WITH MY SISTER BEHIND MY BACK?" Doug growled as he tightened the choke hold he had on me.

I struggled against the arm around my neck, but I couldn't get a word out. The Marines taught their people well.

"I should fucking kill you right now, but I think I'll make it slow and painful instead," he hissed.

I swung an elbow at him to no effect.

He loosened his arm just enough for me to get a few words out. "It wasn't like that."

"How could you? I trusted you to keep her safe, not ruin her."

"I asked her to m-marry me."

He loosened his grip. "What?"

I still couldn't get loose. "I want to marry her."

He let go and shoved me to the deck. "You better not be messing with me," he growled.

"Never."

His scowl softened. "You're serious?"

I got up and dusted myself off. "Damn straight."

He cocked his head. "Then why is she crying her head off to Sam? What the hell did you do to her?"

"The fuck if I know. I asked her to marry me, she said no, and then she split. She's *your* stupid twin sister. You tell me what her problem is."

He ran his hand through his hair. "I got no idea. I got the call from Sam that Brit was in a bad way, and she let slip that you two had been playing house. I took emergency leave and hot-footed it over here to kill you."

"I got that part." I grabbed the garbage bag and trotted down the stairs to dump it.

Doug followed. "You have to have done something."

I headed back to the kitchen door. "Come on inside."

He followed me up the stairs. "You better start at the beginning and tell me what's gone down. Because Sam said things are not good. You messed Brit up somehow."

I gave him the short history, leaving out the R-rated details, and at the end we were where we'd started: both of us clueless.

"I still don't like you sleeping with Brit without asking me."

I noticed that for Brittney he used *sleeping with* her, rather than *fucking* her, which would have been his wording for any other girl.

"And you would have said yes?"

He huffed. "Fuck no."

"That's why, shit-for-brains."

He drank some water. "I guess you're right. So what did you leave out? Why is she crying her fool head off?"

"Got me. I was going to go after her to find out."

He looked me in the eye. "Bad plan with her. You gotta know what's going on first."

"What? You going to go talk to her?"

"No, better than that. We call the one person she's already talked to: Sam."

It made sense to me. I knew my sisters would confide things to one another they wouldn't tell me.

Doug pulled out his phone and dialed. He put it on speaker while it rang.

"Hi, Doug," Samantha answered.

Doug started. "Sam, I've got Zack Benson here with me."

Silence.

"Okay," she said tentatively.

"I want to hear about what has Brit so upset."

Silence again.

"I don't think I can say."

Doug snarled. "Don't give me any of this secret sisterhood shit. This is Brit we're talking about. Zack wants to make it right, and frankly he's a thousand percent better than any of those other A-holes she's been seeing, so spill. What's her problem?"

"It's not for me to say," Samantha answered.

"Yes, it is," Doug told her. "This is Zack we're talking about. You gotta give him a chance to fix this."

"He should talk to her," Samantha said.

Doug's face was getting red now. "Stop giving me the runaround. She's my sister too, for God's sake. Tell me what's going on."

"You should call her," Samantha responded.

"I tried that. She won't answer," Doug said.

"That's because her phone is off, I think," Samantha said.

I raised my hand to stop Doug from making the situation any worse. His combative stance wasn't getting us anywhere.

"Samantha, I'd just like to talk to her and try to understand her problem so I can help fix it."

Samantha was quiet on the other end of the line for a moment. "It's the list of names."

I had no idea what that meant.

"I thought we were past that," Doug said. "She hasn't talked about that in years."

"She hasn't talked about it with you for years. That's because you get like this."

"Like what?" Doug demanded.

"Combative, just like you are now. You didn't listen to her, so she stopped talking to you about it."

I cut Doug off again. "Samantha, what is it about the list?" I asked calmly.

She sighed. "One of the names is your cousin. She hadn't connected the dots before because she'd never heard his name and didn't think he was related."

I leaned closer to the phone. "What does that mean? What is the deal with this list of names?"

"I have to go to work. Doug knows enough to fill you in."

"Thanks, Sam. Be safe," Doug answered.

"Always," she said before hanging up.

I turned to my friend. "List?"

His face showed a mixture of frustration and anger. "That fucking list again. I thought I'd gotten through to her and gotten her to ignore that, put it behind her."

"What is it?"

"A bunch of people… Let me back up. What do you know about Delgado?"

I wracked my brain for a second. "He was a drug dealer she testified against for a murder she witnessed. The guy later killed her boyfriend, Todd—at least she thinks he did—but they never found the body. And so now when he gets out, he comes after her for revenge, and some stupid key he thinks she has, but she doesn't know a thing about. That's about it."

"Well, that's not the whole story," he began. "At first she was too scared to testify against Delgado, so she ran off. Then this piece-of-shit detective laid the list on her. He claimed it was a list of drug ODs that were her fault because she'd held off coming forward to testify. And he told her the list would only grow and be on her conscience if she didn't agree to come to court."

"That's a pretty heavy burden to put on someone."

"No shit."

"So she blames herself for these ODs?"

"That's about the size of it. I thought I'd gotten her past this years ago. But obviously not. So if your cousin is on that list, she's sittin' there thinking she caused his OD."

Now at least I knew what the problem was. "Thanks, man. I owe you."

He punched me in the shoulder. "It's up to you to make this right. If you don't get her to marry you, we'll be right back where we started: you sleeping with my sister and not marrying her. That's fucking unacceptable."

"Got it."

"I'll spread-eagle you in the desert, pour honey on your naked ass, and wait for the ants to do their thing." He laughed.

He might be exaggerating, but because it was Doug, I couldn't be sure. "Thanks for that warning."

"Nothing like proper motivation." He stood. "I think I'll go ask Kelly on a date." It was just like him to turn it around so I got the point.

"Don't you fucking dare," I snarled.

"Just sayin', turnaround's fair. Hey, I haven't gotten any shut-eye since I got the call. You got a place I could rack out?"

"Sure. Upstairs, second room on the right."

He gave me a mock salute and headed for the stairs.

Now I had what I needed.

Brittney was going to learn the truth. She was meant to be mine, and I was going to have her.

No question about it.

ZACK

DAD WAS AT HIS DESK WHEN I OPENED THE DOOR LATE THAT afternoon.

"Zachary, I thought you were taking the day off."

I took the seat across from him. "Maybe more than that, actually."

"I see. Does this have to do with Brittney?"

The family grapevine was working overtime if he already knew, but of course he knew. He always knew.

"Yes. And I've made a decision."

He waited.

I steeled myself for the argument to come. "I'm not going to London."

He steepled his hands and nodded. "Very well."

Very well?

I'd expected a lecture on family obligations instead of acceptance.

"You think she's the one?"

He'd also heard about my proposal, apparently.

"I know it."

"Then go make your argument. She has a say in this too, you know."

"Yeah, that's the problem."

"Why is she reluctant, do you think?"

"It's complicated."

"Then you have your work cut out for you, I would say."

That was an understatement. Combating irrational fears was the hardest.

I stood.

"I think you should call Phillip Patterson."

"Why?"

"His grandfather has a cabin quite near the Covington place."

Serena had told me where Brittney had gone. I shouldn't have been surprised that she'd told Dad as well.

"Thanks. I will, if I need to."

It was too late to make the drive today, so tonight I would plan. Tomorrow I was going after my woman.

CHAPTER 43

BRITTNEY

THE NEXT MORNING I TURNED ON THE TV LONG ENOUGH TO CHECK the day. It was Saturday, the day Zack was scheduled to leave for London.

I opened the door to the deck and smelled the clean mountain air—not a hint of LA smog. The sky was a clear blue, a nice day for flying.

Zack would likely be on his way soon, if he wasn't already in the air. He certainly wouldn't be taking a red-eye. For the briefest second I tried to imagine Zack saying something with a British accent, but I knew he wouldn't. Zack knew who he was, and he didn't change. He wouldn't change for anyone or anything.

I could even remember a fight over his hair in high school. The baseball coach had threatened to kick him off the varsity team if he didn't cut his hair. Every other guy on the team complied, but not Zack. He'd said it was who he was, and he wouldn't change for the coach, or anyone. He got to watch the season from the stands.

No, Zack wouldn't adopt even a hint of the accent to blend in.

He would proudly be labeled the Yank, and they could stuff it if they didn't like it.

I had to stifle a laugh. That was Zack all right, defiantly unchangeable. Except I had gotten him to budge on eating fruit—a small victory.

Mr. Patterson's outboard motor sputtered to life, and I stepped out on the deck with my glass of juice to wave. His little aluminum boat made a small wake on the still surface of the lake. The wind hadn't come up yet to create any waves. I watched as he headed to the end of the lake he swore was the home of the big one—the one he intended to land.

It was another warm day, and yesterday's exercise had helped me sleep a little longer before waking. Back inside, I put the juice down and got on the carpet to stretch my sore leg muscles. If one lap helped a little, two might be better. Two laps of the lake became today's agenda.

After a breakfast of pancakes, I started out. This time I brought more rations: several apples and apricots, plus sunscreen, water, and a towel to sit on while I took a break.

The first lap went pretty much like yesterday, except I found a porta-potty that was surprisingly un-gross at a house under construction on the other side of the lake.

I spent the hike trying and failing to think about things other than Zack. I would concentrate on how Samantha might be coping out east, and that would distract me for a few minutes. Worrying about Doug flying over the open ocean off Okinawa also worked for a few minutes, but my thoughts kept coming back to the same topic—the man that inhabited my mind and my heart, Zack.

Halfway around the second lap, I realized today's mistake. I hadn't put on the right socks for this trek, and I was rubbing a blister on my heel.

It had been hard leaving Zack behind, and it was going to take a long time to get over him. I tried to get excited about finding a Mike, or Matt, or some other half-Zack—a guy who wasn't half as bossy or half as annoying, but the prospect seemed bland, like pancakes without syrup or a topping.

Samantha's advice for getting over a guy—well, pretty much everybody's advice—was to move on to the next. If your cat died, you got another cat. If your boyfriend didn't work out, you traded him in for a different one. But I'd gotten a whiff of the loud life: the roar of the Snake on the freeway, wind whipping my hair, sitting next to a man with enough testosterone to power a freight train. And I'd liked it.

I hobbled the last leg of today's journey, wishing I'd added Band-Aids or tape to my backpack.

Even through my foot pain, my thoughts kept coming back to him. The car he drove epitomized Zack. It was loud, powerful, and didn't let anything stand in its way. It could power around any obstacle. And everyone knew, with just a glance, that it was one of a kind. He was one of a kind.

I rounded the final cove, and the roof of Casa Nelson came into view. I walked past Patterson's dock. His trusty little fishing dinghy was tied up alongside, waiting to take its owner on his evening trip.

I laughed. Patterson went out twice a day to land the big one, and I'd just thrown the big one back.

When I reached Casa Nelson, I turned up the path.

Zack stood on the deck, hands in his pockets, staring at me.

Without an avenue of escape, I had to face him. Again.

He took his hands out of his pockets as I hobbled the last few steps to the deck. "Hi, Sunshine."

"What are you doing here?"

It was a stupid question, but I didn't have anything else to say if I didn't want to cry.

"We need to talk."

I hobbled around him. "I told you already, we did."

He blocked my path.

I stood and stared up at him. I was out of words.

Concern splashed across his face. "You're hurt."

He couldn't know how right he was.

*Z*ACK

I FOLLOWED HER INSIDE THE CABIN AND CLOSED THE DOOR. "Do you have anything to drink?"

"You won't be here that long."

I merely smiled.

She cringed slightly as she realized the bite of her words.

She limped to the fridge. "What would you like?"

"Do you have any orange juice?"

She shot me a questioning look. "Of course." She poured two glasses and brought them over.

We sat on the couch.

I brought out my jewelry box again.

"Put that away," she said.

I set it on the coffee table.

"Away," she repeated.

I ignored the request. "I need to understand why you said no."

She took a deep breath. "Because I don't want to follow you to London."

I settled back in the couch. "Why not?"

"I have a career, and it's here. My certification wouldn't transfer there, and I don't want to just sit around all day."

"And that's the reason?"

She crossed her arms. "Yeah, pretty much."

Her body language said something entirely different. She was antsy. She was holding back, and I knew it. She was trapped by her lie.

Somehow I had to get her to open up about the list so we could talk through it and get it behind her. I might not even need to get Doug or Samantha in hot water…

I tried a different approach. "Good, because I'm not going to London."

Her eyes widened. "But you have to. You told me it was the next rotation you had to do."

She hadn't been prepared for that, which told me how far I had to go in getting her to understand the depth of my feelings.

"It was, but I've told Dad I'm not going. Staying here with you is more important."

"But it's your duty to your family. That's the most important thing. You told me so yourself."

Was she trying to convince me or herself?

"Brit, I want you to marry me and be my family, and that's more important. The family business will be fine without me, but I can't say the same about me without you."

"I can't marry you."

"Why not? You said you didn't want to go to London. Problem solved. We're not going to London."

She fidgeted, caught by her own deception, her own inability to be truthful.

The first step in getting her past her guilt had to be for her to admit it. She had to acknowledge it.

~

BRITTNEY

THIS WAS GETTING WORSE, NOT BETTER. I COULDN'T BE WITH HIM and destroy him when he learned the truth. Having given up every-thing and then learning what I'd done would compound the hurt.

"I can't," I said curtly. I rose from the couch. "Want some more juice?"

I shuffled toward the fridge. Being this close to him was messing with my ability to stay rational. The effect he had on me was magnetic, and the closer I got, the stronger his pull. I knew if I allowed him to touch me, the attraction between us would be a black hole that devoured me whole, never letting me escape to a distance that could keep him safe.

He reached me in two strides. "You sit down, and I'll get it." His hand on my arm was light, but the electric feel of his skin on mine was as strong as before. Dangerously strong. Black-hole strong.

I stopped, my mouth frozen, unable to say anything until he let go of me. I nodded.

"Sprain your ankle?" he asked as he continued to the kitchen to pour us more juice.

I limped to the couch. "Blister."

He poured a glass. "Ouch. Take off your clothes, and I'll take care of you."

"What?"

"I said take off your shoes, and I'll take care of you."

My traitorous libido was playing tricks on me, changing his words to the ones it wanted to hear.

"No. I can do it myself."

"Stop arguing and take off your shoes." Bossy Zack was back.

"No," I repeated, playing with him.

"I'm going to spank you if you don't behave. Now take off your shoes so I can fix that."

I removed one shoe, then the other, followed by my socks.

He brought over the juice and handed me a glass. "Which foot is the problem?"

I lifted my left.

He took one look and scowled. "This is not good. Show me the other."

I did, and his verdict was swift.

"I'll be right back. Lie face down on the couch."

"Why?"

"Sunshine, can you stop arguing for one minute and just do what you're told?"

325

I laid down as instructed. At least we'd gotten away from the question posed by the jewelry box I stared at on the coffee table.

He left through the front door and returned with a first-aid kit. He went into the kitchen where he turned on the stove.

"What are you doing?"

"Sterilizing." He turned off the stove and returned, kneeling by the couch.

I watched as he tore open an antiseptic wipe. The moist pad felt cool on the skin of my heels.

He put tissues under my feet and took sharp tweezers from the table.

"Hold still."

I jerked my foot away. "You're not poking me with that thing."

"I said stay still. Now behave yourself. I know what I'm doing. Teeth are your thing, and blisters are mine."

I put my foot back down. "This isn't fair."

He held my ankle firmly. "Life's not fair."

I didn't look as he brought the sharp end of the tweezers down. "That's one."

I'd only felt a slight tug.

"That's two," he said after he held the other down and repeated the puncture. "This may hurt a little." He squeezed first one heel then the other.

It did sting, but not badly.

"Are you done yet?"

"Not yet." He took Neosporin ointment from his kit and dabbed it on my heels. Band-Aids followed.

I closed my eyes as he unspooled and cut pieces of tape, which went over the bandages.

He lifted my feet, sat, and pulled them over his lap. The gross, wadded up tissues from squeezing the fluid out of my blisters landed on the coffee table. "Now we talk."

I tried to pull away, but he held me down.

"Stay still."

"Let me go."

"After we talk."

"You're not being fair." His idea of a position for talking was distorted.

"What did I just tell you about life?" he shot back.

I huffed and gave up. "Okay, then talk."

"You know what your problem is?"

I snorted. "Yeah, you."

He tickled my foot. "Be serious."

I laughed. "Stop that."

He did after a moment. "You're not honest enough."

"I am too." I tried to pull my feet away to sit up, but he wouldn't let me.

"You are not."

"How would you know?"

"I know lots of things. Tell me something you wish you'd told me earlier."

I couldn't go to the list, so I didn't respond.

"Okay, I'll start." He looked into my eyes. "I love you, Brittney Clark."

The words halted my breathing as they cut through me. "You're just saying that."

"I should have told you sooner."

"We haven't been dating long enough," I said.

"Now you're being stupid. I've known you almost my whole life, and I've loved you for years. Tell me you don't feel the same."

I couldn't lie to him about that. "We can't be together. It wouldn't work."

"Bullshit. We're great together."

We actually had been great. I'd spent all my time walking the lake regretting how great we were together.

"Doug would kill us if he knew."

"I don't think so. Let me handle him."

"So you'd be cool with him screwing Serena or Kelly?"

"Hell no. I'd kick his ass. But I would be okay with him marrying one of them, if it came down to that."

I was getting his drift, but I still worried how Doug would react.

"I told you something I regretted not telling you earlier. Now, your turn."

I couldn't come up with anything. "I like your car."

He tickled me again.

I struggled, but couldn't pull my foot loose.

"I'm serious," he said gruffly.

"It won't work out long-term between us."

"Why not?"

I was running out of options to avoid talking directly about my sins. "Because in the end, you'll hate me."

"Not possible."

"But you don't know what I've done."

"Remember, what you've done in the past is water under the bridge. It's what you do in the present to affect the future that matters."

"You could never forgive me," I blurted. "I killed people. I killed your cousin Jonas."

He shook his head. "You had nothing to do with that."

He didn't get it. My inaction had killed his cousin. "Yes, I did. If I hadn't been scared, he'd be alive today."

"You had nothing to do with it," he repeated.

"Let me up. I need to show you something. Then maybe you'll understand."

He let me get up, and I went to the counter.

I extracted my list from the pink envelope in my purse and brought it over. "This is a list of people that died because I didn't come forward to put Delgado away earlier." I shoved the paper at him. "Read the thirteenth name." I couldn't keep the tears at bay any longer.

He took the paper, folded it, pocketed it, and stood to hug me.

I cried into his shoulder as he stroked my back. "You didn't read it."

"I don't need to. You didn't kill any of the people on the list.

328

Addicts chart their own self-destructive paths. Just as you are responsible for your own destiny, so were they."

"But I could have put Delgado away earlier," I argued.

"Think about this, Sunshine. If an addict moves to a new city, does he stop using because he can't meet with his dealer anymore? No. He finds a new dealer. If Delgado had gone away earlier, they all would have found other sources."

I pondered his logic for a moment.

"Now it's time for you to agree to marry me so I can teach you this every day, until you learn to forgive yourself. Their fates are not your responsibility."

"But he was your cousin."

"You didn't kill him," he said softly into my ear.

"I don't know if I believe that."

"Is that all that's keeping you from saying yes?"

"Isn't that enough?"

He squeezed me tighter and kissed the top of my head. "Is there anything else?"

"No. I just can't live with you knowing that, your whole family knowing that. I don't want you to resent me."

"Well, Sunshine, now you *have* to marry me, because you didn't have anything to do with this death. There's something else you don't know." He loosened his grip and pulled my chin up with a finger. "I have Jonas's suicide note. He killed himself."

My heart stopped for a beat. "What?"

"I said, you have to marry me now. Drugs were just the weapon he used. Jonas took his own life. It didn't have anything to do with you or Delgado. Like I said, if not him, it would have been some other dealer. Jonas's death is not on you."

I blinked back the tears. Tears of remorse for his cousin who'd decided to end his life, and tears of joy that I could remove a name from my list. "You can't just tell me to marry you, though."

"Stop being obstinate. I tried asking, and that didn't go very well," he shot back.

"Well, maybe you should try again."

He let me go, retrieved the box from the table, and took a knee. "Brittney Clark, will you marry me?"

I leaned over to take his face in my hands. "Yes," I said before I planted the kiss on him I'd been holding back.

He stood, lifted me off my feet, and spun me around before setting me down. "You need to see if this fits." He picked up the box and slid the ring onto my finger. "What do you think?"

"It's a little big."

"I can get it sized down for you."

I looked down on the perfect ring, given to me by my perfect man. "No, it fits, and it's gorgeous. It's just the stone is so big."

"Not as big as my love for you, Sunshine."

Lauren had been right. This cabin was built for romance.

He pulled me in for another kiss.

As we intertwined, I drank in his taste and the love I knew he had for me—the love he'd shown me in his own non-verbal, masculine way.

CHAPTER 44

BRITTNEY

ZACK AND I HAD SPENT ANOTHER TWO GLORIOUS DAYS AT CASA Nelson, just the two of us. We wore out the bed and the couch as he lavished attention on me several times a day.

We'd also spent time hiking the nearby trails and around the lake some more. Each time, Zack bandaged and taped my heels to protect them, and they were healing well, in spite of the extra walking.

We'd had old man Patterson over for dinner, and I'd learned the Phil Patterson I'd met at the Habitat weekend was his grandson.

This morning, after I finished checking that we'd left the place clean enough, I closed and locked the door. I kissed my finger, and pressed it to the door. "Thank you for the memories."

Zack stood by the Snake. "Two cars or one?"

For work, I'd need my own car. "Two. And tell me again why we can't stay another few days?"

He hadn't actually said, but I could hope he'd slip up and tell me now.

It didn't work. "You need to meet someone before he leaves town," he said.

Now I knew it was a man, but that wasn't much help.

I'd tried guessing, but gotten nowhere fast.

He got in and started the Snake. The rumble of its idle had me wishing I could ride with him, but that would have to wait till we got back.

The drive was long, but uneventful as my little car tried to keep up with the Snake. I really needed a better car.

He parked in front of his house, and I pulled in just behind him.

The kid he called Piss Boy and an adult were walking our way on the other side of the street. This time the boy didn't give the middle-finger salute.

"Mr. Benson?" I heard the man call as I got out.

Zack stopped and waited for them to cross the street.

I put my arm around Zack when I reached him.

"Mr. Benson, Tommy has something he'd like to give you."

Now we had a name other than Piss Boy.

Tommy offered Zack the folded paper. "I'm really sorry, and I apologize for using the house when I shouldn't have."

Zack smiled. "Very well, but it's this lady you should apologize to. It's her house."

The boy repeated himself, and I assured him it was okay now.

Zack extracted himself from my grasp, leaned into his car, and pulled a cell phone from the glove compartment. He handed it to Tommy.

After a moment the man, apparently the boy's father, said, "And?"

"Thanks, Mr. Benson," Tommy said.

Zack nodded.

The duo left, and Zack turned to me. "Do you think he learned the lesson?"

"Looks like it." I went to pull my bag from the trunk of my car.

Zack started toward the steps. "Doug," he exclaimed. "What are you doing here?"

I turned to see my brother come out the front door.

"Is it true?" His wavering stance said he'd been drinking, a lot. "Have you been shacking up with this A-hole?" he yelled.

I froze. "It's not like that," I protested.

Doug's judgment was the first thing that went when he got drunk, and dealing with him when he got like this was never easy.

"Looks like it to me," he said as he grabbed the railing for support and started down toward Zack.

"It is, and I'm proud of it," Zack said, standing his ground.

My heart stopped. "No," I yelled.

Doug lunged, and Zack grappled with him.

I ran to them.

"I'm gonna kill you," Doug grunted as he and Zack each threw a punch and missed.

Doug grabbed Zack, and they both went to the ground.

"Stop it. It's not like that," I yelled at my brother.

I had no chance of breaking up a fight between these two, and as drunk as Doug was, it could end badly.

Doug started laughing.

Zack joined him, and the wrestling stopped.

Zack got up first.

"Just messing with ya, sis," Doug said as he got to his knees.

"Yeah, he knows," Zack confessed, brushing himself off.

Doug got up. This time he wasn't wobbly. He'd faked being drunk.

I slapped him.

He pulled back. "What the fuck?"

"You gave me a heart attack. You should know better."

Doug laughed. "That's what you get for not talking to me about what's going on." He pointed at Zack. "I almost killed this fucker on Friday when I got back."

"He did," Zack chimed in.

"Well, I didn't think—" I said.

Doug grasped my shoulders. "You sure didn't think. You should have told me." He wrapped me in a bear hug. "Congratulations, by the way. You caught yourself a good one. You just should have let me know."

"Can I come out now?" It was Samantha's voice.

Doug released me, and Samantha hurried down the steps. It became her turn to give me a congratulatory hug.

"How'd you get here?" I asked. I could hardly believe it.

"Zack's dad sent a plane to pick me up. That's the way to fly, by the way. You gotta try it. Super cool."

I turned to my fiancé. "Is there anybody that doesn't know?"

He shrugged. "I thought it was good news. What can I say?"

"Do you have a date?" Samantha asked.

I looked at Zack, who didn't offer any suggestion. "We haven't figured that out yet."

"We're having a barbecue tonight," Samantha proclaimed.

"We are?" I asked.

"We are," Zack confirmed.

"I gotta catch a flight in the morning," Doug explained.

I cocked my head. "Who's we?"

"Family and friends," Zack replied.

Samantha grabbed my hand and pulled me toward the cars. "So you get to take me grocery shopping."

"Hold on," Zack called after us. "You'll need these." He tossed me his keys.

I caught them. Keys to the Snake. "Really?"

"Just be careful."

My eyes widened. "I will. And we'll park at the far end of the lot."

He waved.

"You told me I couldn't drive it, and now you're letting her?" Doug exclaimed.

Zack shrugged as I backed toward the car. "She's family. What can I say."

Samantha followed me. "What's so special about an old Mustang?"

"You'll see," I told her as I unlocked the Snake.

Doug was still grumbling.

Sam climbed in her side. "What's with these seatbelts?"

"Competition belts." I showed her how to buckle them, just as Zack had shown me.

I started the engine.

"It needs muffler work," she said.

I pulled out onto the street and pressed the gas. The engine roared, and the car charged ahead. The tires chirped as I shifted into second and let the clutch out too quickly. I hit the brakes to slow down to a reasonable speed.

Samantha grabbed the seat and braced herself. "Holy shit, what is this?"

"This is a '67 Shelby GT500." I patted the steering wheel and repeated Zack's explanation. "It's a simple car. Nothing but pure, unadulterated horsepower. In its day, it was the ultimate car for turning gasoline into noise, tire smoke, and speed. A simple machine with a simple mission—going fast as fuck."

Samantha laughed. "I think it's super cool he lets you drive it."

I didn't explain how happy this made me, since the original schedule for letting me drive had been the tenth of never.

ZACK

I WAS TURNING OVER THE LAST OF THE HAMBURGER PATTIES ON THE grill when Brittney came up from behind.

She wrapped her arms around me. "How did you get all these people here without me knowing?"

I pulled her arms away. "Careful, I don't want you to get burned."

"Well, how?"

"I slipped old man Patterson a list when we had him over for dinner, and he passed it on to Phil."

"That's sneaky."

"I wanted it to be a surprise."

"It is, and it's great—especially that you brought Samantha out. It's been too long since I saw her."

Phil appeared. "How are the burgers coming? We're running low."

"A few more minutes."

He mumbled something I didn't catch before turning away.

Brittney kneaded my shoulders quickly. "I better get back to mingling, but I wanted to say thank you again for letting me drive the Snake."

"Thanks will be accepted later after everyone has left."

She giggled. "Do you have anything in particular in mind?"

"I'll think of something," I assured her.

She left, and Phil returned again, looking over my shoulder to examine the meat. "I got a plate, if you think they're ready."

I loaded up his plate. We'd cooked all the meat the girls had brought back. This was a hungry crowd. I followed Phil to the table and fixed myself a plate, making sure to snag a piece of Katie's apple pie before it was all gone.

Looking around the crowd, we were still several short of a full family gathering. Mom was still in Paris, my sister Kelly couldn't make today, and Vincent was in Boston.

Dad, Dennis, Serena, my fiancée, the Knowltons, the Covingtons, Phil, and Brittney's brother and sister were here—a ragtag group if ever there was one.

Dad was bending Doug's ear, no doubt talking Marine to Marine. The girls had congregated around Lauren and baby Wendell.

A half hour later, Constance came in carrying a cardboard box. Winston followed.

"We have a present for you," she told Brittney.

Brittney accepted the box and opened it. "My God, my papers." She gave Constance a hug. "How?"

"Winston and I managed a quick trip to San Jose."

Brittney pulled a check from the box. "And a check for the money he took? How did you get that out of him?"

Winston chuckled. "We told him we knew people who could put him on the terrorist watch list."

I couldn't hold back my laugh. That was a good line.

Throughout the evening, everyone made time to take me aside and congratulate me on the engagement, and my choice of bride.

I couldn't have agreed more.

Dad pried himself away from Doug long enough to approach me again about London. "You know, we can keep that position open for a while, so you two can decide if it's the right move for you as a couple."

I patted his shoulder. "Thanks, Dad. I'll talk with Brittney about it, but don't hold your breath."

"I really do think it would be a good opportunity for you, Zachary."

He wasn't one to give up easily.

Phil came from inside the house, a concerned look on his face. "Zack, there's cops at the front door that want to talk to you and your dad."

I started toward the house. "Okay."

"I wonder what they want," Dad said.

Phil followed us.

When we reached the door, we found two sheriff's deputies.

Dad moved past me. "Hi, Ward, what can we do for you?" He shook hands with the older man.

That's when I realized the older one wasn't a deputy. He was the head man, the sheriff himself.

"Lloyd, it seems we've got a situation," the sheriff started. He pointed to a black SUV at the curb with a suited couple standing by it, a man and a woman. "The FBI would like to interview you. I told them I wanted to talk to you first."

"Thanks for the heads up. What do they want?"

"It's about a bank robbery in Maryland, but Lloyd, you need to prepare yourself for a shock."

Dad waved them up. "Let's talk to them, then."

The sheriff looked relieved that he wasn't going to have a showdown of some sort.

The short woman introduced the pair, FBI Special Agents Parsons and Newson.

The woman, Parsons, addressed Dad, "Mr. Benson, there was an after-hours bank robbery two days ago in Bethesda, Maryland."

"Go ahead," Dad said. "How can we help?"

So far none of this made any sense. A bank robbery in Maryland couldn't have any connection to us.

"Sir," Parsons continued, "blood evidence collected at the scene came back a match to a missing person. The parents are deceased, and you are listed as the next of kin."

I dreaded her next words.

"The blood belongs to a Deborah Ellen Benson."

I felt faint. *My missing cousin?*

Dad gasped. "She's alive, then?"

Parsons took a breath. "It would appear she wasn't killed in the abduction as was believed at the time."

Dad wobbled a little, and I steadied him. "Get Dennis for me, Phillip," he said.

Phil rushed off.

"How certain are you?" Dad asked.

"It's a DNA match. We wouldn't be here if it wasn't."

Dennis came up at a run. "Phil said it's news about Debbie?"

Phil returned just after Dennis.

"We have evidence that she's alive," Parsons told him.

"And may be involved in a bank robbery," the other agent added, which earned him a stern look from Parsons.

Dad grasped my brother's shoulder. "Dennis, you're the oldest. You need to go out east and learn everything you can. Get back to me when you have something solid to report."

"Vincent's already in Boston. Why don't we call him?"

Dad's jaw ticked. "You're the oldest. It's your job."

Dad turned to me and Phil. "In the meantime, we have a party to get back to. Not a word of this to any of the others until we know more."

I started to object. "But—"

He cut me off. "Not a word to anyone—not a single, solitary word. Understood? That means you too, Phillip."

We all nodded. Dad's tone said he was serious, and there would be no changing his mind on the subject. A task had been assigned and rules stated—end of discussion.

This changed everything. We'd never known there was an accomplice in Debbie's kidnapping. But there must have been. How else could she still be alive?

Another thing bothered me as I pasted on a smile on the way back to my fiancée. *Why hadn't we gotten another ransom demand if she's been alive all this time?*

EPILOGUE

THE REAL LOVER IS THE MAN WHO CAN
THRILL YOU BY KISSING YOUR
FOREHEAD OR SMILING INTO YOUR EYES
OR JUST STARING INTO SPACE. -
MARILYN MONROE

BRITTNEY

I ROLLED OVER TO FACE ZACK.

He had worked hard yesterday getting the house ready for today's party. He was still asleep this morning, which was unusual for such an early riser. My fiancé's chest rose and fell with the rhythm of waves against the shore—slow and steady. *Steady* was a good word for him.

I'd learned I could count on him for anything, anything at all.

With the heavy comforter over us, I couldn't see if he was as hard and ready as usual, or if I would find him soft and warm for a change because he'd been so exhausted last night.

I grew wet as I contemplated my attack. If I needed to stiffen him up, that would be fun too.

Lying next to him, for the moment I contented myself with watching him sleep, wondering how I had been so lucky to find such a perfect man. It had taken returning to the town I'd vowed I would never set foot in again to find the one for me—the one who'd been in plain sight forever, the one I'd left behind.

When Benji had forced my move back, I'd cursed him for

ruining my life, not realizing his craziness could lead to an outcome like this.

I slipped my hand down under the covers and slowly made my way to my target.

"Morning, sleepyhead," Zack said groggily as he opened his eyes.

I moved closer and brushed my lips against his. "Good morning. But today you're the sleepyhead."

My hand found its destination, and I knew the answer before I asked. "Would you like to?"

"Always, Sunshine."

I stroked his hard length with a light grip and moved down to cup his balls.

He reciprocated by pulling me closer for a kiss. Our tongues tangled, and we exchanged breath. He tried to roll toward me, but I let go of his balls and pushed his hip down firmly. This morning was my turn to be in charge.

Releasing him from the kiss, I moved down to bite his nipple lightly.

He tensed as I did.

I blew on the tender flesh and moved farther down. I gave his cock a long, slow lick from root to tip before taking him in my mouth. A few quick strokes, and he was well lubricated. It was sexy the way his cock jerked slightly as I blew cold air on the wet underside.

I climbed up over him and positioned myself over his super-hard cock.

He kneaded my breasts and thumbed my nipples with the circular motion that always sent tingles through me.

I held his cock and lowered myself slowly, a bit down and then back up, and a little more down, teasing him with my slow approach.

His gentle moans as I lowered myself and his gasps as I pulled up were my guide. I slowly took more of him with each stroke until I reached his root. I rocked into him, and he guided me up and down with his hands on my hips.

He moved to thumb my clit, but I pulled his hand away. Not once, but twice he tried.

"No," I said. "My rules today. You first." I shoved down fully, and his steely cock stretched me.

He was always making me come, and often twice before he did, but not this morning—it was my turn to set the rules. He relented and went back to guiding my hips with his hands, thrusting up into me as he pulled me down, each push seemingly deeper than the last.

I neared my climax and every cell of my body tensed as he thrust into my core. My nerve endings tingled with every lift off of him, but I held on. I had to. I had to make him come first today.

His breathing became shallower as he tensed up, nearing his limit.

I rocked down hard on him and reached behind me to grab his balls. I used the other hand to pinch his nipple as he came, gushing into me with a loud groan and a final deep push.

His legs shook and his cock continued to throb inside me as I ground down on him. He moved his thumb to my clit. His circling pressure quickly took me over the top with a shudder as he pulled me forward to kiss and nibble at my nipples. He truly was the clit whisperer.

I couldn't catch my breath as the spasms shook me and my body dissolved into climax.

He pulled me down farther to hug me tightly. "You can wake me up like this any morning you want, Sunshine."

The smile on his face in the dim morning light was all the reward I needed.

"I know what I'm going to call him," I said.

"What?"

I shifted my hips on his cock.

"Not that again."

"I think I like Lightning."

"Any name is a bad idea, if you ask me."

"You like Rebar better?"

He chuckled. "No way. Where are you getting these?"

"From *Sweet Home Alabama*. It was lightning that brought them back together again."

He pushed me up and cradled my breasts. "Then I get to name these."

"Like what?"

"I'll think of something."

I relaxed against his chest. This was always the best part, the ultimate closeness between husband and wife to-be: the perfect beginning to a new day in our life together.

BRITTNEY

SERENA HELD UP A PINK TOP FROM THE CLOSET. "WHAT ABOUT this one?"

Zack's sisters were helping me play dress-up for the combination housewarming and engagement party we were hosting this afternoon.

Zack's mother had insisted on a proper engagement party with the whole family, and Zack hadn't wanted to do it until at least the downstairs of the house was ready.

This was girl bonding time, and my chance to learn the family episodes Zack didn't want to tell me.

I took the hanger from Serena.

Kelly silently shook her head when her sister looked the other way.

"And then there was the time he tried to drive the old VW bug, before he got his license," Kelly said.

Serena laughed. "It was parked in the driveway. Dad wouldn't let him drive until he got his permit, but Zack decided to get a little practice in before then. Bad idea."

"It was on a hill," Kelly added.

"Every time he tried to put it in gear, the engine died, and it slipped farther down the hill," Serena told me.

Kelly pulled a lower-cut peach top from the rack, trying to control her laughter. "It ended up half in the street, and when Dad got home, he grounded Zack for two weeks."

I joined the laughter and handed the pink shirt back to Serena, holding Kelly's peach suggestion up in front of me.

Serena nodded. "I like it."

I took it off the hanger. "I'll save that one. Do you have any other good stories?"

"A ton," Kelley replied.

I pulled off my T-shirt to try the top.

Serena was already looking through my limited jewelry choices. "What do you have that's gold to go with that?"

I didn't have much in the necklace department that was gold. I slipped into the top they'd picked out while she searched.

She pulled out Todd's heart-shaped pendant. "This would be good. I especially like the chain length."

She meant that it hung enticingly low.

"I'm not sure that's a good one," I told her, not eager to wear Todd's piece.

"Try it on," Kelly encouraged me. "And let's see."

I gave in, and Serena helped with the clasp.

"What does it say?" Kelly asked.

I'd inadvertently gotten it on backwards—the inscription was facing front. "It's a Klingon love poem."

Kelly peered closer. "Cool."

"What does it mean?" Serena asked.

Sheepishly I admitted, "I don't remember."

Actually, I'd never known. Todd had said it was a secret for later, and later had never come.

"We should get Winston or Nick to translate it," Kelly suggested. "They're both super Trekkies."

I undid the clasp to reverse the pendant so the engraving was on the back, and reconnected it.

"That's a good look," Serena said.

Kelly nodded. "Yup."

Checking the mirror, I agreed.

WHEN I GOT DOWNSTAIRS, ZACK'S PARENTS HAD JUST ARRIVED.

"I hear there's a party around here somewhere, but I don't see any food yet," Lloyd joked.

"Try the kitchen, Dad," Zack told him.

Lloyd made his way toward the back.

Zack's mother, Robin, smiled warmly at me. "You look lovely, Brittney."

I felt the heat rise in my cheeks. "Thank you."

"Please excuse Lloyd. Sometimes he has no manners. Now, I hear from Serena that you've gotten Zack to start eating fruit again."

"I'm going to go check on Dad," Zack said before he scurried off.

"Every day," I told her. "He still complains about the kiwis, but I'm working on that."

"It's the seeds, dear. He won't admit it, but he's deathly afraid of them ever since the infection."

Now I was learning something new.

"What infection was that?"

"When he was young, we had an awful time getting him to brush properly. Anyway, he got strawberry seeds caught under his gum line and got a terrible infection that almost cost him a tooth. After that he pretty much swore off fruit."

"Well, that explains a lot."

Lloyd returned with two wine glasses and handed one to

Robin. "You have to come see what Zack and Brittney have done with the kitchen."

When I turned, the house was overflowing with all the guests Zack had invited: the Knowltons, the Covingtons, Phil, and the rest of the Benson family, even Vincent and his wife were out from Boston. Zack had also invited a few dozen coworkers from the company. Samantha had just arrived from Philadelphia, but Doug was still overseas.

Phil was running his hands over the mantle Zack had repaired and refinished. "You know, you do such good work, I might have to hire you."

"You couldn't afford me," Zack replied.

All the work Zack had put into fixing this fine house was now on beautiful display. He was proudest of the hardwood floors, the staircase, and all the intricate millwork. It had been a pain to strip the layers of paint, but the end result was worth it.

"And these floors," Phil went on. "So much nicer than the shit they put down today."

Zack beamed. "The previous owners had glued laminate over this whole place. Twice."

"Fucking idiots," Phil agreed. "What do you plan on doing next?"

Zack nodded toward my and Samantha's currently unoccupied house. "I'll be fixing that one next. After that, I don't know."

Zack and his father had called a truce on the London move, and Zack's next rotation would be here instead, with time off for the house restoration.

I tightened my arm around him. I was *so* looking forward to that project. He was teaching me the joy of restoring a house to its former glory.

I got up on my toes and whispered into Zack's ear. "I have something to tell you."

Phil backed away. "If you guys are getting all mushy, I'm outta here." He turned and left, shaking his head.

"What?" Zack asked.

"You were right all along."

He chuckled. "That's no surprise."

I punched his shoulder lightly. "Cut it out. I'm being serious." I pulled my pink envelope from my pocket and pushed it at him. "I want you to help me with this."

He had reminded me every day that none of these deaths were my fault. As we moved forward with our lives, I needed to put this behind me once and for all.

He took the envelope.

I grabbed a match from the mantle matchbox, struck it, and lit the corner of the envelope as he held it out. The expired match went in the fireplace.

I took the envelope from him and rotated it as the yellow flames curled around the edge and grew. Slowly the paper gave way to ash, erasing this guilt from my pre-Zack life. When most of the envelope had been consumed, I tossed it in the fireplace. I turned my back on the flaming paper, a relic from my previous life, and faced the man that represented my future.

"I'm done looking backwards."

He wrapped me in his powerful arms and kissed me. "I'm proud of you."

I was proud of me too. "Thank you for being you."

I was grateful he was persistent enough to teach me the lesson I needed.

The moment didn't last long. Serena arrived to drag me over to Katie and Nick. "Hey, Nick, we have a question for you. Who's better at Klingon, you or Winston?"

He shrugged. "Depends."

Serena moved behind me to undo the clasp of my pendant, and in a moment she had the inscription visible for him to read.

Nick pointed Katie toward the front room. "Hey, Precious, go get Winston. This one might be more than I can handle alone."

Katie returned with the burly agent in tow.

Winston examined the writing. "Klingon, you say?"

I nodded. "That's what I was told. And the number is the star-date of our first date."

Winston shook his head. "You were sold a bill of goods. This is gibberish, no Klingon here."

Nick nodded his concurrence. "Definitely not Klingon."

Zack wandered over.

Winston examined it again. "Not Romulan either. This is just a monkey banging on a typewriter."

My shoulders fell. Forever I'd thought it actually meant Todd cared for me, but this made no sense.

Zack put his arm around me. "Well, you were going to melt it down anyway, right?"

"Yeah."

"Hey," Nick exclaimed. "This isn't a stardate. The first section here is the routing code for a bank in Miami. I see it all the time in my work. That second number is the right length for an account number, so somewhere in the rest of this crap is what we need." He rubbed his hands together. "Winston, got your laptop handy?"

Winston turned for the door. "In the car. Be right back."

A minute later we were huddled behind Nick, watching him work on the laptop.

He tried several combinations of the words in the inscription, and suddenly he was into the account profile page on the bank's website.

I gasped.

Zack nudged me. "It's a retirement account, and you're listed as the beneficiary?"

"I see it. I just don't believe it." The account was Todd's, but it was the balance that struck me—over eight hundred thousand dollars.

Zack whispered in my ear. "This must be the key Delgado was after."

I nodded.

Nick turned around. "What are you going to do with all that money?"

Phil piped up. "I know a construction company that's looking for an investor."

I knew exactly what I would do. "I think I'll donate it to drug rehab non-profits in Jonas's name."

The money most likely had been earned off the backs of drug addicts, and I intended to give it back to them.

Zack gave me a kiss of appreciation. "That's a great idea, Sunshine."

"Before you do that," Winston said, "report it as found money to the sheriff. If nobody claims it in ninety days, it's yours."

"Do you think Delgado will go after it?" Zack asked.

"How's he going to know? It's not like they advertise it. And besides, he'd have to explain where it came from. To have a chance, he'd have to give up who he worked with, and that would be a death sentence on the inside."

The group disbanded from around the computer after a minute.

An hour later, Zack's parents called everyone together. "Time for a toast to the engaged couple," Lloyd said.

Zack's brothers filled glasses with champagne.

I had Zack on one side and his sister Kelly on the other.

When Dennis tried to add champagne to my orange juice, I pulled the glass away. "I can't."

Zack gave me a knowing smile.

Samantha shot me a sly look. "Can't?"

I nodded.

She leaned close to whisper, "Check with me before you pick a name."

Kelly grinned and whispered to Serena. She hadn't missed the meaning of my words either.

The toast was made, and my man lifted me into a congratulatory kiss to applause from the crowd.

He was mine, I was his, and soon it would be official.

"I love you, Sunshine," he whispered in my ear as he put me down.

Just like in the movie, I'd come back to the town I thought I'd left for good and found my true love, right here where he'd always been—waiting for me.

I'd had to find my way back here before he could show me the way forward.

He'd given me everything: true love, his name, confidence in my future—in our future, and before long, a child.

I stretched up to whisper in his ear. "Will you eat a pomegranate for me, then?"

He backed away. "No way."

Some things weren't going to change.

THE END

THE FOLLOWING PAGES CONTAIN AN EXCERPT OF THE NEXT BOOK IN the series: **Nailing the Billionaire**.

SNEAK PEEK: NAILING THE BILLIONAIRE

CHAPTER 1

JENNIFER

I'D MAKE HIM PAY FOR WHAT HE DID.

My modified headlamp cast a dim glow on the recalcitrant lock.

The file folder needed to be back in place before it was missed. I had my copy, and when the news broke, there was a good chance this file would attract attention.

I stretched my aching shoulders, and the tensioner slipped out of the lock as I pulled the pick tool toward me.

Fuck.

After wiping my brow with my sleeve, I repositioned the tool at the bottom of the key slot to start picking this cylinder again—for the fourth time, or was it the fifth?

Normal file-cabinet locks wouldn't have been this hard, but the company hadn't gone with standard, hardware-store locks. These were a bitch, and the latex gloves I wore didn't make it any easier. The YouTubers made it look so much easier than it was.

The faint sound of a door opening down the corridor caught my attention.

I ducked low and quickly put one hand in front of the light source before clicking it off with the other.

The door closed, and footsteps followed. They came closer, and then stopped for a few seconds before clomping my way.

Shimmying back behind a file cabinet with my bag, I tried to control my breathing, with limited success. The sound of my heart beating threatened to swamp the sounds from the corridor.

Every time this happened, I was more scared than the last. Getting caught in this file room would be something I could explain away during the work day, perhaps. But after hours, with the lights off? No way. It would be out-of-the company time for yours truly, and most likely off to jail as well, and I would fail at my mission.

There were days when jail didn't sound so bad—it would be a lot less stressful, but that was just me kidding myself. I couldn't live with what it would do to Mom and Ramona. Who would look after them if I couldn't? Certainly not Uncle Victor. Although, the thought of Mom and him in the same room was funny. She'd be after him day and night about his drinking, and I'd bet on Mom carrying the day. She didn't lose many arguments.

I halted a laugh halfway up my throat. Silence was paramount until I knew the footsteps were far enough away. It didn't matter how funny my daydreams got, I had to concentrate on tonight's task.

Eventually I judged it had been long enough and struggled to my feet again.

I wasn't tall, but these locks were positioned for people shorter than me. Rolling a chair in here was out of the question, and hunching over for an hour was going to make this a multi-Tylenol evening. *Advil*, I reminded myself. I planned on a glass of wine, and research said not to take Tylenol with alcohol.

I started again on the file cabinet.

Somebody needed to invent an easier way to do this. Movie characters were always past the lock in less than five seconds, but

Hollywood didn't need to be accurate. *Suspension of disbelief,* they called it.

One of those actors should come in here and tackle this lock. That would show them what the real world was like. Just because the script said *and the lock opened* didn't make it so.

Suddenly, the tension tool loosened as the cylinder turned. Another quarter turn and the plug popped toward me with a loud clunk. At least it was open, but this stupid cabinet was all kinds of trouble.

I froze and listened intently for half a minute.

I couldn't detect any sounds, so I slowly pulled out the squeaky bottom drawer. Pulling my notes from my pocket, I checked where I'd originally found it. I pulled the file folder out of my messenger bag and slid it back in the drawer, exactly where it had been two days ago.

Slowly I eased the drawer closed, pushed in the lock plug, and turned the cylinder with my tension tool to the locked position.

Success.

Slipping off the headlamp, I clicked it off before closing it in my bag. With the tools back in place, I pocketed the leather case of my pick set. It was too tall to fit well, but I'd deal with that later.

I shouldered the bag and made my way to the door.

The hallway was quiet, so I slipped through the door and closed it behind me.

Moving quietly, I started left. I couldn't relax until I'd made it out without being spotted.

At the corner, I listened before peeking around the corner of the long corridor.

I pulled my head back quickly.

The bigger of the two night guards was halfway down and coming this way.

I shuffled back the way I'd come as silently as I could.

The first office door I tried was locked, and the same with the second. There wasn't any time to try to pick one, and the file room door had locked behind me.

The sound of the guard rattling a doorknob just past the corner left me no alternative. I pushed my way into the bathroom, grabbed the handle to keep the spring-loaded door closer from doing its thing, and gently shut the door behind me.

I turned. *Shit.*

I'd ended up in the men's room. I tiptoed to the far stall and slid inside.

A cough outside the door got my heart racing. He was just outside. If he came in here, I was done.

The sound of the door opening sealed my decision. With my hands braced against the stall walls, I put one foot on the toilet seat and climbed up, hoping it wouldn't squeak when I put my other foot on the opposite side of the seat and crouched.

It didn't, but as I lifted my other foot, my pick set case came loose and fell to the floor, the light sound masked by the loud closing of the door to the corridor.

I closed my eyes and unsuccessfully willed my heartbeat to slow. Slow, silent breaths were agonizing as my lungs burned for more air.

The footsteps made their way inside and were followed by a grunt and the sound of a zipper coming down.

I opened my eyes, and the sight of my pick set on the floor where it might be visible if he turned only compounded my terror.

More grunts preceded humming and the sound of the guard peeing in the urinal.

A bead of sweat threatened to fall into my eye, but I didn't dare move to wipe it away.

The sound of the stream stopped and started a few times before the humming stopped and was replaced by another grunt as the zipper sound announced he was done.

The sound of flushing followed, then the door thudding shut.

Thankfully he hadn't bothered to wash his hands. If he had, he might have noticed the pick set in the mirror.

Finally able to breathe again, I wiped my brow with my sleeve, stepped off the toilet, and tried to compose myself. After retrieving the pick set and pocketing the latex gloves, I pulled two tissues from the box by the sink to dry my sweaty hands.

Two minutes went by on my watch before I listened at the bathroom door and found the hallway quiet enough to slip out again.

My path to the stairwell exit required a left down the long hallway, a right at the end, and another jog right. The path was clear as I made the final turn, and I could finally relax as I shuffled softly down the concrete stairs to the garage level.

The back of the garage had a separate set of stairs to the street, and no surveillance cameras.

Once back in the safety of my car, I pulled out my iPad, composed the quick email, and sent it.

> To: Hydra157
> From: Nemesis666
> The pony is back in the barn.

CHAPTER 2

JENNIFER
(Four days later)

As I added pins to secure my French twist this morning, I wondered if the bomb would drop today. It had been four long days since I'd put the file back in place. A girl could hope.

I turned my head left and right, and a quick mirror check showed my twist to be perfect. A professional woman always presents a professional image—a habit Mom had taught me.

I ventured out to make breakfast for myself and my sister, Ramona. This meant pouring the Raisin Bran.

"Are you taking me to school today?" my nephew, Danny, asked as I sat down. He'd served himself cereal already.

"No, not today. Your mommy's taking you."

"Why?"

"Because it's Tuesday, and it's my turn," Ramona answered from the doorway.

Danny spooned another mouthful of cereal, seeming content with the answer for a change.

Ramona joined us and dug into her cereal. "Anything planned for tonight?" she asked me.

I swallowed. "Nope."

She was clearly fishing for some sign of a third date with Simon, but he hadn't called again, at least not yet.

She gave up the quest, and ten minutes later, the two of them were out the door.

After the dishes, I gave in and sat down at my laptop.

After it powered up, I logged in to the bank's website.

I unfolded the bill I'd pulled from the drawer, and a double-check showed what I feared. My mouth dried. We'd skipped eating out, but with three mouths to feed, and after also paying Paul's bills, I didn't have enough to cover this today.

My pay wouldn't be direct-deposited until Friday. That meant this would be another late payment to deal with. The envelope went back in my purse, at the bottom this time.

Mom would have figured a way to make this all work, but I wasn't her.

Before I could close the computer, the new-email chime sounded, so I clicked on the icon. It was good news at last.

> To: Nemesis666
> From: HYDRA157
> The balloon is launched.
> Hope you can see it.

I grinned. I needed to hustle if I was going to see his reaction.

I deleted the message, closed the computer, and hefted my purse.

Mom would have been proud of the actions I was taking for our family. Paul's bills were current, Ramona and Danny had a roof over their head, and most importantly, I was avenging Dad.

My little car started with the typical fuss, another thing I needed to spend money on. Money I didn't have. It could use a good cleaning as well. I closed the window when I ended up behind a bus belching the black death of diesel fumes. The state told us we had to get our cars smog checked every two years, but the city busses did whatever they wanted.

The traffic was heavy, but I made it to the Starbucks in time.

Inside, I ordered a tall mocha and took my preferred table. The coffee was expensive, but it couldn't be avoided. When hunting the rich, you had to go where they went.

Nursing my latte slowly, I turned on my tablet to read the news. Now all I had to do was wait for my target.

The table provided me a clear view of the place, but I had to get here extra early to snag it ahead of two old ladies who seemed to think this table had their names on it. It was important to get the chair facing the right direction.

I scrolled through the news on the tablet in front of me as if I were reading it. Each time the door opened, I glanced over.

So far he'd been a no-show.

Fireman Ed was at the register with his daily list of a dozen beverages, and my target usually beat him here. Checking my watch, I fretted that he might already have seen it and decided to skip his mocha before work today. That would be disappointing, to say the least.

I switched back to the *Times* website.

The story was third from the top, and probably would remain there all day. It would serve him right. I'd checked the print version already and knew it was several column inches on the front page below the fold, and it continued on page three. It was guaranteed to get a reaction, and cost him a ton in the stock market. Couldn't happen to a more deserving monster.

DENNIS

I WAS RUNNING LATER THAN USUAL. I SHOVED MY PAPER UNDER MY

arm as I pushed through the door of my building out into the bright, early morning sunshine.

Bad idea.

He stood directly in my path and shoved an envelope at me. "Dennis Benson, you've been served."

I pocketed the envelope without bothering to open it. It was the same ugly yellow as the previous one she'd sent me six months ago. There was no reason to start off the day in as rotten a mood as the contents would certainly create.

Looking through the glass before I opened the door would have been a good idea, but in retrospect, that wouldn't have accomplished anything other than putting off the inevitable.

If I'd ducked out the back, he would have tagged me at work, or back here in the evening. As distasteful as it was, there was no avoiding these legal arrows she sent my way.

My God, the woman could be vengeful. *Hell hath no fury* the quote went, and the writer was understating it in this case. What a bitch.

I set off on my morning ritual walk to get my coffee. Rituals were good; rituals kept me grounded. I'd read that the first half hour set one's mood for the rest of the day, and a brisk walk followed by delicious brew was my way of starting on the right foot.

The California sun on my face brightened my mood with every stride. Exercise and being outside in the sun, if not in nature, was good for the mood and the soul. The smog wasn't as bad as yesterday, and the Santa Monica mountains were visible. Their winter shade of bright green had already given way to summer's duller colors. I forgot about the wretched envelope, and my mind went back to walking the woods and the seashore, camping, and cooking over a campfire. Back-to-basics activities brought us closer to nature and our roots as pioneers.

The Benson family had been early settlers in California, and I was proud to be a multi-generation Californian, not a recent transplant from elsewhere on the continent.

Taking a deep breath, I pulled open the door and entered Starbucks.

The line wasn't long, but the fireman at the counter was reading from a list, and the last time I'd been behind him it had been quite a wait.

Looking around the tables, I saw a lot of regulars, plus three empty tables near the back. Mr. Infinite List ordering now wouldn't take a table, and with only two others ahead of me in line, at least I could catch a table to relax this morning.

The envelope in my jacket pocket was a lead weight on my mood, but I refused to let her have that level of control over me. A good run is what I needed, something to get the endorphins flowing.

~

JENNIFER

AN INCREASE IN STREET NOISE ANNOUNCED THE OPENING OF THE door to the coffee shop.

I glanced over, and there he was. Tall, imposing, with steely gray eyes and a defined, sharp jaw any woman would find attractive. His sandy blond hair was annoyingly in place, and his suit immaculately tailored to span his broad shoulders and taper to his trim waist. The perfection of the man annoyed me to no end.

At least being behind Fireman Ed would annoy him.

He scanned the room.

I looked away and turned to catch the woman to my left eying him.

She was just short of drooling. Her eyes raked his form as she twirled the ends of her hair, and the corners of her mouth turned up. She was probably imagining his touch. She licked her lips. *Yuck*, she disgusted me.

He disgusted me, because I knew what he'd done.

I looked past her and caught another girl ogling.

They probably thought he was Adonis in a suit.

I knew better.

The suit hid the red skin of the devil himself, and the perfect hair hid his horns. One day soon, I would strip away the spit and polish and nail him to the wall, for all to see him as he really was: ghastly, mean, and with an ugly soul.

Mr. Immaculate got in line to order with his newspaper under his arm.

When he reached the register, I listened carefully for the grande mocha extra shot he always ordered.

He chose it again today, which was good. Every hunter knew the predictable prey was the easiest to get. He tipped the barista with a dollar bill as he always did, a subterfuge of generosity meant to conceal his true character.

I hid behind my raised tablet and watched him while he waited for his order.

He didn't check the paper.

When his coffee was ready, he took it to a table in the corner and opened his newspaper. He read with his cup in his hand, taking short sips.

It took thirty seconds or so for his jaw to drop as he found the article. He put the cup down and studied the page before turning to the remainder of the article on page three. His eyes got wider as he went on. His jaw clenched.

I smiled behind my tablet as the story corroded the confident exterior of the man and wild anger grew in his eyes.

His hands balled into fists, as he probably planned his revenge against the writer—something along the lines of a meeting in a dark alley where he could pulverize him. Or would he choose the anonymity of a bullet from long range?

He deserved it all and more for what he'd done to me, what he'd done to my family.

The door opened again, and I glanced reflexively that direction.

363

Martha and Mona had arrived. The M&M girls, they called themselves. They made their way to me.

Martha arrived first. "Good morning, Jennie. Thought we'd come early today to see if you had any luck yet with—"

"Shh," Mona said, interrupting her and cocking her head in Mr. Immaculate's direction.

Martha looked over and put her hand to her mouth as she sat.

Mona took a seat as well. "Thank you for saving our table for us."

"My pleasure," I said. Each time they joined me, I couldn't bring myself to refuse.

Martha leaned over the table to whisper, "Did you approach him yet?"

"Not yet," I whispered back.

Mona adjusted her chair to see him better. "I don't see what the big deal is. I'll go talk to him, if you won't."

I reached out to touch Mona's hand. "Please don't. It's something I need to do myself."

"I agree," Martha interjected. "We're too old to be playing matchmaker."

"Speak for yourself," Mona shot back. "I'm not old; I'm mature."

"You're a year older than me," Martha corrected her.

These two could go at it for an hour, each jabbing at the other in a light-hearted way.

While we'd been talking, Mr. Immaculate had checked his phone and stood to leave.

He folded up his paper, tossed his cup, and headed for the door. His countenance showed the combination of anger and frustration I'd hoped for. The door closed behind him.

A sigh came from the woman to our left who'd been undressing him with her eyes. She had no idea what a total schmuck she was lusting after.

This would not be the last unmasking of his misdeeds. One by one I would reveal the skeletons in his closet, and the world would finally see the real Dennis Benson. His fancy suit wouldn't fool anyone then.

Martha stood. "Do you want your regular?" she asked Mona.

"Yes, please, but less cinnamon this time," Mona replied.

After Martha left for the counter, Mona leaned my way. "You should let me wave him over, and you could introduce yourself."

I had to keep nixing her suggestions because I couldn't tell them my true intentions. "Thank you, but no. I need to do this my way."

She let out a loud breath. "At this rate, you'll be my age before you find the right one."

"There's nothing wrong with your age," I assured her.

That earned a smile. "You're a dear."

Martha returned with their coffees, and I excused myself shortly after that.

CHAPTER 3

DENNIS

THE FLOORS DINGED BY AND THE RED NUMERALS INCREASED UNTIL the uncomfortably hot compartment finally opened on the top floor.

I turned left toward my office, and my phone chirped with a text message. I stopped to check it.

DAD: We need to talk.

Dad was the only one I knew who bothered to make sure his punctuation was correct on a text message. Talking to him was not at the top of my list right now.

My assistant, Cindy, was away from her desk, and before I even reached my office, I could hear Jay Fisher, our general council, and Larry Zerfoss going at it about this morning's article. It would obviously be the only thing talked about all day.

They were standing in my office, and they halted their argument mid-sentence when I entered.

I closed the door behind me and hung up my coat to cool off. "Morning."

"Did you see the *Times* this morning?" Larry asked.

I took my seat and put down the paper. "Just did."

"They make it sound like it's our fault," he complained.

I opened the paper. "I know."

Jay nodded.

"It's not fair, not fair at all," Larry continued. "This is going to tank us."

"What's the damage so far?" I asked.

Larry checked his phone. "Fourteen percent down and still dropping."

The stock market didn't like surprises or bad news, and this was both.

I turned to Jay. "Have you read it?"

He nodded. "Several times and—"

Larry interrupted. "We didn't even own the company when this was going on."

I put a hand up to stop him. "I know."

"Is there anything we can do legally?" I asked Jay.

His face telegraphed the answer. "No. I can't see anything factually wrong, and that means there's nothing to dispute." He turned to Larry. "Unless I'm missing something."

Larry took a breath. "It's just the way they present it—it makes us look like the guilty party here."

"It's America," Jay told him. "Spin is allowed. The First Amendment gives them to freedom to print shit like this, twice a day if they want to."

Jay's answer was the same conclusion we'd come to on the previous article. We had no recourse with the paper.

I pointed to the byline. "Larry, where are we on finding out who Sigurd is?" Each of the articles had been penned by a *Sigurd* —no last name, or no first, whichever it was.

Dad had been the one to point out that Sigurd was a mythical

Norse dragon slayer. Apparently, someone considered us the dragon.

"Nobody's talking, and it seems like maybe nobody at the paper even knows. The last article was submitted online through Romania, which is obviously a ruse."

Just as in the last article, there were details that had to have come from inside the company. We had a mole, and a destructive one at that.

"Better get your talking points sharpened up, then," I told him.

He held up a set of pink message slips. I've got five analysts' calls and counting to return on this."

I stood. "Then you better get going. It's your job to turn this around."

He shook his head. "This isn't going to be easy."

"That's why we have you," I told him. "Just think of them as Eskimos you have to sell a refrigerator to."

The two left, with Larry still grumbling.

If we did have to sell refrigerators in Alaska, he was just the silver-tongued devil for the job.

I followed them out.

Cindy had returned to her desk. "Good morning."

I nodded. "Not from where I stand."

"Your father called."

"I know. I'll call him in a bit." He probably wanted to remind me of the mistake I'd made.

"And Melissa called as well," she warned me.

"You might as well tell me I have a root canal scheduled today."

"I'm just the messenger," she shot back.

I withdrew into my office. The root canal message would have been better news than a call from my ex-wife. If I could ever have a do-over in life, that's one rash decision I wanted to unwind.

Her bitchiness, Melissa, could chill for a while.

I dialed Dad.

"Dennis, thank you for calling back so quickly. I wanted to see how you are fairing with this *Times* nonsense."

"Feeling a little persecuted," I admitted.

"Well, that's one of the problems with deciding to take your company public. You have so many others judging you all the time, and it's rarely fair."

There it was, the lecture about how I shouldn't have insisted on splitting off a portion of Benson Corp. for me to run and financing it in the public markets.

"Dad, we've been over this."

Rehashing my decision to leave wouldn't do either of us any good.

"That's not why I called," he said. "I'm calling to see if there's anything I can do to help."

"Not unless you know a way to get the *Times* to stop picking on us."

He paused. "Dennis, is that who you think you have a problem with?"

"No. I know it's most likely the anonymous writer."

"That's the one you need to find, but in the meantime, this reminds me of your grandfather."

I sighed. I didn't need another down-home, don't-count-your-chickens-before-they-hatch kind of saying today.

"Your grandfather used to say you couldn't add anything to the lemonade to make it more sour, but you could always add sugar to make it sweeter."

"Thanks, Dad."

A lot of good that did.

"I'll bet if you look around, you have some sugar you can add to the news."

My brain kicked into gear, and I understood his message for a change. I had no idea why he couldn't be more direct; it would have made life so much easier.

"Thanks, Dad, that's a good suggestion."

When I was sixteen, I'd been sure my generation was a lot

smarter than our elders. Ever since then, I keep getting reminders that we didn't know as much as we thought, and today was another one.

"Have a good day, Dennis."

We hung up.

I walked to the door and opened it.

Thankfully, Cindy was at her desk. "I need Larry, Jay, and Bob, right now."

∾

JENNIFER

I PASSED THROUGH THE LOBBY, AND EVERYTHING LOOKED AS IT had yesterday.

The elevator disgorged passengers at several floors before reaching the fourteenth, where I got off. Turning right into finance, I could see and hear the hum of gossip as people stopped at each other's cubicles to share what they'd heard, or read, or just guessed at.

I unlocked the drawers of my cubicle and dropped my purse in the bottom one after taking out my phone and putting it on the charger. A dead phone was a useless phone, and mine was losing charge faster these days. I needed to take it in for a battery replace-ment when I got the time—if I ever got the time. Time and money always seemed to be in short supply these days.

I pushed the power button, and my computer slowly came to life.

"Did you see the news?" Vanessa asked breathlessly from behind me.

I turned. "No, what news?"

"You have to check the *Times'* website."

"Is it good? We're due for some good coverage about now."

"This is the opposite. You gotta read it."

"Okay." I turned back to my monitor and logged in. "We're having the worst luck with those guys." I selected the browser and navigated to the *Times* site.

The story was still third from the top. "Oh my God," I said as I read the words I knew so well. I put my hand to my mouth. "Oh my God," I repeated.

"It's terrible." I kept my hand over my mouth to hide the smile that grew as I read. The article took the Bensons and this company down a notch. They deserved that, and much more.

I composed myself. "Is this true?"

"I don't know for sure, but Leo thinks it is."

Leo had been here the longest, and everyone approached him as if he held all knowledge related to Benson Corp.

Vanessa left, and I busied myself with work.

Three other people stopped by throughout the morning to see what I thought of the news. Each time I could only express horror and say it probably wasn't true, and that I hoped for all our sakes it wasn't.

This story had amped up the company gossip mill even more than the last one.

My cell buzzed. It was my sister, Ramona.

"I see there's a story in the news about you guys," she started.

"I can't talk right now," I answered. "Things are kinda busy here."

"I imagine. Talk tonight then?"

"Sure. Tonight," I said

"Hope you're doing okay."

"I'm good, just hunkered down at work."

"Take care, sis."

"I always do." Careful was my middle name.

We hung up, and I went back to the spreadsheet torture in front of me.

Vanessa wandered by a little later. "Sixteen percent," she muttered before she made a throat-slashing motion across her neck and left.

The upside was that the stock slide was hitting my target, Dennis Benson, where it hurt the most, and it couldn't happen to a more deserving toad.

Emailing Hydra, the one person I could share this with, was also off the table. No emails from work—that had been a firm rule from the beginning. I couldn't share the reaction until I got home, another reason to hope this day went quickly. While I attacked my spreadsheets, I had to keep my glee to myself. Nobody here could know I was the source behind these damaging news stories.

Fuck you, Dennis Benson. Someday I'd be able to speak those words to his face. That would be a good day. No, that would be a great day. Vengeance would finally be mine.

I checked the stock price again. Down eighteen percent.

As Shakespeare wrote, "revenge should have no bounds." And I had only just begun.

Printed in Great Britain
by Amazon

26817979R00215